THE OZARKS

Chronicles
OF THE *Ozarks*

Brooks Blevins, General Editor

The
Ozarks

An American
Survival of
Primitive Society

VANCE RANDOLPH

Edited by Robert Cochran

The University of Arkansas Press
Fayetteville
2017

To M.R.

CONTENTS

SERIES EDITOR'S PREFACE

IT WOULD TAKE SOME DOING to convince me that anyone has ever been more connected to a region than Vance Randolph was (and is) connected to the Ozarks. For half a century he chronicled his adopted region, writing about its songs, its stories, its folkways, its dialect, its crimes, its peculiarities—and most importantly its people, without whom those other topics would never have existed. Even now, more than three and a half decades after his death and a quarter century after the last of his posthumous publications, anyone writing anything about the Ozarks has to reckon with Randolph. It would be a stretch to say Vance Randolph defined the Ozarks—but not a great big one. He certainly established the blueprint for analyzing the region and its people, and writers deviating from Randolph's model of the Ozarks and his sketches of the people who encapsulated the Ozark spirit for him must explain their temerity, must account for their foolishness.

I never met Randolph, and I regret that. But I suspect we would not have seen eye to eye—wouldn't have geehawed. Looking back on his life from the vantage point of the early twenty-first century, he strikes me as the kind of fellow who puts too much pepper in his beans. And it wouldn't have taken Randolph more than a few moments to peg me as the kind of stiff-necked academician that occasionally quashed his plans and fuzzed up his life from time to time. And he wouldn't have been wrong. Like most scholars, I've plowed through life—blinders often securely in place—motivated by a desire to discover the *truth*, propelled by the belief that lying somewhere in the distance is an accurate rendering of the Ozarker, both historic and contemporary.

Randolph often educated readers about the region and its people, but his primary motivation was entertainment. He knew a good story. He understood that his adopted region shared many characteristics with an increasingly generic American culture but that readers didn't pay money to discover just how similar Carroll County, Arkansas, might be to Delaware County, New York. Anachronism, uniqueness, and regional distinctiveness sold the Ozarks to the American public, and the *truth* is, there's nothing wrong with that. The Ozark region—the world, for that matter—relies on both approaches to satisfy life's yin and yang or its dialectic or however else we humans characterize the often productive union or resolution of seemingly oppositional forces. Randolph may have embellished from time to time and he certainly cherry-picked his informants, but only rarely did he make things up from whole cloth, for the people who best exemplified the Ozarks for him did in fact exist. They may have represented the last of a breed—the evolving world never stops replenishing the supply of that breed—but they were here, and they were bearers of lifeways that were certainly anachronistic, if not completely unique.

Fortunately for the Chronicles of the Ozarks, Bob Cochran—like Randolph an outsider who has now spent most of his life in the region—knew Vance Randolph personally. I consider Bob's excellent 1985 biography of Randolph just as essential to an understanding of the Ozarks as any of the myriad things written by the old codger himself. In spite of his academic credentials,

Bob is a *character* in his own right, not as crusty and irreverent as Randolph, but fully capable of holding his own with the fellow who almost singlehandedly shaped our perceptions of the region. And no one is more qualified to reintroduce us to the book that started it all back in 1931, Vance Randolph's *The Ozarks: An American Survival of Primitive Society.*

BROOKS BLEVINS

INTRODUCTION

IT'S NOT UNUSUAL FOR A debut book in the field to end up as a benchmark in a celebrated author's career, the point where promise blossoms as performance. But even Vance Randolph must have been pleasantly surprised at the success of *The Ozarks: An American Survival of Primitive Society*. By 1931, when it hit the shelves in late September, the author, who would turn forty at his next birthday, was already an old hand in the writing racket. His first article-length studies of the region's traditional culture had appeared in scholarly journals (*Dialect Notes, American Speech,* the *Journal of American Folklore*) in 1926 and 1927, but he'd been making money with his pen since the early 1920s by turning out booklets on scientific and psychological topics, mostly for Emanuel Haldeman-Julius's Little Blue Books series in Girard, Kansas. *Life among the Bees* and *The Psychology of the Affections,* both from 1924, are representative titles.[1] Randolph churned these out strictly for the money, received a flat payment with no provision for royalties, and garnered no reviews. The scholarly articles, of course, paid nothing at all, and were read only by small bands of professors and regional culture enthusiasts.

Everything changed with *The Ozarks*. In the first place, it was a much bigger book, published in hard covers by Vanguard, a left-wing New York firm established in 1926 as a sort of east coast analogue of Haldeman-Julius's Kansas operation. (Randolph wrote for Vanguard from its beginnings, cranking out such titles as *The ABC of Evolution* and *The Substance of "The Descent of Man" by Charles Darwin*, both from 1926. He turned out a total of six *"ABC"* titles, plus two *"Substance of"* numbers. All went down without a ripple.)

But *The Ozarks* made a real splash, earning the new-minted folklore scholar his first national-level reviews in both the literary and the scholarly worlds. The newspapers and literary magazines were quicker on their feet, with well-known novelist and folksong collector Dorothy Scarborough (her *On the Trail of Negro Folk-Songs* had been issued six years earlier by Harvard) offering up praise in the *New York Times Book Review* and western history writer Stanley Vestal agreeing more lyrically in the *Saturday Review*. Both grabbed the hint of Randolph's subtitle, with Scarborough's review titled "Where the Eighteenth Century Lives On," and Vestal citing the volume's appeal for the reader who "likes the tang of Shakespearian English" or feels "nostalgia for that America which passed so swiftly away at the coming of the machine and the immigrant."[2] (Note "the immigrant"—how quickly they forget!)

The scholarly reviews came in more slowly, and not from all quarters. *The Ozarks* was ignored by the *Journal of American Folklore*, the field where Randolph would eventually gain his greatest acclaim. *American Anthropologist* also failed to take note, but Louise Pound and Robert Redfield, prominent figures both, weighed in with applause in *American Speech* and the *American Journal of Sociology*. It was a heady reception.

He moved energetically to seize the day. Before the next year was out he'd finished a sequel, *Ozark Mountain Folks*, followed up by successive book-length volumes in each of the next three years. *From an Ozark Holler*, a short story collection, was issued in 1933; *Ozark Outdoors*, a collection of hunting and fishing pieces done with fellow Kansan Guy W. von Schriltz, appeared in 1934; and *Hedwig*, a novel, ended the run in 1935. All were issued by Vanguard. It was, for sheer volume and generic variety, a spectacularly fruitful five-year run, matched only by the series of Columbia University Press folktale volumes from the 1950s (with *Down in the Holler,* the Ozark speech study co-authored with George P. Wilson and published by the Oklahoma University Press, mixed in).

Randolph's recollections of *The Ozarks'* origins contrast at several points with the observations of scholars interested in the history of folklore as an academic discipline. His staunchest supporters in the folklore business cheered his prescient anticipation of a "folklife studies" approach—Herbert Halpert's *Journal of American Folklore* obituary praises *The Ozarks* and *Ozark Mountain Folks* as providing "not the first folklife description of a North American region, but certainly one of the richest."[3] By this accolade Halpert means to praise the wide range of Randolph's survey. After first sampling the "great many" topics addressed—"from the settlement of the area and the role of women to descriptions of a singing-school and a farm sale, along with chapters on dialect, folksongs and singers, folk beliefs, witchcraft, etc."—Halpert describes Randolph's approach as "holistic," placing the author "too far ahead of his time" to garner "proper appreciation" from "the few American folklorists of the day." These superannuated gents, trapped in the perspectives of a Eurocentric antiquarianism, were focused on "selective text collecting [read Child ballads] in a few genres [read music and verbal lore]." The new guy on the block, for all his lack of clubby credentials, had left the academics in the dust—"their folklore interests were far more limited than his."[4]

Randolph himself stressed his book's connections to the discipline of anthropology: "I wanted to be an anthropologist," he said in 1980, "to write popular books on anthropology." In the same conversation, he was more specific about his inspirations: "Vanguard asked me to write a book about the Ozarks like Margaret Mead's *Coming of Age in Samoa*."[5] All this is certainly plausible; the two books exhibit similarities sufficient to support the idea that the aspiring anthropologist had at least had a look at Mead's work (published in 1928, three years before *The Ozarks*). Anthropological aspirations were nothing new either; over a decade and a half (from 1915 to 1929) Randolph repeatedly failed to convince Franz Boas at Columbia, the discipline's reigning kingpin, of the worthiness of his Ozark studies as the focus of a doctoral dissertation. (Mead, better connected, not only held a Columbia PhD but sent *Coming of Age in Samoa* to the world fronted by a Boas introduction.)

The most important models for *The Ozarks*, however, came not from far off Pacific islands but the Appalachian Mountains just to the east. The most important of these was Horace Kephart's *Our Southern Highlanders*, first published in 1913, which served Randolph at levels ranging from subject matter and tone down to line-level syntax and phrasing.[6] Kephart, like Randolph, was an outdoorsman and a professional writer, not an academic—*Camping and Woodcraft, Camp Cookery,* and *Sporting Firearms* preceded *Our Southern Highlanders*. Kephart campaigned for the establishment of Great Smoky Mountains National Park and helped lay out the Appalachian Trail. A Tennessee mountain is named in his honor. He never applied to Boas.

Vance Randolph, then, as he bent to his first major book, approached it as a professional writer with ethnographic aspirations, assigned by his publishers to emulate a popular work buttressed by serious academic credentials. The result is a strange and complex mix—the ahead-of-its-time prescience of its sweeping "folklife" range would inspire a generation of later folklorists even as its descents into hokey "these are the last" nostalgias, thumping "real Americans" cant, and (especially) lurid sexual asides would by turns dismay and outrage. The first two clichés mostly caught a pass in the early reviews—neither Scarborough nor Vestal had any problem with nostalgia (and the latter's reference to "immigrants" suggests susceptibility to the "real Americans" note). And Randolph sounds both notes loudly and clearly. He ends his opening chapter with a bizarre portrait of the "Ozark hill-billy" as a beleaguered "genuine American," a remnant figure "neither refined nor corrupted by the influence of European and Asiatic civilizations." "There are not many real Americans left now," he laments, staging the Ozarks as a threatened hideout where "our contemporary ancestors" are making "their last stand."[7]

The closely related "these are the last" note is no less prominent, recurring at intervals throughout the book—it closes the chapters on dialect ("a few more years and the hill people will be talking just like the rest of us"), and the Ozark play party ("another ten years, in my judgment, will see its total extinction in the Ozark country"), and the volume itself closes on a reprise of the imminent extinction of the "real American" himself ("native Ozarkers will soon give place to 'furriners,' and vanish like the Indians and the Bluff-Dwellers").[8]

But these standard clichés of the genre pale in comparison to the more infrequent but incomparably more vivid references to irregular sexual beliefs and practices casually dropped at intervals into the narrative. For example: "Every mountain girl knows that if she puts a drop of her menstrual fluid into a man's liquor he is certain to fall madly in love with her." Here's another sample: "Sexual acts between human beings and domestic animals are rather common in the Ozarks, and nearly every native believes that these unions are sometimes fruitful."[9] Every, nearly every—by such sly insertions, however preposterous the claim, Randolph positions such beliefs not at the relict margin but at the contemporary center.

All this, the bumptious jingoism, the schmaltzy elegiac notes, the kinky sex—they're tabloid fodder, and Randolph knew it. No doubt he thought they would boost sales. But there's also a deeper note, a coolly purposive rhetorical distancing. Born in 1892, he was a child of the respectable middle-class center in Pittsburg, Kansas, his father an attorney and small-town politician (Republican) and his mother a DAR stalwart and long-time head of the public library. But the son declared for the margins early, dropping out of high school for a pool-hall job and initiating his writing career with a stint at the *Appeal to Reason*, the then-famous Socialist Party newspaper published in nearby Girard.

He never really looked back, either, and *The Ozarks* introduces an author careful to present himself as neither native nor academic, a knowing but insistently unaffiliated gentleman visitor with a taste for rustic settings. He fills twenty pages with richly detailed reportage on Ozark dialect, only to sign off with a casual disclaimer: "But these questions must be left to the scientific students of dialect." An entire chapter is devoted in similar detail to "The Passing of the Play-Party," but here too the author exits with a self-effacing wave, leaving "all theoretical and scholarly considerations to specialists."[10] On some topics these moves are more emphatic, the generally sympathetic tone abandoned in favor of caricature—the discussion of a "typical brush-arbor service," for example, verges at several points upon open mockery: "'I'm saved! Praise God!' comes from old Jethro Tolliver, who is converted regularly every Autumn. . . . another brother keeps wringing his hands and yelling 'Jesus, oh, Jesus' in exactly the same tone he uses in calling his hogs."[11]

In *The Ozarks*, then, the Randolph whose enormous body of

work made him "the region's most famous chronicler" is fully on view for the first time. He's a slippery, singular figure, difficult to pin down. At once too rough-edged for the academy's comforts and too scholarly for a wholesale jump to the booster bandwagon, he ended up putting his lack of money where his wiseacre mouth was, spending most of his long span of days as a hand-to-mouth freelance writer. Brooks Blevins's summary assessment is both succinct and accurate, noting both his industry and his finally romantic sense of himself as connected to traditional Ozarkers by a shared marginality: "One cannot classify Randolph as a simple romantic," he concludes, "he was too savvy, even too ornery, for such pigeonholing."[12]

Amen. I first encountered Randolph in 1976, as a newly arrived assistant professor at the University of Arkansas in Fayetteville. I delayed my initial visit, imagining a retired professor and wondering if anything could be duller, but of course what I met was a codger, a self-described "hack writer." He was the merriest of bedridden men, brimming with hilarious tales. Of his soldiering in the First World War, for example, he was eloquent in the description of spectacularly varied illnesses (including mumps and orchitis) that kept him under medical care for most of his four-month tour of duty. "Just a handful of soldiers like me," he laughed, "and the damn government would be brought to its knees." Later on, when I inquired as to who he'd be backing in an upcoming presidential contest, he was gruffly dismissive—"I don't give a tinker's damn who gets elected," he said.[13]

I loved this note, knew at once I was in the presence of a perfect anti-mentor. Even as an oldster I retain a modicum of earnestness—I'll die with it, knowing it renders me gullible, occasionally vulnerable to salesmen (though rarely to politicians and never to clergymen). But I had more then, way too much, and Randolph was just the man to knock out the stuffing. It was joy and emancipation to listen to him, Sancho to a juvenile Quixote. Herds of sacred cows lay slaughtered in his wake.

So here's the "region's most famous chronicler," back again after nearly a century, addressing himself for the first time to the territory he would claim as his own. Thanks to the University of Arkansas Press for undertaking so worthy a project, and to series editor Brooks Blevins for the wisdom of including Vance Randolph's maverick, unmistakable voice.

ROBERT COCHRAN
*Center for Arkansas and Regional
Studies, University of Arkansas*

NOTES

1. The full range of Randolph's published writing is spelled out in Robert Cochran and Michael Luster, *For Love and for Money: The Writings of Vance Randolph* (Batesville, AR: Arkansas College Folklore Archive Publications, 1979).

2. Dorothy Scarborough, "Where the Eighteenth Century Lives On," *New York Times Book Review* (December 27, 1931), 54; Stanley Vestal, "Ridge-Runner Culture," *Saturday Review of Literature* 8 (December 26, 1931), 407–8.

3. Herbert Halpert, "Obituary: Vance Randolph (1892–1980)," *Journal of American Folklore* 94 (July-September, 1981), 346.

4. Halpert, "Obituary." 345, 345–46, 346. Halpert's use of "folklife" as a descriptor is potentially misleading, as the term refers in academic circles to programmatic initiatives originating in Scandinavia, central Europe (Austria, Switzerland) and the British isles (Ireland, Scotland, Wales) in the 1930s dedicated to a cultural anthropological approach to the whole range of traditional culture. New professional associations and regionally based societies and archives were established, new academic journals were founded, open-air museums were constructed, festivals were organized. American scholars, late to the party, were led by Pennsylvanians, who had a Pennsylvania Dutch

Folk Festival up and running in Kutztown by 1950 and the *Pennsylvania Folklife* journal in print by 1957. For a thorough if staidly written account see Don Yoder, "The Folklife Studies Movement," *Pennsylvania Folklife* (July, 1963), 43–56. Randolph couldn't have been less interested; what little he knew of shifts in academic fashion he found comic (though he could speedily assume a donnish tone with editors when it suited his immediate interests). Academic movers and shakers, from Boas in the teens and twenties to Richard Dorson in the fifties and sixties were deeply right to suspect his fundamental lack of serious commitment to their righteous causes. Folk festivals were a big deal in the United States in the 1930s, though even here Randolph's involvement was brief, turbulent, and at last unsatisfying. For the whole (hilarious) story see Robert Cochran, *Vance Randolph: An Ozark Life* (Urbana: University of Illinois Press, 1985), 133–40.

The fundamental accuracy of Halpert's description, however, is highlighted by comparison with David Hackett Fischer's influential *Albion's Seed*, published more than half a century later (in 1989). Fischer's volume tracks "four British folkways" from regional origins in England to their counterparts in North America, describing each in turn according to twenty-four "folkways" (or twenty-six in a second listing) defined as normative systems of "values, customs and meanings." Straightforward lists are provided in the introductory matter. Application of Fischer's "folkways" to *The Ozarks* shows Randolph, though he has nothing of Fischer's systematic approach, addressing himself in some fashion to almost every one. See David Hackett Fischer, *Albion's Seed: Four British Folkways in America* (New York: Oxford University Press, 1989), 7, 8–9, 11.

5. Cochran, *Vance Randolph*, 99.

6. Others in this vein include Josiah H. Combs, *The Kentucky Highlanders* (Lexington, KY: J. L. Richardson, 1913), and John C. Campbell, *The Southern Highlander and His Homeland* (New York: Russell Sage Foundation, 1921). Randolph cited all three in the 1920s; for details of Randolph's borrowings see Cochran, *Vance Randolph*, 115–17. Kephart's volume, like Randolph's (and unlike Mead's) featured photographs of its subjects. Randolph's inclusion of tune transcriptions for his musical selections was cutting-edge practice in 1931—W. K. McNeil singled it out in praising his four-volume *Ozark Folksongs*, which commenced publication in 1946, fifteen years after *The Ozarks*. See W. K. McNeil, "Introduction," *Ozark Folksongs Collected and Edited by Vance Randolph*, Vol. I (Columbia: University of Missouri Press, 1980), 27. *The Ozarks*, incidentally, is sometimes identified as the earliest book-length study of the region. This is mistaken—that honor belongs to Carl Ortwin Sauer (1889–1975), the great Missouri-born cultural geographer whose *The Geography of the Ozark Highland of Missouri* appeared a decade earlier,

in 1920. As his title makes clear, Sauer's Ozarks is centered in Missouri; Arkansas is mentioned only in passing.

7. Vance Randolph, *The Ozarks: An American Survival of Primitive Society* (New York: The Vanguard Press, 1931), 22.

8. Randolph, *The Ozarks*, 86, 165, 310. Speaking of "Bluff-Dwellers," contemporary readers should be warned that many of Randolph sources (and some of his attitudes) have long since been supplanted or discredited. A good presentation of current scholarship on Ozark prehistory is "Native American Prehistory," the second chapter of Jeannie Wayne, Tom DeBlack, George Sabo, and Morris Arnold, *Arkansas: A Narrative History*, 2nd ed. (Fayetteville, University of Arkansas Press, 2013). Randolph's treatment of moonshining should be supplemented by Ben F. Johnson III's *John Barleycorn Must Die: The War against Drink in Arkansas* (Fayetteville: University of Arkansas Press, 2005). Brooks Blevins's *Ghost of the Ozarks: Murder and Memory in the Upland South* (Urbana: University of Illinois Press, 2012) focuses on the spectacular Connie Franklin saga (mentioned in passing by Randolph), but also includes informative discussions of moonshining and the issue of Ozark peonage (both topics addressed by Randolph). Study of the play party has also benefited from more recent scholarship—see Alan L. Spurgeon, *Waltz the Hall: The American Play Party* (Oxford: The University Press of Mississippi, 2005). Randolph was no hater, but his attitudes toward women and African Americans were often patronizing (though he was strikingly philo-Semitic). One cringes today at the easy use of n-word formulations and jocular references to women—there is for example his report on DeSoto's failed searches in the future Arkansas for cities of gold; his party "sacked village after village but got only robes and furs and women for their pains."

9. Randolph, *The Ozarks*, 89, 105. Such tales go way back, and American instances are certainly not concentrated in the Ozarks. Two of seventeenth-century New England's most prominent chroniclers, William Bradford and Cotton Mather, provide vivid accounts of legal proceedings resulting in the execution of two citizens for just such "unions." In both instances the "domestic animals" involved (neither zoophile was monogamous) were also slaughtered, in accordance with scriptural injunction. For details see Cotton Mather, *Magnalia Christi Americana* (Hartford: Silas Andrus & Son, 1853) Vol. II, 405–6 and William Bradford, *Of Plymouth Plantation* (New York: Capricorn Books, 1962), 202–3. Contemporary accounts are available on the Internet—celebrity Arizona sheriff Joe Arpaio busted a Pennsylvania man in 2015 for crossing into his jurisdiction for a tryst with a mare, and Mississippi authorities arrested a Greenwood man in 2011 for "unnatural intercourse" after four "show hogs" came down with vaginal infections. For the former, search under "Pennsylvania man arrested,

Arpaio, horse;" for the Mississippi story, search "Greenwood man caught, show hogs." Finally, for an absolutely titillation-free if strikingly oblique first-person account see maverick preacher Will D. Campbell's riveting memoir, *Brother to a Dragonfly* (New York: Bloomsbury, 2000), 27.

10. Randolph, *The Ozarks*, 86, 141.

11. Randolph, *The Ozarks*, 45, 48.

12. Brooks Blevins, *Hill Folks: A History of Arkansas Ozarkers and Their Image* (Chapel Hill: University of North Carolina Press, 2002), 137.

13. The dismissal of politics is reported from memory; for the remark about wartime "service" see Cochran, *Vance Randolph*, 57.

THE OZARKS

AUTHOR'S PREFACE

THE OZARK COUNTRY AND ITS people cannot be adequately described in any one book, nor can any one writer do justice to the subject in all of its fascinating aspects. I have chosen to write about such matters as seem to me diverting and picturesque, and likely to interest the general reader. This book, therefore, is not concerned with the progressive element in the Ozark towns, nor with the prosperous valley farmers, who have been more or less modernized by recent contacts with civilization. It deals rather with the "hill-billy" or "ridge-runner" of the more isolated sections, and it is based upon some ten years of association with people of this type. Every statement in the book is intended to be taken quite seriously and literally; there is not a line of fiction or of intentional exaggeration in it.

It is impossible to acknowledge specifically the assistance which I have received from a variety of sources, but a special word of appreciation is due Mrs. Isabel Spradley, Van Buren, Arkansas; Mr. Charles J. Finger, Fayetteville, Arkansas; Mrs. Cora Pinkley-Call, Eureka Springs, Arkansas; Dr. F. M. Goodhue, Mena, Arkansas; Mrs. Rose Wilder Lane, Mansfield, Missouri; Mrs. Eloise Chapman, Anderson, Missouri; and Mr. Maurice V. Lamberson, Pineville, Missouri. These individuals have contributed a great deal of valuable information, but they are in no way responsible for my interpretation of the data, nor for the

character of the book in general. Parts of several chapters originally appeared in *The Journal of American Folk-Lore, Ozark Life,
American Speech, Forest and Stream, Dialect Notes* and *The New York
Times,* and I am grateful to the publishers of these journals for
permission to reprint the material here.

V.R.

CHAPTER I.

Old Trails and Campfires

LOOK AT A RELIEF MAP of the United States, and you will see the Ozark country standing out like an egg-shaped excrescence in a vast central plain—the only mountainous region between the Southern Appalachians and the Rockies. The Ozark hills are rugged in places, and extremely beautiful, but they are called mountains only by grace of contrast to the interminable prairies which environ them. They are nowhere much more than two thousand feet above sea level. It is difficult to define the exact limits of the Ozark country, but for our present purpose it begins in southern Missouri somewhere south of Jefferson City, runs east as far as Poplar Bluff, west to the vicinity of Talequah, Oklahoma, and south to a point a little beyond Mena, Arkansas. The hills south of the Arkansas River are called the Ouachitas, and differ geologically from the Ozarks proper, but the natives do not concern themselves with this distinction, and neither shall we. The whole Ozark region, as here defined, is about three hundred miles long and about one hundred and fifty miles wide; a country of scattered peaks and short rocky ridges, smooth pine-clad contours and skylines, winding green valleys and clear, swift streams.

Practically unknown to the readers of guide-books—even the great Baedeker devotes only two short sentences to the whole region—the Ozark plateau has recently come into considerable favor as a summer playground, but the tourists who speed along our splendid new highways and idle about our summer-resorts are really missing the best that the hill country has to offer. For the most interesting features of the region are the people who live here, and the most picturesque of the Ozark natives are seldom seen by the casual summer visitor.

The vociferous individuals who sell hotdogs and gasoline to the tourists are exactly like those who sell similar commodities along the highways of New Jersey and Ohio and California, but the real hillfolk are very different. One has only to leave the broad auto roads and go back a few miles into the hills to find himself in a different environment, among people who have until very recently been curiously isolated from the outside world, and whose way of living has changed very little since their sturdy forbears wandered west from the southern Appalachians more than a century ago. There are men in the Ozarks today who sleep in cord beds and hunt with muzzle-loading rifles; there are women who still use spinning-wheels and weave cloth on home-made looms; there are minstrels who sing old English ballads brought over by the seventeenth-century colonists; there are old settlers who believe firmly in witchcraft and all sorts of medieval superstitions; there are people who speak an Elizabethan dialect so outlandish that it is well-nigh unintelligible to the ordinary tourist from Chicago and points east. The typical Ozark native differs so widely from the average urban American that when the latter visits the hill country he feels himself among an alien people. The hillman recognizes the difference, too, and refers to all outsiders as "furriners", whether they come from North Dakota or South Germany.

When I first came to the Ozarks my mountaineer neighbors interested me not at all, but I was fascinated by the relics
of savage peoples who hunted through these hills in ages past.
Almost every sharp-eyed visitor is struck by the abundance of
Indian artifacts; in almost any ploughed field, after a shower,
one can pick up flint arrowpoints and spear-heads by the dozen,
and at some old village sites the ground is literally covered by
arrow-makers' chips. Numerous flint axes and tomahawks have
been found also, and the rounded stones used as pestles in
grinding maize are not uncommon. Many Indian burials have
been unearthed, some of them containing beads of European
manufacture, and metal ornaments as well as the inevitable flint
weapons. Specialists in these matters believe that the Caddoan
tribes came into the Ozarks from the South about 1000 A.D.,
but the Osages were the first historical inhabitants of the region,
and remained here in considerable numbers until about 1825,
when they ceded the last of their Ozark holdings to the United
States Government and moved west into the Indian Territory.

Centuries before the coming of the Osage Indians the Ozark
hills belonged to a very different people known as Bluff-Dwellers,
whose bones and primitive handiwork may still be found by the
visitor who cares to dig in the shallow limestone shelters or "rock
houses" along the mountain streams. These people passed away
too soon to be mentioned even in the Osage traditions, and
their very existence was unknown until about 1903, when a
party of archeologists under Dr. Charles Peabody unearthed the
first Bluff-Dweller remains in Jacobs Cavern, McDonald County,
Missouri. More recently Mr. M. R. Harrington made a series of
excavations in the vicinity, and his collection of Bluff-Dweller
skeletons and artifacts is now exhibited by the Heye Museum of
the American Indian, in New York.

The Bluff-Dwellers did not use the bow and arrow as modern

Indians do, but flung their flint-tipped spears from a grooved throwing-stick, identical with the *atlatl* found in the Aztec ruins of Mexico. Their favorite meats were vension and turkey, but the bones of bear, elk and buffalo are also plentiful in their refuse heaps, and they did not disdain turtles and many smaller animals. They made hoes of stone and mussel-shells fastened to wooden handles, raised corn and beans and squashes, and ground their grain in sandstone mortars. They gathered acorns, chinquapins, walnuts, hickory nuts and hazelnuts, and stored them in grass baskets or in pits lined with coarse matting. They made water-tight vessels by daubing their baskets with pitch, and also used crude pots of clay, tempered with sand and crushed mussel-shells. The bodies of their dead were doubled up in shallow graves lined with deerskin, and many have been found with clothing, dried skin and mummified flesh still clinging to the bones. Some of them wore robes made of feathers twisted on strings, but many bodies were clad in deer-skin tanned with the hair on, while caps and sandals woven of grass seem to have been the vogue. One puzzling thing about these Bluff-Dweller skeletons is that several skulls show an artificial frontal flattening, probably produced by a tight band about the newborn infant's head—a deformation common in several South American tribes. Except for a few specimens from Vancouver Island, these flattened skulls are the first ever discovered in North America, according to Dr. Ales Hrdlicka of the United States National Museum.

The fossil bones of the great wooly elephant-like creatures called mastodons have been found in many parts of Missouri and Arkansas, but until very recently it was believed that these beasts became extinct long before the appearance of human beings in the New World. The first bit of evidence to the contrary was the discovery in Jacobs Cavern of the mineralized leg-bone of a deer, upon which is engraved something very like a mastodon.

I was fortunate enough to be present when this carving was unearthed, and I notified various anthropologists. Mr. N. C. Nelson and Dr. Clark Wissler, of the American Museum of Natural History, came out from New York to examine the specimen and the cavern in which it was found, as did Dr. Vernon C. Allison of the United States Bureau of Mines. Mr. Nelson, after considering the matter for a month or so, announced his conviction that the mastodon carving was a plain fraud; Dr. Wissler was much less outspoken than Mr. Nelson, but apparently inclined to a similar view; Dr. Allison, after an exhaustive objective study of the artifact and the various cavern deposits, concluded that the engraving is authentic, and has since published numerous articles in defense of this opinion. Several recent discoveries in the vicinity seem to support the claim that the Jacobs Cavern carving is genuine, but it must be admitted that the whole problem is still far from a satisfactory solution.

By far the most important result of the archeological investigation of the Ozark caverns was Dr. Allison's now famous study of stalagmitic growth—the latest scientific attempt to assign actual dates to prehistoric events, and to recover a chronology which will bridge the gap between historic and prehistoric records. This matter has been discussed at length in the technical journals, of course, with impressive charts and graphs and mathematical formulae, but the general principles of the thing seemed simple enough as Dr. Allison described it to me beside the campfire in Jacobs Cavern.

Stalagmites are simply rounded pillars of whitish stone, very common in limestone caverns, and until very recently they did not arouse any particular scientific interest. A stalagmite's development begins when rain water seeps through dead leaves, rotten wood, or any other decaying vegetable matter, until it becomes charged with carbon dioxide—the same gas which produces the little bubbles in soda-water and champagne. Water charged with carbon dioxide dissolves limestone, so that by the time the carbonated water trickles down through the limestone rocks into some subterranean cavern it is strongly saturated with lime. As each drop of this lime-water evaporates it leaves a thin crust of lime on the cavern floor, and thus the stalagmite is built up layer by layer into an inverted icicle of limestone. So much for stalagmites in general.

When Dr. Allison visited Jacobs Cavern with the other archeologists to examine the mastodon carving, he observed that several flint spear-heads, fragments of bone and bits of charcoal were embedded in one of the stalagmites, which proves that human beings lived in the cavern while the stalagmite was growing. Now, quoth he, if it were possible to determine the age of this particular stalagmite, we could tell exactly how long ago these cavemen lived in the cavern! And with this consideration in mind he began his study of the laws which govern stalagmitic growth.

Allison's work with stalagmites growing under laboratory conditions was carried out in an experimental mine near Pittsburgh, Pennsylvania, and represents nearly two years of the most rigid scientific research. The results of the investigation may be summarized briefly as follows: Stalagmitic growth depends upon rainfall, air-movement, temperature, and the amount of lime in the water, so that one can tell by the form of a stalagmite what climatic conditions prevailed during the period of its formation. Moreover, since the air contains more dust in the dry part of the year than it does in the rainy season, and since this dust deposit produces a darker layer in the stalagmite, it is possible to determine the stalagmite's age simply by counting the annual layers, which are very similar to the annual growth-rings of a tree.

When this research was complete, Dr. Allison made another journey to the Ozarks, cut out a section of the Jacobs Cavern stalagmite weighing fifteen hundred pounds, and shipped it back to Pittsburgh, where it was subjected to a more intensive examination. The form of this stalagmite registered a long period of cool, rainy weather, which began very suddenly and gradually gave way to a warmer and drier climate, while a careful count of the annual layers indicated that the rainy season lasted over a period of twelve hundred and thirteen years. However, there was nothing in the stalagmite to show in what year this long rainy period began, nor when it ended, and the indefatigable Allison was forced to seek this information elsewhere.

The key to the problem was at last discovered in the structure of tree trunks-a matter which has been very thoroughly investigated by Dr. A. E. Douglass and his students. Trees not only add a growth ring for every year of their lives, but the rings produced in wet years are thicker than those produced in dry, so that a growing tree records the weather very much as a stalagmite does. A California redwood, which was cut down and exhibited at the Chicago World's Fair in 1892, was found to be thirty-two hundred years old. The rings of this great tree show an indubitable record of a cool rainy period which lasted for slightly more than twelve hundred years. Since Allison knew exactly when this tree stopped growing, he had only to count the annual rings in order to get the limiting dates of this prolonged rainy season; it began in 1226 B.C. and ended about the beginning of the Christian era. Substantially similar records have been found in thousands of other tree trunks, and there is other evidence that this condition was general all over the northern hemisphere; therefore, Allison concluded, it represents the same extended rainy season recorded by the Jacobs Cavern stalagmite.

Human beings certainly lived in the Ozarks long before the

bad weather began in 1226 B.C., but we know very little about
them, except that they were not cave-dwellers. Probably they
lived in bark houses or skin tepees, just as the modern village
Indians do. When the rains came, however, and the cold winds
swept down from the north, the people evidently took refuge in
the caverns. As Dr. Allison pointed out, it is significant that only
those caves which face the south show any evidences of human
habitation. It was the cold and wet weather, according to Dr.
Allison, which caused the Bluff-Dwellers to seek shelter in the
caverns, and it was certainly the wet weather which made the
stalagmites grow. We know that the Jacobs Cavern stalagmite was
growing during the period of occupation because man-made
objects are found at various places in the stalagmitic material,
and their positions relative to the annual layers give us almost
the exact dates of their deposition; as the weather became gradually milder, the cavemen doubtless spent more of their time in
the open, and in the same period the stalagmitic growth proceeded less rapidly. The stalagmitic record carries us down only
to about 13 B.C., since in that year the stalagmite reached the
overhanging roof of the cavern, and the deposits from that time
forward are irregularly distributed and illegible. The cool rainy
period did not come to a sudden end in 13 B.C., however. The
growth-ring record of the big redwood trunk shows that the
weather moderated very slowly indeed, and that it was several
hundred years before the last climatic effects of the great Ice
Age had definitely passed. By the beginning of the sixth century A.D., however, the Ozark summers were certainly drier and
probably as warm as they are today, and the cavemen doubtless
returned to a life in the open. There has been very little stalagmitic growth in this country since the sixth century, and there
is no evidence that any of the Ozark caverns have been contin-
uously occupied since that time.

The Entrance to Saltpeter Cave

This study is by no means complete. There are still many unexplored caverns in the hill country and it is quite possible that some further evidence may be unearthed in the near future. All of these caves and rock shelters should be excavated by competent archeologists, and it is to be hoped that the men and the money necessary for this undertaking may soon be available.

The first Europeans to see the Ozarks were Spaniards, probably the followers of Francisco de Coronado, who are said to have passed through the hill country about 1540, in search of the fabled golden city of Quivera. A brave show they must

have made, too; clad in shining armor, mounted upon richly
caparisoned horses, armed with swords, lances and primitive
firearms, it is no wonder that the poor Indians fled before them
everywhere. They lived very well on venison, turkey and the flesh
of the "humped cows", but found no treasure at all; they sacked
village after village, but got only robes and furs and women for
their pains. Hernando de Soto visited the Ozark hills some years
later, interested chiefly in robbing the Indians and converting
them to Christianity. He fought Osages all through the White
River country, and was defeated in a great battle near the present site of Jacksonport, Arkansas. After this calamity he spent
some time in prospecting for gold in the Boston Range of the
Ozarks, crossing the Arkansas River near Dardanelle Rock. Still
farther south he bathed in "a strange lake of very hot water" at
the place now famous as Hot Springs, Arkansas.

Later on many other Spaniards and Frenchmen came,
among them the redoubtable Du Tisne, whose exploits have
been the basis for so many wild stories. When an Indian threatened to scalp him it is said that Du Tisne pulled off his wig and
threw it on the ground, shouting that he would call down the
fires of heaven on anybody who dared to touch a hair of it. He
did call down the fires of heaven, in a sense, when he ignited
some tinder with a burning-glass, and he astonished the natives
by burning a clear liquid which appeared to be water, but was
really *eau de vie*. Some of these early Frenchmen are responsible
for the name Ozarks, too—it was originally *Aux Arcs*, the name
of one of their trading-posts on the Arkansas River.

The last of the Spanish caravans came up from New Mexico
in 1720, but when the Indians learned that these people were
enemies of the French they killed them all, except a priest who
somehow escaped to tell the story of the massacre. A legend
is still current that just before the attack the Spaniards buried

a vast treasure, which they had obtained from some unknown source, and poor deluded hillmen are still digging for it in many widely separated sections of the Ozark country.

The first American hunters and traders wandered into the Ozarks before 1800, but they were few in number and made no permanent settlements, the nearest exclusively American villages being in the territory now included in Cape Girardeau and Perry Counties, Missouri. The great Daniel Boone himself spent a winter in what is now central Missouri, at a place called Boone's Lick, and is believed to have made several hunting trips into the Ozark hills of northern Arkansas.

It appears that there was never very much serious fighting between American whites and Indians in the hill country proper. The Ozark region was a part of the vast area purchased from the French in 1803, and the Osages relinquished the last of their rights about 1825, most of them moving west into what is now Oklahoma. Then came white settlers in considerable numbers, largely from the mountain districts of Tennessee, Kentucky, Virginia and North Carolina—nearly all old-timers of English stock, descended from the early colonists. Oxcarts and old-fashioned linchpin wagons, with strange boat-shaped boxes, carried their scanty belongings on the long trek over the mountains; flatboats ferried them across the Mississippi. Their material heirlooms were not very numerous, but they brought the manners and customs of their mountain forbears with them to their new homes, and settled down to a sort of life very much like that which they had left in the Appalachians. The Ozark country is, in a sense, only a small edition of the Appalachian highlands, just as the bluegrass region of Kentucky is only a kind of transplanted Virginia.

The early settlers did not bother much about the legal ownership of their land—they just built their cabins where they pleased, without troubling to record an entry, although it appears that they could have obtained perfectly good titles from the government by paying about fourteen dollars, thus securing the land to their children. Fourteen dollars was a lot of money in those days, however, and there seemed to be plenty of land for everybody. Many a mountain boy has discovered on the death of his parents that he did not inherit the old farm at all—it still belonged to Uncle Sam. Some shrewd hillmen homesteaded their land rightly enough, but before the time came to patent it the owner relinquished his rights, and another member of the family entered on the same piece of ground. By these successive entries it was possible for a family to hold land for several generations without paying any taxes. I am told of families still living on farms which they have occupied since the early fifties, without ever having had a complete title!

Many of the pioneers settled on rich valley land at first, but most of them sold out later and moved back into the hills. They were traditional hillmen after all and their wants were few and simple. The hill land was sufficiently productive for all their needs. The only plow in use was the "bull tongue", which has been described as "a sharp stick with an iron rim on it", and this was usually pulled by a yoke of oxen. Some farmers made wooden harrows, but many merely "drug" the ground with a bunch of green boughs. The crop was all cultivated by hand with the hoe, and it appears that the women and children did a great share of the work. Corn was, and still is, the principal crop, but some wheat was grown on the "balds", and most hillmen put in a few rows of "taters" and a little garden-truck and tobacco. The Ozark hillsides are singularly adapted for fruit, and many of the pioneers set out little peach and apple orchards.

Some of them brought pigs, too, and these seemed to thrive and multiply without any care or feeding; when the hillman

wanted pork he took down his rifle and stalked a "razor-back"
just as he would a deer. The early settlers had few cattle, and
kept sheep only for wool; not many of the hillfolk will eat mutton if they can possibly get any other sort of meat. A little cotton
was grown, but only as much as the women could spin and weave
into cloth, and use for filling quilts and "coverlids". These matters were not taken very seriously by the menfolks, anyhow. The
first Ozarker was a hunter and fisherman rather than a tiller of
the soil, and as long as the woods abounded in deer and turkeys
he was accustomed to live largely upon wild meat, and quite willing to wear buckskin if no wool or cotton clothing was at hand.
In fact, the old-timers tell me that they usually preferred the
buckskin, as the rough jeans woven by the pioneer women had
a texture very much like that of fine sandpaper, which did not
make for comfort in a country where underwear was practically
unknown.

As time went on more people came west from Tennessee
and Kentucky, and a few drifted down from Illinois and other
Northern states, until many of the Ozark settlements were more
populous in the sixties than they are today. At the beginning of
the Civil War period the hillmen were predominately Southern
in their sympathies and traditions, but the truth is that most of
them took very little interest in the rumors of war which reached
their isolated settlements. The typical Ozarker in those days was
concerned solely with local affairs. He was always ready to fight
for his personal liberty, and was fiercely loyal to the interests of
his family and his clan but he knew little and cared less about
matters of national policy. The shadowy government in far-off
Washington touched him very lightly, so why should he be disturbed by this talk of secession? And the slavery question was
of even less importance, for the pioneers had neither slaves
nor prejudices against them. Even today there are many grown

men and women in the Ozarks who have never seen a Negro. There were some red-hot secessionists in the hills, of course, and even a few men who openly sympathized with the Union but the great majority of the hillmen went about their affairs quite unconcerned, and paid no attention whatever to the gathering war-clouds.

When the first armed troops appeared in the Ozarks, however, the whole situation was changed at once. Some of the young men enlisted in the regular fashion, but large numbers simply "tuck t' th' hills" and made savage war on Federals and Confederates alike. Ancient feuds broke out anew, and under cover of all this military excitement men shot down their old neighbors, burned their cabins, and stole their property. Reenforced by deserters from both armies, these "bushwhackers" kept the hill country in constant terror all through the war period, and bitter hatreds were engendered between certain families and neighborhood groups which persist even to the present day. These were bad times for the hillfolk, especially for the women and children. The following passages are from a stenographic report of my interview with an old woman near White Rock, Missouri, not far from the Pea Ridge battlefield:

> "Hit shore was mighty hard for us gals endurin' o' th' war. Th' boys had all tuck t' th' hills, an' th' horses was all gone, an' nothin' for we-uns t' eat, nohow . . . Atter while they got t' killin' ol' men even, so Paw he lit a shuck for th' timber, an' bushed up thar till th' war was plumb done. I warn't full growed then, only jest teen-age, but me an' Sis made two craps 'ith a yoke o' cowcritters.
>
> "Plowin's turrible hard on a gal's feet, an' we didn't have no shoes noway, but Sis she kilt a dawg an' made us some big moccasins out'n th' hide. We couldn't make out t' tan th' leather nohow—th' soap was all gone long ago—so

I had t' put them moccasins in th' spring branch at night, t' keep 'em saft like. Gawd, but they shore was cold an' wet of a mornin'! An' stink . . . they was jest plumb rotten!

"I mind when ol' Sterlin' Price was a-raidin', th' Choctaw Injuns was with him, an' they et up ever' last stalk o' sugar-corn even—jest all set down an' peeled it an' chawed it for th' sweet. We-uns shore didn't have no long sweetenin' thet Winter!

"They tuck th' oxens, too, but they left a Injun pony, shot plumb through th' hips an' hurt too bad t' foller. Hit got well atter while, but it warn't no good for plowin'. Hit was willin' enough, seemed like, but it never was broke right, an' bein' raised with th' Injuns thataway, it couldn't understand nothin' we-uns said. Paw he snuck in one day— two big pistols a-hangin' onto him, an' his rifle-gun in his hand—an' tried for t' holp out, but he couldn't make th' critter plow, neither . . .. We did make a leetle crap o' corn thet year, but th' dang Yankees come an' tuck most of it.

"I recollect onct a gang o' bushwhackers rid up, an' one of 'em he says: 'Wal, we run onto your ol' Pappy out in th' hills this mornin'-left him a-layin' thar deader'n a ol' shoe.' An' I says, says I: 'How many o' you-uns did he git?' 'Nary one,' says he. 'Shucks,' says I, 'thet warn't my Pappy, noway!' An' shore 'nough, hit warn't—he crope in for his vittles th' very next night!

"But two o' my own cousins did git kilt right in front of our house. I was a-feedin' 'em, an' they was shot down as they run for th' horses. Th' Yankees they jest laughed an' left 'em a-layin' thar in th' road, so me an' Sis had t' dig graves an' bury 'em . . . Hit shore was turrible, them days."

I think that this is probably a very fair picture of wartime conditions in most parts of the Ozarks, but it appears that there were some backwoods families so isolated that neither troops nor bushwhackers ever disturbed them very much. My grandfather, who fought at the battle of Pea Ridge, Arkansas, in 1862, met men almost within range of the cannon who had never even heard of the War! There are many people still living in the hills who remember these matters quite distinctly. I have met a number of old men who were regularly enlisted in the Confederate Army, and many more who were unofficially active in the guerrilla warfare of the period. Most of these latter, however, are still reluctant to discuss their exploits, and in some neighborhoods there seems to be a general desire to avoid all reference to the Civil War, as a subject uncomfortably close to the still existing feuds and family hatreds which grew out of it.

The last sixty years have brought some changes to the Ozarks, of course, but it is astonishing how insignificant these changes are, as compared with those which have occurred in more enlightened parts of the country. With the possible exception of some remote districts in the southern Appalachians, the "hill-billy" section of the Ozark country is the most backward and deliberately unprogressive region in the United States. It is only in such isolated places that we find the traditional American nowadays, neither refined nor corrupted by the influence of European and Asiatic civilizations. There are not many real Americans left now, and we do not understand them any more. The Ozark hill-billy is a genuine American—that is why he seems so alien to most tourists. In a sense it is true that the American people are making their last stand in the wilderness, and it is here, if anywhere, that we must go to meet our contemporary ancestors in the flesh.

CHAPTER II.

The Hill-Billy at Home

THE MOUNTAIN MAN'S CABIN IS his castle, and even though the door stands hospitably open, it is very bad form for a stranger to approach it unheralded. Usually the barking of pot-licker dogs sounds the alarm, otherwise the traveller is expected to stop a little distance away and "holler" until someone comes out to look him over. However unprepossessing, he is almost invariably invited to "light down an' set a spell", for even the poorest and stingiest of backwoodsmen feels himself bound by the tradition of indiscriminate hospitality.

Once inside the cabin, the "furriner" is usually struck by the untidy state of affairs, and often concludes that the hillman's wife must be a very slatternly housekeeper, but the fault is really in the cabin itself. Log houses are always built of green wood, because it is so much easier to work than seasoned timber, and this sort of material soon warps and sags out of shape. Great cracks appear in the floor, mud "chinkin'" falls out from between the logs, and the clapboards cup and twist so that the roof nearly always leaks. All of the old-time cabins are dirty through no particular fault of the housewife—it is almost impossible to keep such places clean. Recently some summer colonists have built beautiful houses of peeled pine logs and seasoned timber, but such cabins are more expensive than frame dwellings nowadays, and the hillman who has money to spend prefers a "box-house" of sawed native lumber, with a cheap tar-paper roof.

The old settlers built their cabins of good hardwood logs, hewn from virgin timber with patient blows of the choppin'-axe. Every log was notched or "scribed" at the ends, so as to fit closely together when set into position. It was no small task to roll the logs up the skids, and a good "scriber" or "corner-man" saved a deal of trouble by notching the ends so that they slipped easily into place at the first trial, and did not have to be refitted. In the best cabins the logs were fastened together with wooden pins driven into auger-holes, or by big hand-forged iron spikes. The spaces between the logs were filled with "chinkin'", which consisted of sticks or stones set in clay, or in a mixture of clay and moss. The door was of heavy rough boards hung on wooden hinges, fastened by a hard-wood latch. The bar was usually operated by a string, which could be left hanging outside or pulled in through a hole as desired. The roof was made of "shakes" or clapboards, about three times the size of ordinary shingles, and fully an inch in thickness. These were rived out of straight-grained oak with a tool called a frow, the "shakes" being split off as the frow was struck by a wooden maul. These heavy shingles were held in place by pegs or short nails, and were always laid in the dark of the moon, since every hillman knows that "shakes" put on in the light of the moon will warp and cause the roof to leak. Most of the old cabins have puncheon floors—a puncheon is a log split in two, with the flat side up—but I have lived in several which had no floor at all save the rocky ground.

Few of the early cabins were provided with porches or "galleries" as the hillfolk call them, and many were without windows.

Such windows as they had were very small, and covered with heavy wooden shutters. There was no glass, but sometimes the hillman scraped a piece of rawhide thin and stretched it tightly over the opening; when this rawhide was well greased it was weatherproof, and admitted a considerable amount of light. The old-timers say that a wildcat skin, boiled in lye to render it translucent, was really better than glass, because no skulking enemy could peep into the house, or locate the occupants unless they passed between the window and the light. I have seen more modern cabins with glass window-panes, but even today the builder seldom bothers to fix the window so that it can be opened; he just nails the sash fast to the wall, and lets it go at that. The typical log cabin has only one room, but sometimes a lean-to of rough boards is added later, and some of the larger houses have lofts, accessible by means of a rude ladder nailed against the wall. Children sometimes sleep in the loft, which is also used to store dried fruit, peppers, beans, onions and medicinal "yarbs", all strung and suspended from the rafters. Occasionally one sees two cabins built close together, and connected by a roofed-over gallery or "dogrun", but this type of architecture is not as common in the Ozarks as it is farther South.

The most conspicuous articles of furniture are the beds, usually of the cord type, in which a rope does duty for springs, with a featherbed or tick filled with cornshucks serving as a mattress. I have seen a few really beautiful bedsteads of cherry or walnut, with massive turned posts, but most of the oldest ones are crude homemade affairs. Sometimes there are little trundle-beds for the smaller children, so arranged that they can be slipped out of sight beneath the big beds in the daytime. Next in importance are several straight-backed chairs with split hickory bottoms, a rude table and a shelf or two for the water-bucket and provisions. A rough mantel-piece or "fire-board", several wooden pegs upon which to hang clothing, two forked sticks or deer

A Typical Mountain Cabin

antlers for the inevitable rifle, and the simple furniture of the mountain man's castle is complete.

The great fireplace is located at one end of the cabin, and occasionally there are two chimneys, which provide a fireplace at either end of the house. Nearly all of them are built of carefully selected limestone slabs—the Ozarker does not favor the stick-and-mud chimneys so common in other parts of the South. Many of the oldest chimneys were made with a large piece of slate or shale at the base, but I have never been able to find out just why this material was preferred. In the Winter time the fireplace provides light as well as heat, and in Summer the hillfolk go to bed at dusk, so that the problem of lighting troubles them very little. Nearly every cabin nowadays has a cheap kerosene lamp, however, for use in emergencies. Rusty candle-molds are to be found in many old houses, but the only candles I have ever seen used in the Ozarks were brought in by newcomers. Not long ago, however, I visited a home in which the only artificial light was a "slut"—simply a dish full of grease, with a twisted rag stuck in to serve as a wick.

Many of the hillfolk use cheap cookstoves nowadays, chiefly because these consume less wood, but the old-timers still prefer to cook their food at the open fireplace. Nearly all of the cooking is done in pots or kettles set upon the coals, or suspended from the potrack, which is a straight bar of iron built into the chimney; the swinging crane so common in old New England houses was never widely used in the Ozarks. Cornbread is usually cooked in heavy skillets or "Dutch ovens." The so-called johnny-cake is baked slowly on a grease-soaked "johnny-board" set up before the fire. In Winter time many people like "cracklin' bread", which is simply cornbread seasoned with bits of crisp brown pork.

Some of the pioneers ground their corn in the Indian fashion by placing it on a hollowed-out rock and pounding it with a stone pestle. I have seen several large stone mortars, said to have been made by the early settlers, but I suspect that they are of Indian manufacture, although the white hunters may have used them on occasion. In some cases the pioneers built "sweep-mills" in which the pestle was attached to a spring pole, but all such makeshifts soon gave way to little grist-mills run by water power, some of which are still in use. Another primitive means of converting corn into meal was by the use of a grater—a piece of tin roughened by a great number of nail-holes, and fastened

to a board. The housewife stuck one end of the board into a
kettle, and rubbed an ear of corn across the pierced metal until
she had meal enough for dinner. The grater is still used in some
places, particularly at the season when the corn is too tough for
roasting-ears but not quite hard enough to grind well, and the
"grated bread" made from this sort of meal is very good indeed.

Cornbread is the staff of life in the hill country, but wheaten
"light bread" or "biscuit bread" is sometimes provided for visitors, and enjoyed by the family on certain special occasions.
Many hillfolk are fond of hominy, which is made by soaking
shelled corn in lye-water. Just outside the cabin is the ash-hopper,
a sort of square funnel built of heavy boards, and provided with
a wooden cover. The housewife fills this thing with ashes from
the fireplace, and then pours in water, which comes out at the
bottom as an amber liquid containing lye. She soaks the corn
in this to remove the "skin" from the grains, and then rinses
it in clear water to eliminate most of the lye. After a big batch
of hominy is made the whole family eats nothing else for days,
until everybody is tired of it—"jest plumb burnt out on hom'ny."
The lye is used in making soap, too, and for this purpose it
must be concentrated by boiling slowly in large kettles. Then
pork scraps and bits of refuse grease are added and the mixture
stirred and boiled until the "saft" soap is produced—a bluish,
jelly-like, stinking mess which many old settlers prefer to the best
"store-boughten" laundry soap.

The Ozarker's table is often a shock and a despair to the
hungry traveller. Many mountain families have neither milk nor
butter, and when they do have butter it is often flaky and rancid.
I have heard that this is because the woman heats the churn at
the fireplace, or pours hot water into it to make the butter come
more easily. The hillfolk nearly all prefer sour milk to sweet, and
if one wants the latter he must say so in no uncertain language. I

once asked a woman for a glass of milk, and she replied that she had none, although I had just seen her carry a big pail of it into the cabin. This being indicated, she said: "Oh yas, we got plenty o' *sweet* milk, if you-uns want t' drink *that*!" Most Ozarkers do not care much for fresh vegetables, and they seldom eat raw fruit, but prefer to make pies or cobblers of it, or stew it into what they call "sass". There is no convenient way to keep food fresh, in the absence of any sort of refrigeration; even the spring-house is a luxury enjoyed by comparatively few, since many families depend upon shallow wells for their water.

I have never been able to find out just why the typical hill-man does not build his house conveniently near his water-supply, but it is a fact that he seldom does so. Even when the spring is on a higher level than the cabin, so that water could easily be piped into the house, or the "spring branch" diverted so as to flow directly past the door, the hillfolk still seem content to carry water all their lives. Often the cabin is located a hundred yards or more from the spring or well, and the only explanation I ever heard was that of an old woman who attributed it to the hillman's laziness and general lack of consideration for women. "A man allus puts th' house whar th' ground's level, an' whar he kin git th' logs easy. He don't keer how fur off th' spring is, cause hit's allus th' womenfolks whut has t' tote th' water." There is doubtless some truth in what the old lady said, but her explanation does not altogether satisfy me. I know a man near Southwest City, Missouri, who has hauled water in barrels from a spring more than a mile distant, for nearly twenty-five years. There are several grown sons in his family, and they could certainly dig a well near the house in a few days' time, but the idea of doing so seems never to have occurred to them. A "furri-ner" in my neighborhood once built a summer cottage directly above a spring, so as to have a stream of ice-cold water always flowing through his basement; this seemed to me to be an ideal arrangement, but the natives all shook their heads, with vague predictions that no good would come of it.

Except for a little fish and game, and an occasional chicken, the typical hillman has no meat other than pork—he does not care for beef or mutton even on the rare occasions when these are available. The word *meat*, in the Ozarks, means bacon or salt pork, and if one wants to indicate any other sort he must use a specific name. Killing and butchering hogs was a big job in the old days, when the average family killed as many as twelve or fifteen porkers for their Winter's meat. The neighbors all gathered on the appointed day, and unless there was a very large spring nearby they repaired to the nearest creek and built a great fire of logs, in which a number of large stones were heated. Having no vessels big enough to scald hogs in, they diverted the stream into a suitable hollow or pit among the rocks, and heated the water thus impounded by throwing the hot stones into it. When the hogs were scalded everybody helped to scrape and gut the animals, which were then cut up by the most proficient butchers in the party. At noon the women provided a big dinner, with fresh pork of all kinds, and the host set out a jug or two of corn whiskey. In the evening there was another big feed, followed by a dance or a play-party. A certain creek-bottom near Eureka Springs, Arkansas, is still known as "Hawg Scald", because it was a favorite place for these hog-killing festivals.

The meat was packed away in salt for several weeks and then hung up in the smokehouse—a tight log building with a dirt floor and no chimney. There was usually a small pit lined with stones, or an old iron pot to build the fire in. The little fire of hickory chips was kept burning for about two weeks; some families used corncobs rather than hickory, in the belief that this gave the meat a better flavor. The smoking process completed, the pork was covered with ashes, to keep the skippers out of it. Nowadays many people just smear the outside with a mixture containing cayenne pepper, instead of using the ashes. Sausage was usually put up in cornshucks—the old-timers did not fancy the intestines of pigs as containers for sausage, and they had no stuffers, anyway. It is easy to pull an ear of corn out of the shuck without damaging the latter, put the sausage inside, and tie the ends of the husk together. These "shuck-sassages" were hung up in the smokehouse and smoked with the other meat, and were usually left hanging there until needed. It was not considered necessary to pack sausage in the ashes, since the cornhusks and the spices are sufficient protection from the skippers.

Many hillfolk are fond of "greens" or "wild sallet" composed of the tender leaves of pokeweed, thistle, wild lettuce, dandelion, pepper-grass, lamb's-quarter, mustard and several varieties of dock. This is really very palatable if boiled until tender and then warmed in a pan with olive oil and a little garlic. The native will have none of this, however, but simply boils his greens in a pot with a bacon-rind or a bit of salt pork, and serves the whole mess very moist, with vinegar and raw onions.

It is said that there were many sugar-maples in the Ozarks at one time, but maple-syrup and maple-sugar are quite unknown to the hillfolk nowadays. Wild honey is obtained sometimes by skilled bee-hunters, who "line" bees in flight and so locate bee-trees. To see these fellows fell a bee-tree and rob a colony of wild bees is a most interesting experience, but the fine points of the bee-hunter's craft are quite beyond me, and I shall not attempt to describe his methods here. Until very recent years there was no beekeeping worthy of the name in the hill country; some farmers kept a few colonies of black bees in rude "bee-gums" made of hollow logs, and sold a little "chunk" honey to their neighbors, but that was all. Many people grow a little sugar cane,

and when "'lasses-makin' time" comes they squeeze out the sap
in sorghum-mills of their own construction, usually operated
by a horse or mule. Despite generous lubrication with soap or
tar these presses emit ear-splitting squeaks and groans which
can sometimes be heard nearly a mile away. The juice is taken
off into large kettles and boiled down to the consistency and
sweetness of ordinary commercial molasses. This is the standard
"long sweetenin'" of the mountain table, and is used in all sorts
of cooking. Granulated sugar is called "short sweetenin'", and is
still regarded as a luxury in some isolated sections.

The old-timers had no way of preserving fruit save by drying
it, and many of them still prefer to dry their peaches and apples.
The pared, sliced fruit is spread on an old quilt placed on the
roof, or upon a rude platform built for the purpose. When a
storm comes the housewife picks up the quilt by the corners and
carries the whole thing indoors. Instead of using the quilt, some
hillmen make drying-trays of thin boards, to hold about thirty
pounds of apples—light enough for the womenfolk to handle!
Some people prefer to dry their fruit in the loft or attic, but this
is unsatisfactory for several good and sufficient reasons. All fruit
dried in the open is black with flyspecks, of course, and must be
thoroughly washed before it is fit for the table. Occasionally an
unusually progressive family is provided with a kiln or dryer—a
tight little building with a sort of fireplace at one end, and trays
for the fruit in the upper part of it. The early settlers had no
fruit-jars or cans, but nowadays most women "put up" great
quantities of tomatoes, wild black-berries, gooseberries, huckleberries and plums, together with various sorts of preserves and
fruit-butters. One favorite preserve is made of watermelon rind,
and another from the reddish fruit of the prickly pear, a kind of
cactus which is common on rocky slopes in the Ozark foothills.
There are big stone jars of pickled cucumbers, too, put up in

a soured mixture of water and molasses, and a sort of pickle made of shredded turnips, called "turnip-kraut" to distinguish it from ordinary sauerkraut. Some hillmen have outdoor cellars, or little holes in the ground under the puncheons, but most of the women keep their canned goods in the cabin. Usually, for some reason or other, they prefer to store it under their beds.

The hillman of today eats very much the same sort of food that his "fore-parents" ate, but he has made considerable progress in the matter of clothing. In the old days buckskin was gradually replaced by homespun, and now the homespun has given way to cheap calico and "duckins". Only a few years ago the spinning-wheel and loom were seen in every mountain cabin, but nowadays most of them have been destroyed, or relegated to the loft or to an outbuilding. When one considers the amount of labor involved in the use of these things it is no wonder that the hill women are glad to see the last of them, and prefer to buy their clothing at the crossroads store. Some few old women still spin and weave, however, and the craft seems to have a fascination for people who are unfamiliar with it.

The wool is clipped from the sheep by means of clumsy hand shears, and is always incredibly dirty and full of cockleburrs, which must be picked out by hand—an almost interminable task. The burrs removed, the wool is washed and dried, and then the fibers are straightened and separated by drawing the stuff between two "cards", which are simply brushes of fine wire, set in leather and provided with rough wooden handles. In spinning yarn, the woman takes a large bundle of carded wool into her lap, and feeds it slowly into the spinning-wheel. She twists each bit between her fingers as it is drawn into the mechanism, where it is converted into a coarse yarn and wound on a spool. This spinning is not nearly so easy as it looks; I tried it once, myself, and found that I either broke the thread at once,

or else supplied the material unevenly, so that the yarn was not
of uniform diameter. Some of the old-time Ozark women are
very expert. Mrs. Ada Check, who lives near Sulphur Springs,
Arkansas, is one of the best spinners I have ever seen, and her
finished product looks exactly like a very superior grade of
"store-boughten" yarn. The material thus produced is used in
knitting socks, mittens, mufflers and the like, and in the old days
was woven into cloth and made into clothing, but weaving is now
a thing of the past in most parts of the country. "Grandmaw"
Check, however, still uses her loom to make homespun cloth,
and she showed me a very fine blue-and-white counterpane as
one of the best examples of her work.

"Grandmaw" Check's spinning-wheel is a small one, which
the operator turns by means of a treadle, but most of the Ozark
spinners use large wheels of a different type. In spinning with
the big wheel the woman stands up and turns it with her finger
or with a short stick held against a spoke, and as the thread runs
out she steps back just far enough to give it the proper twist.
A few spinning-wheels were brought out from Tennessee and
Kentucky in the early days, but most of them were made right
here in the Ozarks. A man named Cleveland, who lived near
White Rock, Missouri, was an expert maker of wheels, and many
beautiful examples of his work are still to be found in the neighborhood. Happy indeed was the bride who received a Cleveland
wheel as a wedding-present!

Cotton from the little hillside patches was also used in
making cloth, the seeds being picked out of it by hand in the
absence of any sort of gin. The cloth known as "jeans" was woven
of wool with a cotton chain, and the famous "linsey-woolsey"
consisted of a cotton warp and a woof of wool. "Linsey-woolsey"
was much in demand for Winter clothing, and it is said that
some pioneer women could weave five yards of it in a single day.

Most of this cloth was colored by steeping it in a tea made of butternut or maple bark, or walnut hulls, which gave it a warm brown color. Hickory and black-oak bark were used for yellow, while madder and indigo made good reds and blues. Green was obtained by scouring yellow cloth, and then dipping it into weak indigo, according to one of my aged informants. I have seen woolen garments reputed to be more than a hundred years old, in which the colors were still fresh and bright, but it seems that the secret of these fast vegetable colors has been lost since the introduction of cheap synthetic dyes, which long ago replaced the old-time colorings even in the remote hill country. I know a few old women who still make and dye homespun occasionally, but most mountain weavers nowadays confine themselves to the manufacture of rag carpets and the like.

Most of the homespun garments that I have seen were badly cut, and sewed together with rather coarse homespun thread, although it appears that machine-made thread was introduced very early. Some large metal buttons were brought into the Ozarks by the early settlers, but most of their buttons were homemade, being whittled out of wood and covered with cloth to match the garment. I have seen old buttons made of buckeyes and persimmon seeds with holes punched in them, and others cut from the shell of a gourd.

One of the things which impresses the Summer visitor at an Ozark cabin is the absence of screens, but the hillman is accustomed to having his house full of flies and other insects, and does not appear to mind them in the least. At mealtime one of the little girls is told off to "shoo th' varmints off'n th' vittles", which she does by waving a green bough slowly to and fro over the diners' heads. There are no facilities for bathing, and few mountain people seem to care much for water, anyhow. Men and boys go swimming in the Summer time, but the streams are very cold, and many grown girls have never been "wet all over" in their lives. The majority of hill women never wet their hair, but comb it for hours on end and are very proud of it. Even in scrupulously clean cabins there is no knowledge of the most elementary principles of hygiene and sanitation. Sick people and well people sleep together, and make use of the same scanty toilet articles. There are no dentists in the hills, but every country physician is provided with a forceps of sorts, and can extract an aching tooth on occasion. There are also a few of the old-time "tooth-jumpers" who do their work surprisingly well with a specially made punch and mallet. Most hillmen's teeth appear to be in very good condition, considering the fact that toothbrushes are practically unknown.

A Canadian tourist, in speaking of the Ozark country, once told me that he remembered it as a place where "the natives are too lazy to put up backhouses, you know, but just go out and defecate all about on the ground like dogs!" He used a shorter word than *defecate*, but otherwise the above is an exact quotation. It is a fact that very few of the old-time Ozark cabins have any sort of toilet facilities, and even a rough outdoor privy is sometimes regarded as an indication that the owner is "puttin' on airs". Indoor water-closets and lavatories are altogether unknown, and I have seen mountain children, brought into a modern hotel, utterly refuse to make use of such strange devices. A friend of mine, building a fine log bungalow in the Ozark foothills, was working from a blue-print nailed to a tree, and this was examined with great interest by an aged "ridge-runner". "Whut's thet ar ring mean?" he asked, pointing to a circle which represented the stool in the bathroom. When the matter was explained to him the old man was astounded and shocked. "Shorely," he gasped, "you-uns don't aim for t' dung right in th' house!"

One of my old neighbors lived in a big log house with many

modern conveniences; he had a good cookstove, and a kitchen sink, and a gasoline lamp, and a mail-order phonograph— probably the finest country home in a radius of twenty or thirty miles. However, there was no toilet at all, not even the rude "backhouse" so common in the Ozark villages. This man told me that his parents and grandparents had lived long and happy lives without toilets, and that he felt that there was something unclean and degrading about a group of people urinating and defecating in the same spot. In town, he said, water-closets were doubtless necessary, but in the clean woods the situation was very different. Filth, he added, should be scattered rather than collected.

The picturesque log cabin and its primitive equipment fit perfectly into the Ozark landscape, and a sort of romantic glamour still hangs about a home of this type, but beauty and romance are by no means synonymous with health and comfort. Romantic novelists to the contrary notwithstanding, the simple life of the mountaineer in his snug little log cabin is not without its disadvantages, and the truth is that most of the comfortable houses in the hill-country proper are owned and occupied by "furriners".

CHAPTER III.

Womenfolk and Social Life

THE OZARK HILLMAN IS STILL living in the eighteenth century, and this is nowhere more evident than in the subordinate position occupied by the women of his household. Men and boys are frequently idle for long periods, particularly in the Winter, but there is precious little leisure for the women at any season. Mountain girls and women do all the cooking and housework and laundry as a matter of course, often carrying water for the latter purpose from distant springs or streams. If the family is lucky enough to have any chickens, the women take charge of them; if there is a cow, it is the woman's business to do the milking and to make butter for the market— if there is any market. Women usually cultivate the garden, and are expected to work in the fields on occasion, sometimes hoeing corn or cotton for weeks at a time. Only the other day I saw a woman, with ropes somehow fastened to her shoulders, pulling a little homemade plow as her husband guided it through the "gyarden-patch"! This is not typical, however. Most hillmen leave their wives to manage the garden as best they can, and a man who milks the cow, or does any other sort of "woman's work", is regarded as a weakling by his neighbors. The widow of a prosperous farmer told me that she had always supported the family, even buying "his" clothing and tobacco, during the whole of her married life! Her husband saved the money that he earned, or invested it in more land and livestock. The woman who cannot supply the family table with vegetables, and sell enough produce to provide clothing for herself and her children, is considered an improvident slattern.

The mountain woman always gets up first in the morning, and hastens to "pack" the wood and water into the house, build the fire, and cook breakfast against the rising of her lord and master. If there is only one chair the man of the house occupies it, while women and children stand. At mealtime the men and boys always eat first, and the womenfolk take what is left. Almost from the cradle the male child lords it over his sisters, even those who are considerably older than himself; he studiously avoids any outward show of deference to the weaker vessel, and maintains this attitude of superiority throughout his life.

The "furrin" custom of lifting one's hat to women seems ridiculous and affected to the hillfolk—no real backwoodsman would do such an undignified thing. He looks at it just as the average American regards the European practice of kissing ladies' hands. Several times I have absent-mindedly removed my hat upon meeting women in the hills; the gesture is nearly always regarded with surprise and ill-concealed amusement. In fact, many hillmen have a singular antipathy to taking off their hats at any time, either indoors or out; I have often noticed that my nearest friends appear somehow strange when I meet them in court or in the church-house—it is simply that I am not accustomed to seeing them without their hats. In the old days it was customary for people to walk the narrow trails in single file, the man ahead with his rifle, and the womenfolk trudging several paces in the rear. The women carried the bundles, too, leaving

The Old-Time Corn Grater

the man's hands free to use his weapon. The rifle is generally left at home nowadays, but the woman still walks behind her lord, and she still carries the bundles.

I do not know that the mountain man's family life is a particularly happy one, but it is fairly quiet and free from bickering at any rate. The husband and father is the last word in authority always, and takes orders from no one. He frequently consults with his wife about household and business problems, and may even ask the older children's opinion occasionally, but his final decision is law. Certain other matters, however, the hillman is usually content to leave in feminine hands, and the religious and social life of a mountain settlement is very largely dominated by the womenfolk. A minister of the gospel once told me that the hill people are instinctively and deeply religious, and that there is something about it rugged environment and primitive ways of living which turns men's thoughts to God and immortality. It is certainly true that the typical Ozarker is very fond of attending religious meetings but it seems to me that this is due rather to the poverty of his social life than to any deep religious feeling. Almost the only opportunity for young people to meet one another in some particularly strait-laced settlements, is at funerals, prayer-meetings, Sunday schools and preachings; it is not surprising that the boys and girls in such an environment are profoundly impressed with the importance and utility of the religious life.

In the early days very few of the Ozark villages were able to build churches or support resident pastors, but each settlement was visited at intervals by a circuit-rider or "saddle-bag preacher". At present, however, there is some sort of a "church-house" in every mountain hamlet, and many have regular ministers, usually of the Baptist or Methodist persuasion. Infinitely more diverting, however, are the itinerant evangelists known as "bresh-arbor preachers", who do not come to the village churches at all, but hold forth in the traditional fashion at the campgrounds. A revival at the old campground is a sort of picnic for the young folk, and is the real social center of the whole region for the time being. A typical campground is a sheltered cove near a big spring, where a large brush-arbor or "tabernickle" has been set up in a little clearing. There used to be a famous camp-ground near Forsythe, Missouri, where it is said that the joyful shouting of the converts could often be heard for more than two miles. The place is still known as "Happy Holler"! The tabernacle is usually nothing more than a framework of rough poles, roofed over with leafy branches, and lighted by crude gasoline flares or torches.

Inside the tabernacle are two groups of rough wooden benches, without backs or arms, separated by a broad aisle; the men are supposed to sit on one side of the aisle, and the women on the other. The pulpit is built upon a little platform at one end of the arbor, flanked by two or three benches reserved for the most influential and devout Christians of the neighborhood— this place is called the "amen corner". Just in front of the pulpit is a long, low seat known as the "mourners' bench". There is usually a bucket of water and a gourd at one side of the platform, and men and women file solemnly up to drink, even during the prayer. These meetings are usually held in the Autumn, as it appears that the hillman is in no mood for revivals until his corn crop has been taken care of. When the news of a camp-meeting is "norated round", whole families come in covered wagons, on horseback and afoot, bringing bedding and cooking utensils, with sufficient food to last several days.

A typical brush-arbor service begins by the parson calling out to an influential worshipper: "Brother Whatley, spos'n' we-all sing a couple o' hymns". Whereupon Brother Whatley rises from his seat in the amen corner, spits carefully over the edge of the platform, and says: "Brethern an' sistern, th' parson asts thet we-all sing a hymn or two, an' hit shore is a pleasure for me t' lead you-all at this hyar meetin' tonight. Less sing one o' them good ol' songs we all know—'How Teejus an' Tasteless th' Hours.' Harumph! Do mi sol do! Do mi sol do!" And with this he waves his arms vigorously at the congregation, and all sing at the top of their voices. How these people manage to sing with their mouths full of snuff or tobacco has always been a puzzle to me, but they certainly do it, apparently without the least difficulty. They all stamp their feet in unison, too, even the preacher. I have seen a woman "give tittie" to her babe, chew tobacco, pat her foot and sing lustily all at the same time, and all with a singular grace and ease of performance which was fascinating to observe.

After the singing of two or three hymns the preacher requests another loud-voiced brother to lead in prayer, which he does at considerable length, with the various deacons calling out "Amen!" and "Bless th' Lord!" and "Gawd grant it!" at appropriate intervals. When the prayer is over the evangelist steps forward and swings into his sermon, which is regarded as the most important part of the service. Mountain preachers generally consider themselves above all worldly graces, such as dignity and restraint, and particularly resent what they call "book larnin'." An old Arkansas circuit-rider once said to me: "Mighty few o' th' wise an' learned are called. Gawd's a-lookin' for pure hearts an' sanctified sperrits, not heads full o' worldly knowledge." In the old days a man who felt "called" to preach was examined in doctrine by the elders, and if they were satisfied as to his orthodoxy and enthusiasm he was ordained—the examiners were not at all concerned with his intellectual or educational status. Naturally, these fellows are fundamentalists to a man, and most of their sermons are of the hell-fire-and-brimstone sort—exhortations to discard all newfangled follies instanter, and return to the good old-fashioned religion of our sturdy fathers. I have stenographic reports of several of these hill-billy sermons, but there is no space for long quotations here. The following paragraph is chosen almost at random from a brush-arbor denunciation of the higher learning:

> "Some folks sets a powerful store by this hyar eddication, but I tell you-all right hyar an' now thet readin' an' writin' an' cipherin' aint never got no sinners into Heaven yit, an' don't you never fergit it! . . . Hell's chuck full o' school-marms, an' they aint no lack o' doctors an' lawyers an' other eddicated fellers thar, nuther ! . . . I got a purty good eddica-tion myself, an' I kin read th' Word, but larnin' is a mighty juberous gift, now, brethern an' sistern. Hit shore is!"

And so on for some two hours and a half.

The typical mountain preacher concludes his fiery sermon abruptly, and immediately calls for another hymn. Brother Whatley leads off with a mighty shout of "Bless th' Lord!" and then swings into "The Old-Time Religion" or "I'm Bound for the Promised Land". "Sing!" he yells, and claps his hands together with a noise like a pistol-shot. Somewhere a woman screams, and overcome with a sudden sense of sin comes stumbling down to the mourners' bench. Weeping, moaning, begging her Savior for mercy. . . . "Hi-yoop! I'm saved! Praise Gawd!" comes from old Jethro Tolliver, who is converted regularly every Autumn. Struck by the power of the Lord, another brother keeps wring-ing his hands and yelling "Jesus, oh, Jesus!" in exactly the same tone that he uses in calling his hogs. A little later he begins to cry that he hopes to meet his dear old parents in Heaven, and to call out "Paw!" and "Maw!" looking up meanwhile as if he expected to see them clinging bat-fashion to the interlaced

boughs over his head. Suddenly he shouts: "Oh, Gawd, Maw,
I know I'm a-goin' t' meet you-uns over thar! Dang it, I bet ye
a dollar I meet you-uns over thar!" . . . Finally the evangelist
decides to end the meeting. "Ef thar aint no give-outs, brethern
an' sistern, less all be dismissed. Stand up! . . . An' now may th'
grace o' Gawd an' th' communion o' th' Holy Sperrit rest an'
abide with us one an' all, we ast it for Christ's sake, amen."

At most of these meetings there is no instrumental music at
all, but occasionally a rather daring pastor makes use of a little
portable organ. The piano is considered altogether too frivolous
to be played in connection with religious services, and a violin
or other stringed instrument would never be tolerated in the
house of God. I recall one misguided schoolteacher who tried to
educate her patrons by arranging a "lecture course"; the various
"entertainments" were held in the Methodist church, and all
went well until one of the entertainers undertook to play a cello.
Several men arose immediately and marched out, followed by
their wives and children, and the liberal element in the church
was quite overwhelmed by the storm of criticism which swept
the village. One old woman remarked the next day: "I hyeerd
feet a-pattin' all round me, whilst thet 'ar fiddler was a-fiddlin',
an' it seemed like you could jest see th' ol' Devil a-standin' right
thar in th' church-house!"

The foregoing account gives a glimpse of the ordinary
uneventful brush-arbor worship, such as a casual tourist may
see for himself in almost any of the more isolated sections of
the Ozarks. There are, however, occasional meetings of a much
more sensational type, and if one wished to emphasize the outlandish and fantastic side of the Ozarker's religious life he would
have no difficulty in collecting plenty of data for the purpose.
Even in the comparatively conservative Baptist and Methodist
churches there is no lack of hysterical "shouting" which can be

heard for half-a'-mile or so, and at some of the "branch-water" revivals there is even less decorum and restraint.

Some of these backwoods Christians experience what is called the "gift o' tongues", and go about shouting a wild gibberish supposed to be one of the languages used "way back in Bible times". Occasionally a shouter falls into a sort of cataleptic state, and on recovering lies in a semiconscious condition for hours, apparently with a complete loss of memory for the night's doings. Others dance about with a strange wild gleam in their eyes, apparently oblivious of their surroundings, but are often brought back to this world immediately by some untoward accident. I remember one woman dancer who was crowded off the low platform and fell upon a stray foxhound; the snapping and howling of the frenzied beast sobered the entire congregation at once; and the fact that the woman was not bitten was attributed to God's own mercy! Mountain ruffians sometimes break up these meetings by throwing live snakes or skunks or a "hot" hornets'-nest into the arbor, and on such occasions all religious activities are abandoned at once, and the "unknown tongue" gives way to everyday Ozark English, with short and ugly Anglo-Saxon terms predominant.

Once I heard of an evangelist who was accustomed to bring poisonous snakes into the pulpit, where he suffered them to bite him on the wrists, declaring that God would protect His servant from all harm, and quoting various Biblical references to such matters. I went to see this man, and was shown two large copperheads in a cage in his wagon, but the man of God steadfastly refused to handle them in my presence, although I offered to make a substantial contribution to the church. He said that he claimed no immunity for himself, but that a temporary immunity was sometimes given him by God Almighty for the purpose of impressing His poor sinful children, and added:

"I don't believe in temptin' Providence, an' I don't never tetch no sarpints only when I feel th' Power a-comin' on."

The mountain boys do not often accompany their girls to the meetings, but stand about just outside the arbor, where each asks the lady of his choice if he may "see her home". This procedure is not conducive of harmony among the jealous, half-drunken gallants of the hills, and there have been many bloody fights almost under the brush gables of the House of God. Some revivals are so notoriously immoral that "camp-meetin' baby" has come to mean an illegitimate child, but on the whole I think that there is no more sexual irregularity at religious meetings than at the ordinary dance or "frolic".

The young hillman may do a little "tomcattin' round" occasionally, but when he "sets up" to one particular girl he usually means to marry her, and his suit must be taken seriously. For a boy and girl to go to church together, in some localities, is equivalent to announcing their engagement, and is so regarded by everybody. The young man from the city will do well to inform himself about these matters before paying any marked attention to a mountain damsel; I have known several "furriners" who became involved in serious difficulties because of their ignorance of such local customs. Courtship is still regarded as an important matter in the Ozarks, and the girl who is "talkin'" to one young man must accept no attentions from others. A young woman who trifles in this regard is very likely to get somebody killed, and this adds nothing to her repute or desirability as a wife. The mountaineer is almost insanely jealous, and it is quite out of the question for two young men and one girl to go together to any social function—neither boy would be willing to have people think that he was "playin' second fiddle" or "takin' a back seat".

A hill girl's suitor may call at her parents' cabin without any previous engagement or understanding, but he is usually expected on Saturday or Sunday, or both. On these occasions he takes at least one meal with the family, and in many remote districts it is not considered a breach of etiquette for the young couple to remain together all night, "sparkin'" before the fireplace. One must remember; however, that most of the cabins have only one room, and that the girl's parents are sleeping only a few feet away. A self-respecting mountain man would never permit his daughter to go "traipsin' round" the country roads at night with any young man, nor tolerate the indiscriminate "lallygaggin'" which he sees so often among the tourists. The lack of privacy in mountain homes, together with the tradition of promiscuous hospitality, is probably responsible for much of the sexual irregularity that exists in the backwoods districts. A condition which forces men, women and children of all ages to sleep together in one small room is hardly conducive to sexual morality.

Once married, a woman is expected to "settle down" and attend to the business of keeping house and bearing children. A young married woman who uses "face whitenin'", or exhibits the most casual interest in her personal appearance, is regarded with suspicion by her neighbors. A respectable young matron is not supposed even to talk with men except on business, and then only if her husband is not present to speak for her. For a married woman to go riding or to attend a party with any man other than her husband is quite unthinkable, and would cause immediate and serious trouble. It has been said that the hillbillies' wives are the most virtuous women in America, and it may well be true—they certainly have very little time or opportunity for infidelity.

The respectable hill people condemn all illicit sexual relations as a matter of principle, but in practice they are curiously tolerant of many things. Certain of the sex perversions are perhaps less prevalent here than in more sophisticated communities, but incestuous relations are common enough, and seem to arouse very little moral indignation. The illegitimate child is not held in any particular contempt, either, and usually takes the mother's name, particularly if she continues to live with the parents. The fact that most mountain folk pronounce Miss and Mrs. exactly alike is confusing to the stranger. Lawful wedlock is supposed to cancel all previous laxities, anyhow, and a mother whose child is born a month or two after her marriage does not appear to lose caste.

The truth is that a great many of the pioneer weddings were not legal marriages at all, since the "saddlebag preachers" who officiated had no authority to perform the marriage ceremony. This fact was dimly recognized even then, and many respectable men and women lived together and raised families without any pretense of legal sanction. The old settlers tell of a backwoods couple who came to town and asked for a marriage license, while their ten children waited outside the clerk's office. Asked why he had not attended to this formality sooner, the old man said: "Wal, you see, th' roads has been so turrible bad . . ." This is only a story, of course, but it is a fact that some isolated "hollers" in the early days were not visited for years on end by anyone qualified to read the marriage service, and that illegal unions under such conditions carried no social stigma whatever. One of my friends told me that his own parents, who lived in a very backward section of the Ozarks, were never married until he was about twenty years old, and then only because they wanted to sell the old farm and had some legal difficulty about the title. This man has attained a very prominent position in the community, and both he and his parents seem to be asked everywhere, and received on an equal footing by their neighbors.

Nowadays, however, these extra-legal marriages are frowned

upon by the better element among the hillfolk; no self-respecting mountain girl would consider entering into such a union, nor would her male relatives permit it. Men and women who live together without the formality of legal marriage are now looked down upon by their neighbors, and a notoriously promiscuous woman—particularly if she happens to be poor and friendless— is in danger of being "run out'n th' country," or even thrown into jail upon some pretext or other. I know of one young woman who caused so much trouble in a backwoods settlement that the neighbors decided to "drum her out". About thirty men and women appeared at her cabin one morning, firing pistols, beating tin pans, and yelling at the top of their voices. The cause of all this disturbance said not a word—simply ran down the road as fast as she could, with the mob trailing along behind her, drumming vigorously. They followed her about a mile and then, convinced that she was really leaving the neighborhood, quietly returned to their homes. I was particularly interested in the reaction of the girl's kinfolk to all this, half expecting her male relatives to take down their rifles and wipe out the insult in blood. Several of her brothers had, I was told, engaged in desperate battles over matters which seemed to me of much less consequence. In this case, however, they were sorrowful and humiliated rather than belligerent, and made no attempt to protect or avenge their erring sister.

The mountain man uses the word "whore" to mean any woman who has illicit sex relations, but there are no real prostitutes in the hill country, except such as have been imported by the summer-resort people. Some of the hill girls are promiscuous enough, certainly, but they do not sell their favors directly for money. Dance-hall beauties from the mining towns used to come in covered wagons sometimes, camping just outside the villages, but the mountain boys have very little money to spend, and such caravans are seldom seen nowadays. The traveller will find a few daughters of joy in our new tourist-camps and hotels, but they are Summer visitors only; they ply their trade among the tourists and "furriners", and have nothing to do with the poverty-ridden people of the hills.

Early marriages are the rule in the hill country, and many mountain girls are wives and mothers at fifteen or sixteen. A girl of twenty is well past her first bloom, and not likely to get a desirable husband; when she reaches the age of twenty-five she is on the "cull list", and at thirty she is definitely an old maid. The lot of the spinster is hard indeed in the Ozarks, since she is universally regarded as a failure, and must depend upon the charity of her male relatives for support. This usually means that she does all the household drudgery without any compensation except her board and lodging. Very rarely is there any opportunity for her to "work out" or "take in washin'", since even the most indulgent of mountaineer husbands would never think of hiring another woman to do his wife's work!

Mountain boys and girls generally follow their own inclination in choosing their mates; most parents seem little disposed to interfere in these matters, and all of the hillfolk are so poor that financial considerations are less important than elsewhere. Elderly people, however, are frequently brought together by the curious practice of "recommending", as when the friends of a homeless widow "recommend" her to an elderly bachelor who has a house and is in need of a housekeeper. In such cases the wedding often takes place within a few hours of their first meeting, and is regarded as a business arrangement, without any pretense of sentiment. These marriages are often called "made up weddin's", and many of them appear to turn out very well indeed.

There are no church weddings in the hill country—the cere-

mony always takes place at the home of the bride's parents, and
is followed by a dinner and "frolic" which often lasts until dawn.
Usually the newlyweds do not sleep together on their wedding
night, since many hillfolk feel that this is somehow indelicate,
as placing the union upon too obvious a physical basis. On the
day after the marriage the wedding-guests assemble at the home
of the groom's parents for the "enfare", which is another feast
and jollification.

The shivaree—the word is a corruption of *charivari*—is a sort
of mock serenade, the object of which is to force the groom to
"set 'em up" to his friends and neighbors. It always occurs at
night, as soon after the wedding as possible. The shivaree party
consists of men, women and children, supplied with guns, tin
pans, cowbells and other noise-making equipment. The company usually selects a captain, who walks on ahead with a cane,
feeling about for cords or wires which the groom sometimes ties
across the paths, in order to hamper the advance of the shivaree party. The captain comes forward slowly until he is close to
the building occupied by the newlyweds, and then fires a single
shot from his revolver, upon which all the rest rush forward and
begin their noise-making. According to the old tradition, if the
husband should slip out of the house and fire his own pistol
before the captain of the shivaree party can discharge his, the
joke would be on the latter and the groom would be under no
obligation to stand treat.

When the noise begins the happy couple are expected to wel-
come everybody and set out food and liquor for their entertainment. This is sometimes a real hardship in our poverty-stricken
hills, but nevertheless a well-attended shivaree is a testimony to
the newlyweds' prominence and popularity, and the absence of
any shivaree at all is a sign of their social unimportance. If the
groom does not "set 'em up" promptly and bountifully he is,

according to ancient custom, supposed to be thrown into the river; this is actually done in some cases, and several years ago in Arkansas a poor countryman was drowned by reason of some drunken clumsiness in connection with a shivaree.

On the occasion of my own marriage, my wife and I were staying with friends in one of the Ozark towns; we had made no preparations to entertain a shivaree party, and the best I could do was to supply the celebrants with cigars, candy, ice-cream cones and the like from the village drugstore. Thus I escaped the river, but mine was a poor hospitality as compared with that offered by many native bridegrooms; at some shivarees the guests are served with great platters of fried chicken, fruit and cakes prepared days in advance, with plenty of corn whiskey for the gentlemen. This latter is usually enjoyed outside the house with a great show of secrecy, since the Ozark men and women do not drink together in public. Every respectable woman in the hill country is assumed to be a teetotaler, whether her breath smells of moonshine or not. At social functions the women almost invariably make an elaborate pretense of not knowing that their escorts have any liquor, although the whole place may be reeking with the penetrating odor of new corn whiskey!

Large families are almost universal among the hillfolk, and most farmers seem to desire at least five or six children. This sentiment is easily understood when one recalls that boys and girls are expected to help with the chores almost as soon as they can walk, and at ten or twelve years of age are a distinct asset rather than an expense to their parents. The women seem to be resigned to this point of view, feeling somehow that the bearing of children is a sacred duty. One old woman of my acquaintance did say, in a moment of exasperation, that she "wisht t' Gawd th' mumps had a went down" on her husband when he was young, but this reaction is far from typical. Modern contraceptive measures seem to be very little known, and many of the religious hillfolk do not believe in such things. Abortion as practiced by the "granny-women" is dangerous and unsatisfactory, and is not much favored in the backwoods districts.

The expectant mother goes about her work as usual, with no concessions to her condition except one—she is always careful to avoid anything that might "mark" the child. She gets very little care in childbirth, for the hill-country doctors are ill-trained and over-worked, and many of the hill women will not have a doctor "cunjurin' round" at this time. There is usually a volunteer midwife in attendance, but these "granny-women" are incredibly dirty and ignorant and superstitious. It is a matter of pride, too, for the mother to be up and about as soon as possible after the child is born; I have seen a woman milking a cow, while her four-day-old babe slept on a flat rock nearby. It is no wonder that the mountain women are old at thirty!

Since the mountain people rear large families and do not move far away from the old homestead, there are many consanguineous marriages, and nearly every hill-man is somehow related to almost everybody else in the neighborhood. Due to this complex relationship, the newcomer is often struck by the lack of variety in proper names. There may be a dozen Ab Yanceys, for example, in a radius of ten or twelve miles, differentiated chiefly by adjectives descriptive of their personal characteristics. The original Abner Yancey, let us say, had eight sons, the eldest being known as Little Ab. Little Ab's first-born was called Young Ab. A brother's second son, named for his grandfather, is designated as Dave's Ab. When another cousin, also named Ab Yancey, had his eye pecked out by a captive heron, he acquired the name One-Eye Ab. Another baby fell into a pot of hot soap, burning himself very severely, and was thereafter known as Cripplin' Ab.

Naturally the Abs were still more numerous in the next generation. Young Ab's son inherited his mother's swarthy complexion, and hence was called Black Ab, while a cousin of florid features and auburn hair was always Red Ab. Came also in the course of time Long Ab, Puny Ab, Freckle Ab and Big Ab—some of these names proving ridiculously inappropriate in later life. Thus Long Ab was a very lean, lanky baby, but became quite portly in early manhood, while Puny Ab, who weighed only four pounds at birth, grew much taller and heavier than his second cousin Big Ab, although the latter was a truly gigantic infant. Some of the Abs grew up without any specific "handles", but were named because of some outstanding characteristic which appeared in later life. Ab Horse was a famous horseman, Parson Ab once aspired to the ministry. Devil Ab was a reckless, murderous ruffian, Roarin' Ab was inclined to be noisy in his cups. Roarin' Ab's eldest son was always known as Tiger Ab, for no reason at all so far as I was able to discover. All this is further complicated by the fact that any one of these men, in his old age, may be Uncle Ab or Daddy Ab to the whole countryside.

Many visitors to the Ozarks have reported a very high percentage of defectives among the hillfolk, which they usually attribute to inbreeding—the practice of intermarriage within the family group. In this connection one must remember that mental defectives are much more conspicuous in the hill country than elsewhere, because the mountain people can seldom be induced to send their feebleminded or insane relatives to state asylums if they can possibly be kept at home. Many an "eediot" who would never be permitted his freedom in the city is allowed to run at large in the backwoods, and even to marry and produce a large family of defectives.

Divorce is rather unusual among the real old-time hill people; there are separations sometimes, but legal sanction for

the "parting" is not much in favor. In better class mountain circles, a woman never definitely "leaves" her husband; she goes
to visit her kinfolk, and puts off returning time after time, until
finally everybody is accustomed to the situation, without any
open scandal.

It is only in her old age that the mountain woman is treated
with any great consideration, and rarely even then—the mountaineer has no particular reverence for age *per se*. I have known
several old women, however, who ruled whole families and clans
in truly regal fashion, and whose opinions were deferred to
everywhere. In one case "Gran'pap" was obviously in his dotage,
but "Granny" was regarded as a chimney-corner oracle, and her
grown sons and grandsons consulted her about many matters
which they did not even mention to their wives. Illiterate and
superstitious she was, and filthy and disgusting in her personal
habits, but there was yet a kind of magnificence about her, a
sort of courageous pessimism, and a certain shrewd judgment
of human character and motivation.

Funerals are invariably well attended in the hill country,
largely because they afford the women an opportunity to get
together in a social way. I have known groups of young people to
drive many miles over incredibly bad roads to be present at the
"buryin'" of a man whom they scarcely knew by sight. The old-
time funeral sermon was seldom preached in a church, and there
was no ceremony at the home of the deceased—the whole thing
took place at the cemetery. The pioneers were buried in coffins
of rough boards, made with the widest part at the shoulders,
and tapering toward the head and feet. The coffin was hauled
to the graveyard in a wagon, resting on a little heap of straw or
hay. The procession moved along as slowly as possible, but never
stopped until the open grave was reached. It is very bad luck to
halt a funeral procession, and the hillfolk always send men on

ahead to open gates and clear away any possible obstructions. The grave was dug amply wide and long until almost at the bottom, where it narrowed into the so-called "vault"—a smaller hole into which the coffin fitted rather closely. This left wide shelves of earth at either side, a few inches above the coffin. After the coffin was lowered to its proper place, rough boards were laid across on the shelves of earth, and the dirt shovelled in on top of the boards. The funeral sermon was preached and the hymns were sung as the coffin lay beside the grave. When the burial finally took place, the preacher and the mourners stood about and wept loudly until the last clod was thrown into the grave—to leave before the rites were completed would have been a gross breach of pioneer etiquette. When everything was over, the preacher thanked the people in behalf of the bereaved family and dismissed them with a benediction, just as at a church service.

There was no embalming in those days, and bodies must needs be buried at once. There were no automobiles or hard-surfaced roads, either, and it was impossible for relatives who lived at a distance to get together at short notice. Thus it was that the actual "buryin'" frequently proceeded with no ceremony other than a short prayer at the grave, and the funeral sermon was preached six months or a year later, when all the kinfolk could be present to hear the minister of their choice. These deferred funeral "preachin's" were held in the church-house and the mourners did not go to the graveyard at all. Such a ceremony occurred near my cabin about five years ago, when a great number of people gathered to hear a country preacher eulogize a woman who had been dead and buried for more than a year. I have heard of one case in which the funeral of a man's first wife was attended by his second spouse, who sat beside her husband and wept with him for the loss of her predecessor!

Religious meetings, weddings, enfares, shivarees and funer-

als are the most important occasions of social intercourse among
the old-timers; the only holidays which they take seriously are
New Year, the Fourth of July and Christmas. There are still many
old people who speak of "new Christmas" and "old Christmas",
the latter being celebrated on the sixth of January. There are
many children in the Ozarks who never heard of Santa Claus,
and have only a vague notion of the Christ story, but they all
know that cattle kneel down and bellow at midnight on the eve of
"old Christmas". This matter of two Christmas dates puzzled me
until I remembered that all Christendom celebrated the birth of
Jesus on January sixth until the institution of the Gregorian cal-
endar, which was not adopted by England and her colonies until
the middle of the eighteenth century. The hillman's ancestors
were buried in the American wilderness when the change was
made, and paid scant attention to the newfangled notions of the
mother country, so that within the memory of many men now
living the Ozarkers had their Christmas regularly on January
sixth, just as Chaucer and Shakespeare did.

In the old days the merchants of an Ozark village donated
a quantity of gunpowder on Christmas Eve, and the blacksmith
"fired anvils" with a terrific racket until about midnight. Then
a group of serenaders started out, firing pistols, blowing horns,
beating tin pans, ringing cowbells and so on. When they came to
a house they marched three or four times around it, singing and
yelling and making as much noise as possible. The occupants
invited them in, and served them with apples or cake, washed
down with whiskey or whatever liquor they had. One favorite
Christmas beverage was known as "stew"—a mixture of whiskey
and ginger and hot water. It was very bad form for the serenaders to miss a single cabin, although some of the people were so
poor that they could not "set up" more than a few walnuts, or
perhaps a little tobacco or dried fruit. Only a very unpopular

house was ever overlooked, and a family which was not visited on Christmas morning had no social standing whatever.

In addition to the social opportunities provided by these holidays, the young folk get together now and then at clearings, log-rollings, house-raisings, cornhuskings and other "workin's", and mingle at an occasional candy-breaking or box-supper or church "sociable", but the most interesting of all their lighter social diversions is the so-called "play-party"—a function which is discussed at considerable length in a subsequent chapter.

CHAPTER IV.

The Ozark Dialect

T HE LONGER I LIVE IN the Ozarks the more difficult it
is for me to understand how Professor George Phillip
Krapp and other eminent scholars ever happened to
conclude that there are no dialects in the United States. Even
H. L. Mencken thinks that there are no real local dialects, but
only a general common speech, a vulgate, a *sermo vulgaris*, a
Volkssprache which serves the entire country. "There may be," he
writes, "slight differences in pronunciation and intonation—a
Southern softness, a Yankee drawl, a Western burr—but in the
words they use and the way they use them all Americans, even
the least tutored, follow the same line. . . . A Boston street-car
conductor could go to work in Chicago or San Francisco without
running the slightest risk of misunderstanding his new fares.
Once he had picked up half a dozen localisms, he would be, to
all linguistic intents and purposes, fully naturalized."

Mr. Mencken is doubtless right enough about his street-
car conductor; I have lived in Boston and Chicago and San
Francisco myself, and had no difficulty with the language.
But the Ozark Mountain region of Missouri and Arkansas is a

different proposition altogether. For the past ten years I have spent a large part of my time in the Ozarks, and I am still, linguistically speaking, a "furriner"—an *outlander*.

Whatever the eminent scholars may think about it, every layman who travels much in the Ozark country knows that some of the older natives do speak a peculiar jargon, derived doubtless from the dialect of the southern Appalachians, containing many words and phrases which are almost unintelligible to ordinary people from other parts of the United States. Some of the difficulties are due merely to grotesque mispronunciation, and a few of the peculiar syntactical arrangements may be a bit puzzling at first, but the chief differences between the Ozark dialect and the standard American speech are differences in vocabulary.

The following passage is a fair example of English as it is spoken by the old *residenters* in the more isolated parts of the Ozark highlands:

> "Lee Yancey allus was a right work-brickel feller, clever an' biddable as all git-out, but he aint got nary smidgin' o' mother-wit, an' he aint nothin' on'y a tie-whackin' sheer-crapper noways. I seed him an' his least chaps a-bustin' out middles down in ol' man Price's bottom t'other ev'nin', a-whoopin' an' a-blaggardin' an' a-spewin' ambeer all over each an' ever' whilst thet 'ar pore susy hipped woman o' hisn was a-pickin' boogers out'n her yeller tags, an' a-scrunchin' cheenches on th' puncheon 'ith a antiganglin' noodlehook. D'reckly Lee he come a-junin' in all narvish-like an' tetchous, an' rid th' pore ol' trollop a bug-huntin'—jes' plum bodacious hipped an' ruinated her. They never did have nothin' on'y jes' a heap o' poke sallat an' a passel o' these hyar hawg-mollies, but he must a got hisse'f a bait o' vittles some'ers, 'cause come can'le-light he geared up his ol' piedy cribber an' lit a shuck fer Gotham

Holler. The danged ol' durgen—he should orter be bored
fer th' simples!"

Such talk as this is difficult to understand simply because it
is full of strange words and phrases; it is not, as Mencken seems
to think, separated from standard American English merely by
"slight differences in pronunciation and intonation." Every word
of the above paragraph is commonly used in the Ozark country, and every one of them is duly recorded in the lists of the
American Dialect Society, but I fancy that even those gentlemen
who contend that there are no dialects in America might stumble
a bit if required to make a sight translation into standard English.
And I doubt very much if there is a single street-car conductor
in Boston who could make head or tail of it. Even the hillman's
ordinary English words are very frequently used with some outlandish connotation; the adjective *clever*, for example, has no
reference to intelligence, but means accommodating or generous—one of the *cleverest* men in my neighborhood is definitely
feeble minded! To *carry* means to lead or to accompany, as when
one of my friends "*carried* his hull family plumb t' Bentonville."
The hillman does not carry an axe—he *totes* or *packs* it. The word
strut means to swell, as in the sentence: "Doc, my foot's plumb
strutted this mornin'—jest swole plumb t' a *strut!*"

A *stew* is not a dish of meat and vegetables in the Ozarks, but
a drink made of ginger and hot water and corn whiskey; a *taw* is
not a marble, as it is to children in the North, but a girl—a man's
partner at a dance or a play-party. A *scorpion* is not a scorpion,
either, but a little blue-tailed skink, quite harmless—the real
scorpion is known as a *stingin'-lizard!* *Ashamed*, when used with
reference to a child or a young girl, does not mean ashamed
at all, but merely timid or bashful. The word *gum* means a bee-
hive or a rabbit-trap—when the hillman wants chewing-gum

he calls for *wax*! When a typical Ozark native says *several*, he doesn't mean two or three or four, but a large number; a hunter once remarked to me that he "seen *several* squirrel, but only kilt fourteen of 'em." Country editors very often report that a party or a dance was attended by *several* people—meaning perhaps twenty-five, or even fifty. The word *foreign* is used in a peculiar local sense—a person from Iowa is just as surely a *furriner* as a man from Leningrad or Berlin.

Name is ordinarily used as a verb, meaning to mention, but as a noun it means self-respect or reputation. The defendant in a murder case, explaining that the slain man had repeatedly assaulted and humiliated him, cried out: "He wallered me in th' dirt, Jedge, right afore my fambly, an' I lost my name right thar!" The noun *judge* or *jedge*, by the way, is regularly used to mean a fool or a clown, and there is even an adjective *jedgy*—which gives a diverting insight into the hillman's attitude toward courts of law and justice. The verb *enjoy* is used in the sense of entertain, and one of my neighbors remarked, just after a number of unwelcome guests had left his cabin: "We done our best t' *enjoy* 'em, but they shore was th' sorriest comp'ny I ever seen!" On another occasion the same man said with reference to a similar situation: "We-all ben a-havin' too dang much comp'ny—th' ol' woman's jest *hosted* plum t' death!" The word *lavish* is used as a noun, meaning a large quantity, as in the following sentence: "If them Hammonses come down hyar a-lookin' for trouble, they'll shore git a *lavish* of it!" *Misery*, to the Ozarker, is nothing more than physical pain—"I shore have got a turrible *misery* in my back." *Portly* as applied to a man means handsome, and carries no reference to corpulence. A *bat* is a disreputable woman, and *out* is used as a verb meaning to defraud—"thet ol' feller don't need no pension, he's jest a-tryin' t' *out* th' Guv'ment!" *Fine-haired* means aristocratic, and the word *heir* is used as a verb—one of my friends recently "*heired* a mighty good farm off'n his Pappy." As a matter of fact, many of the strange words and phrases which fall from the hillman's lips are merely survivals of older English usages, formerly common to England and to all of the American colonies, but which are now seldom heard except in isolated mountain regions such as the Ozark country. Only the other day one of my neighbors remarked that he *admired* a flood which had ruined his crops—meaning simply that it astonished him. The superior summer colonist smiles at this, but Milton and his contemporaries used the word in exactly the same sense, and Samuel Pepys tells us that Charles II "is so fond of the Duke of Monmouth that everybody *admires* it, that is, wonders at it."

When a hillman says that someone has *bored* him he means that he has been ridiculed—not at all what the word means to the ordinary American from beyond the mountains. The Ozarker is much nearer to Beaumont and Fletcher, who used bored in the sense of insulted or imposed upon. The Ozarker very often says *argufy* instead of argue, and the "furrin" schoolmarms laugh at him for it, but argufy was formerly quite respectable in England.

The facetious hillman frequently says *buss* when he means kiss, which recalls Shakespeare's sentence: "And *buss* thee as thy wife," also his use of *buss* as a noun—"Thou dost give me flattering *busses*." Spenser uses the same word on occasion, although he usually spells it *busse*. The word *contrary* is used as a verb in the Ozarks meaning to contradict or to antagonize, and it seems to have carried the same significance in Chaucer's day. Chaucer also used the adjective *contrarious*, and this word is still heard occasionally in the Ozark country.

Disremember, meaning to forget, is no longer used in England, or in most parts of the United States, but it is still common in the hill country of Missouri and Arkansas. The hillman's word *dauncy*, which means particular or fastidious about food, is derived from *daunch*, a term common in fifteenth-century England.

When an Ozarker threatens to *feather into* somebody, he means that he is about to shoot this individual, or at least to attack him with murderous intent. Horace Kephart has traced this expression back to the days of the longbow in England, when to *feather into* a man meant to shoot him with such force that the feather at the butt of the arrow was buried in his body.

Fernent, meaning beside or against, is seldom used in the more enlightened parts of America, although still common in the Ozarks. It is still heard in Scotland, however, and in the south of Ireland. *Fraction*, in the Ozarks, means a quarrel or fight, just as it did in Shakespeare's day. The word *generation*, as used in the Ozark country, has nothing to do with temporal succession, but means a race or breed; the King James Bible, printed in 1611, makes Jesus of Nazareth refer to "a *generation* of vipers," meaning simply a crowd, a large number.

In the gales is the Ozark dialect for "in a good humor"; the word *gale* is an old English term used to denote a state of pleasant excitement or hilarity. *Gaum*, to soil, was once common in England but is now obsolete or provincial; it is still commonly used among the hillfolk, usually in combination with the adverb *up*, which intensifies the meaning of so many of our best Ozark verbs.

When one of my neighbors described his mother-in-law as a *pore hippoed critter* I was at a total loss, and there was nothing for it but to ask what the word *hippoed* meant. He explained that the woman was suffering from some imaginary ailment, brought on by "readin' of them fool doctor-books!" This word is doubtless quite old; Tucker, in his book on American English, says that "hypochondria was vulgarly called the hypo" in England as long ago as 1711, and probably much earlier. *Heap* is used by Chaucer

Grandmaw Check and Her Spinning-Wheel

in exactly the Ozark manner when he mentions "the wisdom of a *heap* of learned men." Only the other day one of my neighbors remarked: "My least chap he's kinder puny-like," meaning that his youngest son was not well. *Least*, in the sense of the smallest, is common in Shakespeare and .other Elizabethan writers.

The use of the word *misdoubt*, meaning to suspect or distrust, is a typical Ozark barbarism, but it is used at least once by Shakespeare, who also used *mind* in the sense of intend, exactly as the hillman employs the term today. *Middling*, in the sense of moderately well, is also a good old English word, mentioned by Bailey and used by Dryden. The word *misling*, which the hillman uses with reference to cool and foggy weather, is found in John Evelyn——"a mild and calm season, with gentle frost and little *misling* rain." In ordinary conversation the Ozarker refers to a married woman as *Mis'* or *Miz*, but in formal speeches, such as funeral sermons, he pronounces the word *Mistress* very distinctly, just as the Elizabethans did.

Nigh means near in many parts of the United States, but the comparative *nigher* is now heard chiefly in the southern Appalachians and the Ozarks, I think. It is quite common in the writings of Spenser and many other old English authors. Spenser also used the word *needments*, which still means necessities in the Ozark country. The word *nation* means simply a large amount, and was used with the true Ozark connotation by Lawrence Sterne when he wrote: "And what a *nation* of herbs he had procured to mollify her humours!"

A necklace is sometimes called a *pair o' beads* in the Ozarks, which phrase seemed utterly strange and meaningless until I found in Chaucer's Prologue a reference to the *peire of bedes* worn by the Prioresse. The use of *plumb* as an adjective, as in *plumb crazy*, is another English archaism, and the hillman still calls a sermon a *preachment*, just as Shakespeare did.

A bag or sack is still called a *poke* in the Ozarks, and the word is said to be the source of the French *poche* or pocket—whence comes *pouch*. Shakespeare tells of someone who "drew a dial from his *poke*," and there are many similar passages in other early writers. Chaucer quotes an old proverb about "pigges in a *poke*"—an axiom still current in both England and America, although the word *poke* is seldom heard in ordinary talk save in the backwoods regions of the South.

The use of *right* in the sense of very is not much heard nowadays in most parts of the United States, except in a few set phrases such as "Right Reverend," but it is still very common in the Ozarks. The use of *right* as an intensive is now regarded as archaic in England, but many examples of this usage are found in Shakespeare, who refers to "a *right* good husband" and uses such sentences as "*right* glad I am he was not at this fray."

Reckon, as used in the Ozarks, is not heard in England today except in some northern dialects, but it was once very good English, and is found in the King James Bible. To *red up* a house means to clean it and to set the furniture in order; it is an old English phrase which occurs in many ancient proverbs. The hillman often says *ramping* when he means raging; the word is used in Shakespeare and is evidently connected with the adjective *rampant*, which is still good English. The Ozarker's use of *ruinate* for ruin seems fantastic at first, but it is found in both Shakespeare and Spenser.

Shakespeare uses the word *race* in its original meaning of root—"nutmegs seven, and a *race* or two of ginger"; very few Americans use the word in this sense today, but a *race o' ginger* is still perfectly intelligible to the Ozark housewife. The hillman's adjective *resty*, meaning indolent, is another Shakespearian survival.

Sorry means poor or inferior in the Ozark dialect, as in Shakespeare's "a *sorry* breakfast" and John Evelyn's "*sorry* beds", and is not etymologically related to sorrow at all, but was originally sorey—covered with sores. The Ozarker very often says *soon* when he means early, as in the sentence: "You-all better git a right *soon* start in th' mornin'." This usage is common in many early English writers, including Shakespeare. One of the hillman's emphatic negatives is No *siree*! It has been suggested that *siree* is derived from *sirrah*, which is described as "another and more vehement form of *sir*."

When the hillman says that a certain man and woman are *talkin'* he means that they are contemplating matrimony, and we find the word used in a similar sense by Shakespeare. *Tote* means to carry in the South, but its derivation is not clear; Noah Webster thought that it might be of African origin, but the preterite *toted* is used in *Piers Plowman*.

Tole, to entice, is a rather unusual word in most sections of the United States, but is heard very frequently in the Ozark country. It is found also in many old English writers, as in the following passage from Fletcher:

> "Or voices calling in the dead of night
> To make me follow, and so *tole* me o'n.
> Through mire and standing pool to find my ruin."

The verb *use* means to frequent, or to loiter, and when it is said that "th' dang revenuers air *a-usin'* round" some particular locality the Ozarker understands the significance of the remark without difficulty. The same usage occurs in Spenser and in Fletcher. *Weddiners*, meaning the guests at a wedding party or "enfare" celebration, is a common word in the Ozark country—a very old English term, found in John Stagg's poems in the Cumberland dialect. The word *zany* is often heard in the Ozarks, too, and still carries the meaning of clown or buffoon exactly as it did in Shakespeare's day.

One of the most interesting peculiarities of the Ozark hillman's speech is the extraordinary character of his conversational taboos—the singular nature of his verbal reactions to sexual and scatological matters. The truth is that sex is very rarely mentioned save in ribaldry, and is therefore excluded from all polite conversation between men and women. Moreover, this taboo is extended to include a great many words which have no real connection with sex, and which are used quite freely in more enlightened sections of the United States.

In general, it may be said that the names of male animals must not be mentioned when women are present—such words as *bull, boar, buck, ram, jack* and *stallion* are absolutely taboo. Some writers think that *buck*, meaning a male goat or deer, is not generally objectionable, but I cannot agree with them. It is a strange thing, however, that *Buck* is quite admissible when used as a man's given name, and in this connection may be pronounced freely by men and women alike. The same thing is true of such compound substantives as *buck-shot, buck-ague, buck-brush*, and *buck-skin*.

Many Southerners use *ox, male-cow*, or even *gentleman-cow* instead of the English word *bull*, but the Ozarkers in my neighborhood usually say *male, cow-critter*, or *cow-brute*. It was only a few years ago that two women in Scott County, Arkansas, raised a great clamor for the arrest of a man who had mentioned a *bull-calf* in their presence! Even such words as *bull-frog, bull-fiddle* and *bull-snake* must be used with considerable caution, and a preacher at Pineville, Missouri, recently told his flock that Pharaoh's daughter found the infant Moses in the *flags*—the poor man didn't like to say *bull-rushes*! The hillman sometimes refers to animals merely as the *he* or the *she*, and I have heard grown men use such childish terms as *girl-birds* and *boy-birds*.

A stallion is sometimes called a *stable-horse*, and very rarely a *stone-horse*, the latter term being considered unfit for respectable feminine ears. Such words as *stud* and *stud-horse* are universally barred. The male members of most species of domestic animals are designated simply as *males. Cow, mare, sow, doe* and *ewe* are used freely enough; but *bitch* is taboo, since this last term is often applied to loose women. *Whore-bitch* is a common Ozark term for prostitute. To call a hill woman a *heifer* is to call her a meddlesome gossip, and a *sow* is simply a slatternly housekeeper; but neither term has any particular sexual or moral significance.

The male fowl is usually called a *crower*—the word *cock* is altogether impossible, since it is used to designate the genitals. The word *rooster* is also used as a substitute for *cock*. I have seen grown men, when women were present, blush and stammer at the mere mention of such commonplace bits of hardware as *stop-cocks* or *pet-cocks*, and avoid describing a gun as *cocked* by some clumsy circumlocution, such as *she's ready t' go* or *th' hammer's back*. Such expressions as I *roostered my ol' hawg-leg* are not at all uncommon in this latter connection, and when a hillman says "*I pulled back both roosters*" he means only that he cocked both barrels of his shotgun. The word *peacock* is very bad, since it is supposed to suggest micturition as well as the genitalia. Even *cock-eyed, cock-sure* and *coxcomb* are considered too suggestive for general conversation, and many natives shy at such surnames as *Cox, Leacock, Hitchcock* and the like.

The Ozarker very seldom uses such words as *virgin* or *maiden*, since these terms carry a too direct reference to sex. A teacher of botany tells me that he is actually afraid to mention the *maidenhair* fern in his high-school classes. *Decent* is used to describe women who have no sexual experience outside of lawful wedlock, but the term is not used in polite conversation between the sexes. "Fifty years ago," writes H. L. Mencken, "the word *decent* was indecent in the South; no respectable woman was supposed to have any notion of the difference between *decent* and indecent." *Decent* is still indecent in the Ozarks. *Ravish* and *ravage* always mean rape in the hill country, and are not mentioned in polite conversation. Even the word *bed* is seldom used before strangers, and the Ozark women do not go to *bed*—they *lay down*.

There are no crabs in the Ozarks, but the word *crab* is used to designate a tiny pest which the entomologists call *Pediculus pubis*. Since this parasite is usually confined to the areas about the sex organs, the name of it has acquired an indecent connotation. The tourist may talk of shrimps and prawns and lobsters without let or hindrance, but the first mention of *crabs* is greeted by an awkward silence, or by embarrassed efforts to change the subject.

Even the apparently innocent verb *alter* is never used in the presence of women, because *alter* in the Ozarks means to castrate, and is never used in any other sense. *Rim* means to desire sexual intercourse, and is applied particularly to swine; it is never used in general talk between the sexes. *Stag*, meaning a gentleman who appears at a social function unaccompanied by a lady, is a new word brought into the country by tourists— the natives regard it as vulgar. *Cagey* and *horny* are the ordinary words for sensual, and are never used in polite conversation. *Balled-up*, according to Mencken, was once improper, but is now making steady progress toward polite acceptance. This is doubtless true in the more sophisticated sections of the country, but *balled-up* is still bad taste in the Ozarks.

A paper bag is always a *sack* or a *poke*, since *bag* means scrotum in the hill country, and is too vulgar for refined ears. The sex organs in general are frequently known as the *prides*, and the word *pride* has thus acquired a certain obscene significance. When a hillman says that he *got him a piece* he means that he has had sexual intercourse and thus an intrinsically harmless term like *piece* has become unfit for refined society in the mountains, and must be used with considerable caution. The word *parts*, too, is so often used to mean genitals that it is no longer decent in the Ozarks.

When the word *ill* is applied to a woman it usually means that she is bad-tempered, but sometimes it refers to menstruation, and *unwell* is always used in this sense—a man or boy could never be described as *unwell* in the Ozarks. The individual who is afflicted with a serious disease is neither *ill* nor *unwell*, but *sick*. The term *flowers* is also used with reference to catamenia;

Dr. Morris Fishbein has noted this, and regards it as a modern slang term. It is found in Webster's New International however, and in the King James version of the Bible.

Another doubtful word is the proper name *Peter*. This is so universally used by children and facetious adults as a name for the penis that it never quite loses this significance. Very few natives of the Ozarks will consider naming a boy *Peter*. I recall an itinerant evangelist from the North who shouted out something about the church being founded upon *Peter*—he was puzzled by the flushed cheeks of the young women, and the ill-suppressed amusement of the ungodly. Another preacher, a real Ozark circuit-rider, after talking about Peter's denial of Christ, suddenly called out, "*How many Peters air they hyar?*" There was no laughter or snickering—the people were simply horrified, and the poor preacher almost collapsed when he realized what he had said. This happened almost thirty years ago, but it is still remembered and commented on whenever this preacher's name is mentioned. *Petered out* means simply exhausted, and has no particular connection with sex, but I have several times noticed that a native stumbles and hesitates over this phrase in the presence of strangers, particularly women. He feels somehow that it is just a trifle off color—not quite the thing to say *right out before folks.*

Pregnancy is another thing which is never mentioned when both, men and women are present, even among fairly intimate friends. If no women are within hearing, a hill-man may remark to a comparative stranger that his wife is *ketched,* or *knocked up,* or *in a family way,* but these phrases are not for use in mixed company. A pregnant woman is expected to stay at home and keep out of sight as much as possible, never intimating to any man except her husband that she has the least inkling of her own condition. The word *slink* must be avoided, too, because it means to abort or to miscarry. A midwife is always called a *granny-woman*, and *granny* is often used as a verb, designating the actual delivery of the child. It is sometimes employed with reference to the lower animals, and I have heard a hillman speak of *grannyin'* a cow. These terms are never used in general conversation between the sexes.

Many of the hill people still shy at the word *leg*, and usually say *limb*, particularly if the speaker is a woman, or if the member under discussion is feminine. The general idea is that since women's legs are concealed by their garments they should not be exposed in speech. The younger women no longer conceal their legs, but something of the old taboo still lingers in the common speech; legs are to be seen, perhaps, but should not be talked about. *Stockings*, too, are considered rather indelicate—it is much better to say *hose*. Something of the same sort has occurred in connection with *breast*, and the word *bosom*, which is not common in ordinary American conversation, is still the proper term in the Ozarks.

Even *love* is considered more or less indecent, and the mountain people very seldom use the term in its ordinary sense, but nearly always with some degrading or jocular connotation. If a hillman does admit that he *loved* a woman he means only that he caressed and embraced her—and he usually says that he *loved her up*. Such terms as *passion* and *passionate* are never used save in connection with sexual desire, and must be avoided in polite conversation. The hillman sometimes eats sheep's testicles, which he calls *mountain oysters*, but these are believed to contain a powerful aphrodisiac, and must not be mentioned when ladies are present. No modest mountain woman would ever admit publicly that she is particularly fond of eggs, because eggs also are supposed to excite sexual desire. The word *tail* is frowned upon for some reason or other, and *shirt-tail parade* is regarded as indelicate even at the University of Arkansas, *night-shirt parade* being considered much more refined!

The noun *ass* must be avoided because it sounds exactly like the Southern pronunciation of *arse,* and even *aster* is sometimes considered suggestive. I have seen one of our solid citizens painfully embarrassed because he inadvertently said *manure* in talking with a mountain schoolmarm, and sly allusions to this devastating *faux pas* followed the poor devil for years. A casual mention of the game called *hockey* will paralyze any Ozark audience, for *hockey* means nothing but dung in the hill country. Any mention of laxative drugs is considered in very bad taste, and I shall never forget the country druggist who was horrified when I called for Pluto-water while he was selling candy to some young girls. I remember also a grown-up mountain woman, the mother of several children, who blushed scarlet when she heard *physics* mentioned as part of the high-school curriculum.

The word *bastard* must not be used in ordinary talk, of course, but *woodscolt,* which means exactly the same thing, is not prohibited. A woman who would be highly insulted if the word *bull* was used in her presence will employ *Gawd-a-mighty* and *Jesus Christ* freely as expletives; these words are not regarded as profane, and are used by the most staunch Christians in the backwoods districts. Women of the very best families *give tittie* to their babes in public, even in church, without the slightest embarrassment. Such inelegant terms as *spit* and *belch* are used freely by the hill women everywhere, and I have heard the wife of a prominent professional man tell her daughter to *git a rag an' snot thet young-un*—meaning to wipe away the mucous matter from the child's nose. On another occasion she remarked to a total stranger that her husband had *done got drunk ag'in an' plum benastied hisse'f.* This same woman would never use such words as *leg* and *breast* in the presence of strange menfolks, and would blush to hear of *gonorrhea* or *syphilis*.

So much for prudery in the Ozark dialect. Perhaps a century or so of isolation is responsible for an abnormal development of this sort of thing, or it may be that the mountain people have simply retained a pecksniffian attitude once common to the whole country. But these questions must be left to the scientific students of dialect. The present influx of tourists and summer-resort people is rapidly wiping out the old folk-speech—a few more years and the hill people will be talking just like the rest of us.

Meanwhile, it is probably worth while to record such data as are now available, to be mulled over later by the lexicographers.

CHAPTER V.

Signs and Superstitions

T HOSE WHO HAVE STUDIED THE folk-beliefs of many different peoples in many different parts of the world tell us that the superstitions which still persist in the American hinterland have nearly all come to us from the Old World, "scattered remnants of the folk-thought of the illiterate Middle Ages", when princes and peasants alike were incredibly ignorant and superstitious. The material in this chapter is what I have collected myself, in my odd moments, over a period of about ten years. It evidently represents only a small part of the great body of folk-belief which still exists in the Ozark country. If the superstitions listed in the following pages are merely "scattered remnants", it is difficult for me to conceive of the mental confusion which must have prevailed in medieval Europe.

Nearly every hillman of my acquaintance disclaims all superstitious belief, but an investigation invariably shows that he is superstitious to a remarkable degree. No single individual accepts all of the items listed in the following pages, but every one of them is credited by hillfolk within my own circle of friends and neighbors. The man who laughs at witchcraft and supernatural warning is found to be a firm believer in the moon's influence upon crops, while the woman who doesn't believe in evil spirits takes the question of prenatal "marking" very seriously indeed.

One would expect to find a definite negative correlation between superstition and educational progress, or at least between superstition and intelligence, but this does not seem to hold true in the territory which has come under my observation. Perhaps the most famous "water-witch" who ever lived in my section of the Ozarks was a physician, a man of really extraordinary attainments, while one of the most credulous and superstitious hillmen I have ever known was sufficiently intelligent to learn surveying, and had sufficient education to enable him to teach the district school with unprecedented success.

Superstitions relating to love, courtship and marriage are legion in the Ozark country. Many hillmen still believe in love-powders and potions, and this belief is encouraged by the country druggists, who sell a perfumed mixture of milk sugar and flake whiting at enormous profits. There used to be a patent preparation called "Wonderful Sportine", too, which was highly recommended. These materials are dissolved in a girl's coffee or fed to her in candy, and are said to be quite efficacious. Many mountain damsels carry love charms consisting of some pinkish, soap-like material, the composition of which I have been unable to discover; the thing is usually enclosed in a carved peach-stone or cherry pit, and worn on a string round the neck. Every normal adult is supposed to have a peculiar erogenous area, quite apart from the sex organs, which produces the wildest sort of sexual excitement when caressed. In a man it is usually the back of the head, or the neck, but in a woman it may be the throat, breast, buttocks, or even the ears.

Every mountain girl knows that if she puts a drop of her menstrual fluid into a man's liquor he is certain to fall madly in love with her. Whiskey in which her fingernail trimmings have been soaked is said to have a very similar effect. These beliefs are taken so seriously in the Ozarks that the victim of a love charm or philtre is not held morally responsible for his actions, and many a deserted wife is comforted by the reflection that her man did not leave of his own free will, but was "conjured off".

When a girl's apron is unfastened accidentally, or her skirt turns up, or her stocking falls down, or her shoe comes untied, she knows that her lover is thinking of her. If she stubs her toe against a stone she kisses her thumb, and rests happy in the knowledge that she will see her sweetheart within twenty-four hours. By cleaning her fingernails on Saturday she can force her lover to visit her on the following day, and if a redbird flies across her path she is sure to be kissed twice before nightfall. If a girl puts salt on the fire for seven consecutive mornings, it will bring her absent lover home, whether he wants to come or not. Or she may place her shoes together on the floor at right angles, so that the toe of one touches the middle of the other, and recite:

> "When I my true love want to see,
> I put my shoes in th' shape of a T."

This is said to be particularly effective when the recreant swain is married, or has become entangled with a married woman.

If the fire which a man kindles burns brightly, he knows that his sweetheart is true to him, but if it smolders, she is likely to prove unfaithful. As a further test, he may go into a clearing and bend down a mullein stalk which points toward her cabin; if she loves him the stalk grows up again, but if she loves another it will die. The girl has only to put a bit of dodder or love-vine on a growing weed; if it flourishes, her lover is faithful, and if it withers he is not. Or she may pluck a hair from her head and draw it between her fingers-if it curls he loves her, if it remains straight he does not. If she burns the cornbread it means that her sweetheart is angry, and if she finds a cobweb in the cabin she fears that he will never visit her again. Cold hands are generally believed to be associated with a warm heart, and are often regarded as a sure sign that one is in love. A hill girl often names a match for a boy whom she admires, and then lights the match; if it burns to the end without breaking, she is assured that the boy loves her. My neighbors' daughters once used up half-a-box of matches in this search for knowledge, an extravagance which was very harshly rebuked by the frugal parents.

Marriage is still regarded as a serious matter in the Ozarks, and there are many singular superstitions connected with the choice of a mate. The typical hillman is determined to marry a virgin at any cost, and is firmly convinced that he can detect virginity at a glance. The theory is that every female child has a tiny cleft or depression in the end of her nose, and that this depression immediately disappears after sexual intercourse is effected. Many hill women, too, are firmly convinced that a man's virility is indicated by the length of his nose, and a girl who "keeps company" with a very long-nosed man is subjected to the good-natured raillery of her friends.

A girl who sits on a table, or allows any one to sweep under the chair in which she is sitting, will not marry for a year at least. At a quilting-party, there is always a scramble among the girls to see who will be the first to wrap herself in the newly completed quilt, for she is certain to be the first one of the group to marry. It is said also that a girl can tell when she is to be married by listening to the whippoorwill—every repetition of the bird's call representing a year which must elapse before the happy day arrives. The worst possible fate that can befall a mountain girl is to be a spinster, but it is almost as bad for her to marry a widower. As a young girl in my neighborhood once said: "If I caint be tablecloth, I shore don't aim t' be dishrag!" There is a prevalent belief that a girl who sings while cooking, or while doing any sort of work about the fireplace or cookstove, is doomed to wed a "widder-man".

A very popular way to find out which man one is to marry is to sleep in a strange room, and name each of the four corners for one of the possible candidates. The corner that is first seen in the morning represents the groom-to-be. Or a girl may write the names of nine boys on a slip of paper, and put the paper between her breasts at night—she is certain to dream of the one who is to be her husband. The same result is obtained by placing a mirror, or a thimble full of salt, or a piece of wedding-cake under her pillow. Some mountain girls catch a glimpse of their future husbands by peering into a well at high noon on the first of May, while others address the new moon:

"New moon, new moon, tell to me,
Who is my true lover to be?"

and then go home and wait for the new moon's answer to come to them in a dream. One of the simplest and most sensible methods that I know is to hang the wishbone of a chicken over the door-the first single man to enter is destined to be the lady's mate. If a woman has the habit of resting her thumb inside her clenched hand, everybody knows that she will be ruled absolutely by her husband, while if her thumb is habitually extruded her husband will probably be henpecked.

The best dates and seasons for weddings are determined in part by the changes of the moon and the signs of the zodiac, but the interpretation of this material varies widely. However, marriages in May are always unlucky, and so are those celebrated in rainy or snowy weather—bright, warm wedding-days are best. It is very bad luck to marry a man whose surname has the same initial as one's own:

> "Change the name and not the letter,
> Marry for worse and not for better."

The wedding day is called the bride's day; if it is bright and pleasant her wedded life will be happy. If the morning is fair and the afternoon rainy, the first part of her married life will be happy, and the latter half unhappy. The day after the wedding, when the "enfare" dinner is held at the home of the groom's parents, is known as the groom's day, and the same weather-signs indicate his future happiness or unhappiness. To postpone a wedding is very bad luck, however, an almost certain indication that one of the contracting parties will die within a year, so that when a certain date is once decided upon the ceremony must be performed, no matter what the weather conditions may be.

For some reason which has never been made clear to me, a hill woman is always very careful not to exhibit any of her wedding garments until she has worn them, or at least tried them on. They are never shown to any but her most intimate friends until the morning of the ceremony. I recall a girl who was about to show her mother the new pink "weddin' slippers" which had just arrived by mail, but caught herself just in time, reminded by her sister's agonized outcry. The entire family trembled over her narrow escape from some nameless calamity!

There are many outlandish and outworn notions about physiology, hygiene and therapeutics. Regular physicians are not very numerous in the Ozarks, and a great number of unaccredited persons are practicing illegally, encouraged rather than hindered by the authorities. Most of them are men who have had a year or two of training at some Southern medical college, or who have "picked up doctorin'" by assisting some old physician whose practice they have inherited. These mountain healers save the regular M. D. many a long night ride, and are therefore protected and assisted whenever possible.

There are also the "yarb" doctors, and the "chills an' fever" doctors, who know nothing whatever of modern medicine, and make no pretense of scientific treatment, but rely upon a few simple roots and herbs. Catnip tea is their best remedy for colic, hoarhound is indicated in coughs and colds, sassafras is an excellent spring tonic, mullein leaves are smoked for asthma, pumpkin-seed tea is used to expel tapeworms, slippery elm bark cures all sorts of intestinal trouble, and so on.

Healers of still another type do not attempt any general practice, and seldom accept money for their services, but are endowed with a mysterious "power" to cure certain specific ailments. Some of them, usually old women, can cool fevers merely by the laying on of hands; others draw out the fire from burns by spitting or blowing upon the inflamed areas, while still others claim to heal more serious lesions by some similar hocus-pocus. One old lady who specializes in burns says that she always mutters a few words which she "l'arnt out'n th' Book"—the Bible, that is—but refuses to tell me what particular text is used. I know an old man and his wife who "charm fire" by touching the burned area with a moistened fingertip, and at the same time muttering an "ol' sayin'". The mystic words must not be revealed to any outsider or they will lose their efficacy, and they are passed on in the family or the clan in accordance with certain definite rules; the eldest son and the first son-in-law are told, also some other relatives, but each individual must get the "sayin'" from a person of the opposite sex. Other healers draw the pain out of a burn or scald by holding the injured area close to a hot fire; I have seen the leg of a screaming little girl held almost in contact with a redhot stove, until the child suffered nearly as much from the treatment as from the original burn.

Any posthumous child can cure the croup simply by blowing in the patient's mouth; one of my neighbors happened to be born several weeks after his father's death, and although he ridicules the healing power himself, is frequently called out of his bed at night by distracted parents who want him to treat their children. The same treatment is said to be a sure cure for the "thresh"—a white cotton-like eruption which sometimes appears in a child's mouth. If this doesn't work, one can always cure "thresh" by applying water from the heel of an old boot which has been left out in the rain. There is no excuse for a properly reared mountain baby ever having this trouble, however, since it can be prevented by carrying the new-born babe to a small hole in the wall or chinking, and allowing the sunlight which streams through to enter the child's open mouth.

A wart or boil or sty on the posterior is said to be caused by urinating or defecating in a path, and the hillman sums up the situation in a neat little couplet, which unfortunately is unprintable. The consequences of fouling a path, however, may be avoided by shouting, "I got a sty, it's a lie!" just as the offending act is completed.

One way to cure a wart is to wrap it in a dirty dishrag—the dirtier the better—spit on the rag, and then bury it under the doorstep. As the rag decays the wart gradually disappears. Or you may cut notches on a sycamore stick, as many notches as you have warts, and throw the stick into a stream of water. One of my neighbors tells me that he rid himself of forty-two warts in a fortnight, simply by washing his hands in "spunk-water"— rain-water which falls into the hollow of a rotten stump. Another method of treating a wart is to pick it apart with a needle, and then rub the place with seven different green leaves; it makes no difference what leaves are used, so long as they are from seven distinct species of plants.

One of my best friends professes to be a "wart-taker"; I have seen him treat a wart simply by pressing it a bit with his fingers, rolling his eyes heavenward and assuming a rapt expression the while. This particular wart seems quite unchanged after a period of several months, but the "wart-taker" has a local reputation, and is said to have accomplished some remarkable cures. Another hillman of my acquaintance heals warts, ulcers, "risin's" and the like in this wise: he reaches behind him, picks up a stone without looking at it, and spits upon it. Stirring the saliva about with his finger, he repeats the words:

> "What I see increase,
> What I rub decrease—"

and with that he rubs a little spittle on the wart, which is supposed to disappear in a week or so. All this must be done, however, when the moon is waning; if it should be attempted before the full moon the wart would grow larger and larger instead of wasting away. There seems to be widespread belief that things in general increase or decrease with the moon, and this principle is very seriously considered in connection with certain agricultural activities. An epileptic hillman tells me that he never has a seizure in the light of the moon, and an old "granny-woman" contends that venereal disease is much less likely to be acquired when the moon is in the last quarter than at any other time.

Besides the moon's phases, there are also the signs of the zodiac to be considered, and almost every hill farmer can make out these signs in the almanac, even though he cannot read a line of ordinary print. Each one of the zodiacal signs is supposed to control some particular part of the body, as indicated by the diagram in the almanac, and many hillmen believe that the sign has a great influence upon disease. Stomach trouble is most likely to be acquired or aggravated when the moon is in Cancer, diseases of the throat during the sign of Taurus, venereal infections in Scorpio, and so on. Many people, if forced to undergo a surgical operation, are careful to postpone it until the moon is in the proper constellation, and not a few mountain physicians encourage them in this practice.

The hill people have singular notions of the best means of preventing disease. Many children in the Ozarks wear little flat leather bands or woolen strings around their necks, or tiny bags of asafetida, or little stones sewed into their garments, to protect them from the common diseases of childhood. A buckeye fastened about a man's neck is reputed to prevent the mumps from "falling" or "going down on him"—a calamity to be prevented at all costs. In one settlement I found the children wearing little round pieces of porous stone tied around their necks; it is said that these objects are taken from the entrails of deer, and protect the wearer against disease, financial losses and violence at the hands of enemies. Every hill woman knows that the wearing of gold or amber beads will reduce goitre, and many mountaineers wear heavy cartridge-belts to prevent rheumatism, while a dirty woolen sock tied around the neck is recognized as the best remedy for sore throat. A piece of black silk wrapped about a child's throat is generally recognized as a preventative of croup. I have known hillmen to spend hours and even days in searching the rivers for large "craw-pappies" in order to get the two circular "lucky-bones" found in their bodies, which are carried in the pocket to ward off syphilis. The bigger the bones the better, it is said, and really large lucky-bones are hard to find.

Late Autumns are always unhealthy, the hillman thinks—"a green Christmas makes a fat graveyard." Never allow anyone to step directly in your tracks, particularly in wet or muddy weather, as this will cause severe headaches and even blindness. If a baby's eyes are sore, the mother's milk is the best possible wash for them, just as fresh urine is the best lotion for chapped hands or chilblains. Cow-dung is used as a poultice for all sorts of sores, as well as a dressing for sprains and fractures, and an infusion of sheep manure is much in favor as a remedy for earache. As for insect stings and snake bites, any child in the hill country knows that a piece of freshly chewed tobacco will draw the "pizen" out. In snake bite, however, the main thing is to kill the snake and burn it; this is always done before any other treatment is thought of. Some hill people bind a piece of the snake's flesh to the wound, instead of the tobacco mentioned above.

The pain of bee stings is relieved by applying the crushed leaves of three plants—any three will do, so long as they are of different species—to the parts affected. A skin disease called tetter is always treated with "spunk-water". Sprains are relieved by a poultice of red clay and vinegar, while a piece of fat pork, tied on a wound, is supposed to prevent blood-poisoning. A boil or "risin'" is "drawed to a head" by applying a mass of boiled peach-leaves, or a poultice of hot cornmeal mush. A rusty nail puncture is treated by tying a very old corroded penny over the wound—a treatment calculated to draw the "pizen" out, and prevent tetanus. Lacking the penny, the next best thing is to burn old woolen rags in a copper kettle, and hold the injured member over the thickest part of the smoke.

"Pneumony" is conquered by a poultice of hot fried onions, applied to the chest and between the shoulders with a thick woolen blanket over all. In severe cases the poultice must be renewed every thirty minutes, day and night. Mare's milk is a certain cure for scarlet fever and an infusion of chimney-soot is good for "chills an' fever". Another excellent treatment for "malary" is to tie as many knots in a woolen string as the patient has had chills, and fasten the string about the trunk of the biggest persimmon tree in the vicinity. It is easy to stop night sweats by putting a pan of water under the patient's bed. A child with the colic may be relieved almost instantly by blowing tobacco-smoke up under its clothing, and the best way to cure a pain in the side is to pick up a flat stone, spit in the place from which it was removed, and then carefully replace it. The approved treatment for earache is to prick a "betsy-bug" with a pin, and put a drop of its blood in the ear; people subject to earache often keep a few betsy-bugs alive in a glass jar, to be used as needed. Water drunk from a green gourd is somehow cleansed of all impurities, and some people regard it as a specific for rheumatism. To cure summer-complaint, the hillfolk make a tea by mashing sowbugs and steeping them in boiling water; some mountain healers give large doses of this concoction to sick babies.

The body of a buzzard is somehow used to cure cancer, but this must be done secretly, for the killing of a buzzard means seven years of crop failure for the whole countryside, and the man who shoots one of these birds is naturally unpopular. Dr. Oakley St. John, of Pineville, Missouri, tells me that a farmer who killed a buzzard some years ago, to treat his daughter's cancer, so enraged his neighbors that there was serious talk of lynching him, and several people came into town to see if he could not be punished by the county officers!

To cure sore eyes, the hillman goes to the nearest crossroads exactly at midnight, in the dark of the moon, and shouts:

> "Sty, sty, leave my eye,
> Go t' th' next feller passin' by!"

Another almost universal idea is that venereal disease may be relieved simply by communicating it to another person—a theory responsible for untold and needless misery in the hill country. It is generally believed also that all "bad women" are diseased, and that any woman who has sexual intercourse with seven different men will acquire a "bad sickness", even though all of the men were free from disease! Nearly all of the old-timers believe that gonorrhea and syphilis are simply two different stages of the same ailment, and that the former will gradually turn into the latter if not properly treated. Ginseng root, according to the old settlers, is a powerful aphrodisiac, and I have known several very old men who claimed to have restored their sexual powers by the use of it.

If a patient is suffering from a bad cut or knife-thrust, the first thing to be done is to burn the sole of his shoe, and apply the ashes to the wound. Several old women that I have met profess to stop profuse bleeding by repeating a verse from the Bible, but they will not tell me what verse is used, for I am not a Christian, and the charm would be broken if the words were revealed to an unbeliever. When a mountain man cuts himself accidentally, he always hastens to thrust the knife deep into the soil, as this is said to prevent excessive bleeding.

Dew, or dew and buttermilk, or various mixtures of honey and buttermilk, are generally recognized remedies for curing skin disease and restoring a clear and youthful complexion. And everybody knows that if the hair is cut at the time of the new moon it grows very rapidly and luxuriantly, particularly if treated with the sap drawn from wild grapevines in the spring. It is proverbial among Ozark women that the winds of March are particularly bad for the complexion:

> "March winds an' May suns
> Make clothes white an' maids dun."

Many mountain women believe that to eat chicken hearts raw will make any girl beautiful; I know one poor girl who has eaten them for years, but without any benefit, so far as I can see.

Nearly all the hill people think that night air is somehow

poisonous, and they shut every door and window as tightly as possible, even though an entire family sleeps in a single small cabin. If it were not for the chinks in their clumsily built shanties, and the draught created by the great fireplace, they would certainly be suffocated.

Only a few of the many signs and omens relating to pregnancy and childbirth can be recorded here. Every mountaineer's wife knows that if a baby's diaper is accidentally left in her house by some visiting mother, she herself will very shortly become pregnant. It is well known also, that a child begotten immediately before the menses will be a girl, and that one conceived directly after the menstrual flow is invariably a boy. When a pregnant woman has a craving for some particular article of food, every effort is made to satisfy it, because otherwise the child is very likely to be "marked". I have seen birthmarks which were supposed to resemble strawberries, cherries, sweet potatoes, prunes, eels, and even hams—all of which owed their existence to the mother's unsatisfied cravings for these things. Even if the child has no external marks, his mind is likely to be affected, and he is sure to be "a plumb glutton" for the particular food that could not be obtained for his mother.

Children are also said to be marked by some sudden fright or unpleasant experience of the mother, and I have myself seen a pop-eyed, big-mouthed idiot whose condition is ascribed to the fact that his mother stepped on a toad some two months before his birth. In another case, a large red mark on a baby's face was caused by the mother seeing a man shot down at her side—the discharge of the gun threw some of the blood and brains into the woman's face. Another woman in my neighborhood saw two large snakes fighting or copulating, and when her babe was born some months later it had two writhing serpents in place of a head, according to local testimony! I recall a young farmer who had been worsted in a drunken fight, and appeared in the village all covered with blood and dirt. Instantly everybody sprang to prevent the injured man's pregnant wife from seeing him, and one old man shrilled out, "Git Emmy away, folkses—she'll mark thet 'ar young-un shore'." However, a woman who does not lose her head can usually prevent the marking of her babe at such times, simply by laying her hand upon a growing tree.

The editor of a local newspaper tells me that during the Civil War some bushwhackers killed a man near my home; they cut off one of his ears and threw it into his wife's lap as she sat on her little front porch. The woman was pregnant at the time, and when her child was born one of his ears "warn't nothin' but a wart." This latter part of the tale is true enough; I have seen the man myself. The people here nearly all believe that this is a classic case of "marking"—a positive proof that prenatal influence is a fact! Death is said to be the penalty for a pregnant woman who crosses running water, and she will go to great lengths in order to avoid doing so. When a mother crosses a stream with a babe in her arms, she is careful to carry the child so that its head points upstream; if the child's head points downstream, there is grave danger of death by drowning in later life.

Sexual acts between human beings and domestic animals are rather common in the Ozarks, and nearly every native believes that these unions are sometimes fruitful. Women giving birth to litters of puppies, mares bringing forth colts with human heads, and a great variety of similar phenomena are related and very generally believed. I have never been able to locate a hillman who has actually seen any of these monstrosities—"th' folks allus puts 'em out o' th' way," as one old man told me.

The Ozarker is not especially enthusiastic about bathing at any time, but the belief is almost universal that if a woman bathes at the time of her menses she is likely to be paralyzed. Although

menstruating women go about their house-work as usual, and
even work in the fields, there is one thing that they cannot do, and
that is to pickle cucumbers. As any old woman can tell you, the
pickles would always turn out soft and flabby instead of properly
crisp. To return to the subject of bathing, it is generally believed
that a woman must not bathe for at least nine days after her child
is born, or she will not "do well". Another strange notion is that
the afterbirth must always be buried—if it is burned or thrown
into water, the mother will not make a proper recovery. The same
thing is true in a measure of amputated limbs, although here the
belief is that the owner will return after death, and be forced to
search for the lost member through all eternity.

If a child is born with a caul or "veil" the membrane is always
carefully dried and given to the child after it reaches maturity—
otherwise the youngster is condemned to a life of perpetual misfortune. The series of calamities which befell one of my neighbors is accounted for by the fact that she was born with a veil,
which the "granny-woman" in attendance very properly hung
on a bush to dry; this woman forgot to bring it to the house,
however, and a great storm blew the precious tissue away into
the hills, from which several searching-parties failed to retrieve
it. In case the afterbirth or the veil falls into the hands of an
enemy of the family, the child will be more or less in this person's power all of its life, and may be forced into all sorts of evil
deeds through no fault of its own. Another important thing to
be remembered is that the band which protects the navel of an
infant must always be turned over three times before it is washed
or burned; some people regard this as a safeguard against witchcraft, while others think that it simply prevents the child from
having back-ache later in life.

Instead of the usual story about the stork or the doctor's
little black bag, the Ozark child is often told that babies come

out of knots in the trees, or from cabbages. Little girls are often morbidly interested in knots or excrescences on trees, and the daughter of one of my fellow-villagers was given a severe whipping because she cut up a lot of cabbages in a futile search for a baby. When a woman has a hemorrhage during the ordeal of childbirth, the mountain midwife or "granny-woman" kills a chicken and fastens the warm lining of its gizzard over the affected part. If the baby has trouble in teething, the father catches a fish, rubs the baby's gums with it, and then returns it alive to the water.

The signs of the zodiac must be considered in many operations connected with childbirth and the care of infants. For example, a child should never be weaned except under Aquarius, "when th' sign's in th' laigs," although just what would be the penalty for violating this rule is not clearly understood. Misfortune would certainly be the portion of a child should the moonlight fall upon the bed at the time of its birth, and even an adult who sleeps much in the moonlight is likely to go blind or crazy, or both. Women and cattle alike, according to the wise men of the hills, usually give birth to young when the moon is changing, rather than at other times. A baby born at the time of the new moon will be very strong, and the fourth child is always the brightest one of the family. It is very bad luck to make or buy a cap for a babe before it is born, and if some ignorant person gives an expectant mother a child's cap she hastens to burn it.

There are several methods of determining what a child's future life is to be. One of the commonest is to offer a boy baby a bottle, a Bible and a coin. If he grasps the bottle first, he will be a drunkard; if the Bible, a preacher, or at least a religious man; while if he chooses the coin, he will engage in some mercantile pursuit. A child born on Friday is certain to be hanged, however, and one whose fists are conspicuously clenched at birth is very likely to be a thief. The mountain midwife never washes the palms of a child's hands for several days after birth, lest its luck should be washed away, and it is always best to take a boy baby out of doors as soon as possible and show him the cabin, so that he will not be a rover in later life.

Many trivial happenings are regarded as presages of an approaching death. A bird flying into the house, or a ringing in the ears, or a cock crowing in the doorway, are all sure signs that some member of the family is about to die. Cattle bawling in the night, or horses running about and neighing without any apparent cause, are also regarded as death signs. The falling of a window-sash at night, or the spontaneous breaking of any object when no one is touching it, is a sure sign of death and doom in the house. The famous death-watch or death-tick, a sharp snapping sound sometimes heard in log houses at night, is supposed to mean a death in the building within a few days. This noise is similar to the sound made by cocking a pistol, and is said to be produced by a beetle with a singular gift of divination.

A bat in the house is even worse than a songbird, but a screech-owl alighting on the housetop is worst of all. One cry from this bird, and the mother jumps instantly to throw salt on the fire, while the older children, usually crying, begin to tie knots in a string. If there happens to be a sick person in the house, someone makes every effort to kill the owl, so that its dead body may be laid warm and bleeding on the patient's chest—otherwise he or she will surely die. If a clock that has not run for a long time suddenly begins to strike, there will be a death in the house within the number of days, weeks or months that the clock strikes hours. If a baby loses one of its shoes, and the shoe cannot be found, the child will never live to maturity. When a turtle-dove alights on a house and coos, many people feel that it is a sign of sickness and death, while to carry peacock feathers into a cabin is always a hazardous proceeding. If a cock sits on the fence with his tail toward the front door and crows, it means that a coffin will soon be carried out of the house. Never sweep under a sick man's bed, or tear down a cobweb in a sickroom—the patient will certainly die if you do. I know an old fellow who would not let anybody sweep under his bed for more than a year, and he finally recovered, although the doctor had "plumb give him up." Never make new garments for a sick person—he or she will never live to wear them.

Very few hillmen will plant a willow tree, or transplant a cedar, because nearly every man believes that as soon as the tree grows large enough to shade his grave, he will die. The mountain housewife never borrows salt if she can possibly avoid doing so, and if she does borrow it, is careful never to pay it back. When a woman borrows a cupful of salt she replaces it with an equal amount of sugar, or molasses, or some other household staple—*never* salt.

When a hillman happens to tread upon a grave, he jumps back across it at once, as otherwise a member of his family will die. If he sneezes five times in rapid succession he knows that he will soon hear of a friend's death. If a man bathes just before starting on a journey, he will be drowned. If one feels a sudden chill without any obvious reason, it means that someone or something is walking over the spot which will ultimately be his grave. If a cat licks the door it is a sure sign that somebody in the house will die. It is very bad luck to cut a new window in an old cabin, and the man who makes the saw-cuts will soon lose his dearest friend or relative by death.

If a hillman inadvertently steps over a spade lying on the ground he is seriously disturbed by the belief that it will shortly be used to dig his grave, and to carry a hoe into the house will certainly cause the death of a near relative within the year. If a garment is made on Friday, the owner will never live to wear it out, and if anyone imagines that he hears the crash of glass, when no breakage actually occurs, the head of the house will meet with a violent death before the year is out. To step over a person lying on the floor is a sign that he or she is not long for this world, and if done intentionally is almost equivalent to homicide. Every mountaineer knows that to burn sassafras wood will cause the early death of one's mother, and although sassafras makes very fine charcoal, no native will burn it, or even cut or haul it to the kiln, unless his mother is already dead. The Ozark children are told that if they defecate in a path or public road their sisters will die. If a mountain woman imagines that she sees the face of an absent friend in a mirror she expects to hear of this person's death, and if a young girl sees any coffin-shaped object reflected in water she is sure to die before her next birthday anniversary.

Every mountain bride is careful to wear her wedding garments on certain definite post-nuptial occasions, and every hill woman knows that cloth contaminated with menstrual discharge must be buried in the ground—to disregard these simple rules is to court death in some particularly terrifying form. If a child less than a year old is permitted to see its reflection in a mirror, it will either be cross-eyed, or die before its second birthday; if its fingernails are cut with a metal blade, it will either die within the year, or become a thief in later life. Most mothers take no chances—they *bite* the child's nails off! When cocks crow or dogs howl or foxes bark near a sickroom, or the patient begins to pick at the coverlet, or to slide down toward the foot of the bed, or to emit an odor like that of crushed pumpkins, his death may be expected at any moment. What is more, the last person upon whom the dying man's gaze rests will be the first among those present to follow him to the grave.

When a death finally occurs, one of the bereaved relatives rises immediately from the bedside and stops the clock.
Everybody knows that if the clock should happen to stop of itself
while a corpse is lying in the house, another member of the
family would die within a year, and it is considered best to take
no chances. The next thing to be done is to cover every mirror
in the house with white cloths, which are not removed until after
the funeral. This is done out of consideration for those who may
come in to view the body, for if one of them should happen to
see his own reflection in the house of death he will never live to
see another summer.

The hillfolk have a veritable mania for washing dead bodies; the moment a death occurs the neighbors strip the corpse
and begin to scrub it vigorously. A man may be dirty all his life,
and in his last illness his body and bedding may be so foul that
a visitor can hardly stay in the cabin, but he goes to his grave
clean, so far as water and soap can cleanse him. All of the work
connected with a death—washing and dressing the body, making the coffin, and so on—is done by friends and neighbors. Not
one of the near relatives of the deceased will have any part in
these doings, except in cases of the direst necessity.

Whatever happens, the body must never be left alone for a
single instant, for fear some animal should get at it; if a cat, for
example, should so much as sniff at the corpse, some unspeak-
able calamity would overtake the whole famliy. The belief that
cats will mutilate a dead body seems to be widely accepted in the
South, but appears to have little or no foundation in fact—cats,
ordinarily, do not eat carrion. Several young couples are usually
invited in to serve as a death watch, and at least two persons
are supposed to remain beside the body, while the others may
be kissing in a dark corner, or eating the elaborate lunch supplied by the sorrowing family. A jug of corn whiskey is sometimes

provided for the men-folks, but there is very little drunkenness
on these occasions. If an owl hoots or a wolf howls in the vicinity the watchers are seriously disturbed, because these sounds
signify that one of the group will die before the year is out.
Even the professional undertakers in the Ozark towns hesitate
to leave a corpse alone in their buildings; a light is left burning
all night, and some idlers are hired to stay with the body if no
friends or neighbors offer their services.

Rainy weather is nothing short of calamitous on a wed-
ding-day, but at a funeral it is the best possible omen since it
means that the dead man's soul is at rest, and even a few drops
of rain at this time go further to comfort the bereaved family
than anything the "preacher-man" can do or say. Every Ozarker
knows the little verse:

"Happy is the bride that the sun shines on;
Blessed are the dead that the rain falls on."

If a funeral takes place in the forenoon, another member of the family will die within the year. One must be careful at
funerals to avoid counting the vehicles in the procession, since
an early death is invariably the portion of the thoughtless individual who does the counting. To cross a funeral procession is
regarded as almost equivalent to suicide. The grave must always
be dug on the day of the funeral, since to leave it open over
night would bring about the death of one of the dead man's
relatives. This belief is taken very seriously in some parts of the
Ozarks, and I have known county officials to fail of re-election
because they had callously permitted a pauper to be buried in
a grave dug two days previously. It is customary also to bury the
body with the feet toward the east, and an old woman told me
solemnly that this was done in order that the dead man may rise
and face the east on the day of resurrection.

Although the manufacture of moonshine whiskey is the chief industry in the wilder parts of the Ozarks, agriculture is still important enough to make the weather a matter of considerable import to the natives, and its prediction plays an important part in the Ozark folk-lore. A rain on Monday morning is regarded as a sure sign that it will rain every day of that week, and if it rains on the first Sunday in the month, every hillman expects showers on the three Sundays following. A rainy Easter, also, is said to be followed by seven wet Sundays. Should the sun set clear on Tuesday, it will surely rain before Friday. The belief that early morning showers are of short duration is recorded in the couplet:

"Rain before seven,
Shine before eleven."

A cock's persistent crowing at nightfall is regarded as a sign that there will be rain before morning:

"If a cock crows when he goes to bed,
He'll get up with a wet head."

This jingle is evidently very old indeed, and is one of the very few phrases, in the Ozark speech, in which the male fowl is called a cock. A storm is expected, too, if the chickens go to roost earlier than usual, and the voices of tree-toads and rain-crows forecast a shower at any time of the day. When chickens stand with their tails to the wind, so that their feathers are ruffled, or the leaves of a tree turn up so as to show the under sides, the hill people always look for a shower within a few hours.

The "set" of the moon's horns also tells of coming wet or dry weather, but there seems to be no general agreement about the interpretation of this sign. When lightning-bugs cling close to the ground it means that there is a big rain coming; when they fly very high, the hillman expects a long drouth. When snake-trails are seen in the dusty roads, or when owls hoot in the day-time, it will certainly rain within forty-eight hours. When a mountain man sees a pig with a bit of wood in its mouth he prepares for a terrible storm, and when a heron flies up the river and returns immediately, the hillman knows that the water in the stream is about to rise.

In very dry weather, when the corn patches are suffering, the hillfolk often meet in the church-houses, where their ministers lead them in prayers for rain. Bathing a cat in sulphur-water is said to cause rain, also, and hanging a dead snake belly upward on the fence is a rain charm favored by many. Some of the old settlers claim that burning driftwood along the creeks is the best way to produce rain, and in times of drouth they often fire a great number of drifts simultaneously, so that a haze of smoke hangs over the entire countryside for days. Snowfall is somehow dependent upon the age of the moon, and many hillmen believe that if the moon is ten days old when the first snow comes, it means that there will be ten more snows before Spring. When cats sit with their tails to the fire it is an indication of very cold weather. If clouds are seen moving rapidly, or if quail are found sunning themselves in coveys, or if the brush-rabbits are lying in shallow, unprotected forms, the Ozarker feels safe in expecting two or three days of pleasant weather. The latter sign in particular inspires great confidence, and I am almost persuaded that there may be something in it. At any rate I have often seen farmers go out and flush two or three rabbits, and examine their nests carefully before deciding to go on a journey. Nearly all of the old-time hillmen say that the fourteenth of February, and not the second, is the real Groundhog Day, and are firmly convinced that if it is cloudy and cold on the fourteenth there will be six more weeks of winter weather. Another common belief is that there are always exactly as many frosts in May as there are thunder-claps in February, and that frogs always come out and are "froze back" three times before spring is really here. A sure sign of spring, however, is the arrival of the turkey-buzzards—all the old-timers declare that there is never any freezing weather after the first buzzard is seen.

The changes of the moon and the signs of the zodiac are very important in determining the best dates for planting certain crops. In general, it is said that vegetables which are desired to grow chiefly underground, such as potatoes, onions, beets, turnips, radishes and peanuts, are best planted in the dark of the moon. Plants which bear the edible part above ground, such as corn, beans, tomatoes and peas, are best planted in the light of the moon. Garden truck in general should be set out on Good Friday, but lettuce is planted on St. Valentine's Day, and turnips are always sowed on July twenty-fifth. Potatoes are planted when the sign is in Virgo, or on the seventeenth of March, or on the one hundredth day of the year, and must be dug in the light of the moon, as they will rot otherwise. Beans are always planted when the sign is in the arms; plant them in Virgo and you'll get fine large plants and plenty of bloom, but no beans at all. Bunch-beans must be sowed on Good Friday, and all beans are planted in the morning rather than in the afternoon. Beans planted in May never amount to much. Cabbage is sowed when the sign is in the head, cucumbers when it is in the twins, and corn in Scorpio. Fruit trees are set out in one of the fruitful signs and pruned in the light of the moon. Some farmers contend that one should always drive an old-fashioned handmade nail into an apple tree in order to get the best results. Transplanted trees must always be set out in their old positions relative to the points of the compass-the north side of the tree must continue to face the north star.

There is a widespread belief that on a certain day in August one can kill large trees merely by touching the trunk with the blade of an axe, but there is so much difference of opinion about the proper date that no practical use is made of this information. Nevertheless, nearly all of the older people are firmly convinced that there is something in the idea. In general, the hillman kills weeds and deadens trees between the first and twentieth of August, in the dark of the moon, in the sign of Virgo, or Gemini, or Leo. However, if sprouts are cut on the ninth or tenth of May, it is well known that they will never grow again. One of my neighbors insisted upon clearing his garden-patch on these two days, although his wife and child lay dying only a few yards away.

Shingles or "shakes" rived out in the dark of the moon lie flat, but if made or put on during the moon's increase they warp and turn up. Rail fences are subject to the same principle; if the rails are split and laid in the light of the moon they are sure to curl and twist, and decay much more rapidly than if they are cut when the moon is dark. Even seasoned planks, if laid on the ground in the light of the moon, invariably warp or cup, while in the dark of the moon there is no such difficulty.

Corn is best planted when the oak leaves—or the hickory buds, according to some hillmen—are as large as squirrels' ears. If one laughs while planting corn, the grains on the cob will always be irregular and too far apart. Never pull a pig's tail, or the animal will fail to fatten. A farmer must not have his hair cut too often during the growing season, or his crops will mature very slowly. No hillman kills a toad intentionally—he believes that it would cause his cows to give bloody milk. The farmer who burns the hulls of his seed peas or beans will get no crop from the seeds, according to the mountain soothsayers.

Every hillman knows better than to castrate pigs without

A Sorghum Mill

considering the signs of the zodiac, for animals cut when the
sign is in the heart are almost sure to become infected and die.
The best time for this operation is "when th' sign leaves th'
privates an' is a-startin' down." There is no doubt whatever that
thunder sours fresh milk, even in the winter, and kills chickens
in the eggs. Every child knows, too, that if a hen is set on Sunday
the chickens will all be roosters. Eggs carried in a woman's bonnet, however, invariably hatch pullets. Akin to the superstition
regarding prenatal influence and the "marking" of babies is
the idea that a horse-breeder can color a colt to suit his taste
by hanging a cloth of the desired color before the mare's eyes

when she is bred. Since live stock is not confined in the Ozarks, but merely marked or branded and allowed to roam the hills at will, the matter of finding one's horses or cattle is often a serious matter; however, one has only to consult a harvestman, or daddy-long-legs, and it will immediately crawl in the direction of the strayed animals. The hillman's notions about the proper treatment of sick animals are too complicated for discussion here, but I must mention the fact that colic in horses is relieved by blowing salt into the nostrils, and that a cow with "holler-horn" is relieved by splitting her tail open and applying a mixture of salt and vinegar. I once saw a hill farmer thrusting walnut hulls into the rectum of a bull as a cure for some obscure ailment.

Another belief which is still almost universal in the Ozarks has to do with the location of wells. In every mountain settlement there is at least one water-witch, or "witch-wiggler"—a person who walks about with a forked twig, which is supposed to move in the hands when he walks over a hidden stream of water. I have seen several of these "witch-wigglers" at work, and there is no doubt that they themselves are firm believers in their singular power. They seem to satisfy their neighbors, too, and very few of the old settlers would think of digging a well without calling in one of these fellows to "witch" their land. An unusually able and intelligent physician who lived near my home was a firm believer in "witch-wiggling"; he practiced it himself for many years, and tried to defend it on scientific grounds. Some water-witches seek for treasure, too, by fastening a bit of gold or silver to the crotch of the twig, but apparently without any very conspicuous success.

When a native woman drops a comb she always puts her foot on it and makes a wish—a wish carefully considered, because she is confident that it will come true. The same may be said of a wish made on seeing the first star of the evening, or when one walks on strange ground for the first time. If a young girl happens to put on any garment wrong side out, she must not remove it with her own hands, but may call in some person not related to her; the wish expressed by this individual as the garment is pulled off is sure to be realized. Upon seeing a redbird in a tree one should always make a wish; if the bird flies upward the wish will come true, but if the bird flies downward the desire will never be satisfied. Another view is that on seeing a redbird it is only necessary to make a wish and then shut the eyes, or turn the head away-if you do not see the bird again your wish will come true.

When a woman sees a spotted horse she makes a wish, and if she refrains from looking at the animal again, and tells some one about the occurrence as soon as possible, her desire will be realized. When a girl sees the new moon unobscured by branches—"cl'ar o' bresh", as the saying is—she looks over her left shoulder and makes a wish. When she sees a white mule, or a load of hay, or a woman wearing a man's hat she does the same thing, being careful not to look at the object again after the wish is made. In breaking a wishbone or "pulley-bone" for luck, it is the person who pulls the *short* piece whose wish comes true—in most parts of the country the individual who gets the long portion is the fortunate one.

The signs and superstitions connected with the ordinary activities of the household are usually concerned with matters of no great import, but they are very seriously considered none the less. When a woman drops a dishrag she knows at once that some dirty individual is coming toward the cabin; if the cloth falls in a compact wad the visitor will be a woman, if it spreads out upon the floor a man is to be expected. To drop the towel used in drying dishes means that a stranger will arrive very soon, and if the towel is dropped twice it means that the newcomer will be hungry, and a meal must be prepared. When the wood in the fireplace suddenly falls down, or a rooster crows thrice before the door, or a butterfly hovers about the doorstep, the housewife prepares for company. A redbird to the left of the door means an unexpected guest, as does a fit of sneezing at the table, while an itching nose foretells the arrival of a poor man, according to the old saying:

"If your nose itches, if your nose itches,
Somebody comin' with a hole in their britches!"

No hillman ever thinks of giving a steel blade to a friend—such a gift is sure to sever their friendship. He is careful also to leave a neighbor's house by the same door through which he entered, knowing that to violate this simple rule may cause a serious quarrel. The host, on his part, always politely turns away as a guest leaves his cabin—if he were to watch a departing friend out of sight he feels that they would never meet amicably again.

The Ozark housewife is careful not to sing before breakfast, for this is a sure sign that she will weep before midnight. She never allows any one else to stir the dough which she expects to bake. If a basting is left in a garment it means that the cloth is not paid for, and to find a hole in one's stocking signifies that a letter is waiting at the post-office. Never mend a garment while the owner is wearing it, for there will be as many lies told about this person as there are stitches in the mended part.

If a kerosene lamp is used, it is always best to put a piece of red flannel in the oil to keep it from exploding. If the fire spits and sputters without any apparent cause, it means that two members of the family will quarrel within twenty-four hours. Never look straight into a fire that is being kindled—if you do it will not burn properly, and will bring bad luck to the entire household. Some hill people become furious if a guest persists in staring straight into a stove or fireplace, whether the fire is burning well or not! The child who sings or whistles in bed, or while urinating or defecating, is certain to get a whipping before nightfall, besides bringing down some nameless misfortune upon the heads of his family. To eat in a toilet is described as "feedin' th' devil an' starvin' Gawd." Woe to the boy or girl who walks about with only one shoe on; the hillman punishes such offenses very severely, since they hazard the fortunes of the entire household. Two persons who dry their hands upon the same towel at the same time are almost certain to quarrel, the hill people think, unless they hasten to twist the towel between them. When one gives an Ozark family something to eat or drink, the housewife is always careful to return the vessel unwashed, since to send it home clean is a sure sign of an early quarrel with the donor. I have known women in the hill country deliberately to smear a pot or kettle before returning it to a neighbor, in case the vessel had been washed by mistake.

Nearly all of the hill people are firm believers in ghosts and wandering spirits, although very few of the men and boys are willing to admit such beliefs to strangers. The following tale is told of one of my neighbors, and believed by practically everybody in the settlement. A woman was very unkind to her stepchildren, and one day, as she sat alone in the cabin, a violent blow knocked her flat on the floor, and a loud voice cried out: "Be good to my children!" This story is confirmed by the woman herself, and several of her friends swear that they saw the print of the invisible hand on her face several hours after the attack.

Not far from my cabin, according to the old-timers, a man was captured years ago by a band of night-riders, who hanged him with his own "galluses" until these broke, and then finished the job with a hickory withe. Some women living nearby buried the body, but it was dug up later by dogs, which carried some of the bones down into the road. Not liking the spectacle of human bones being gnawed by dogs, the ladies gathered them up and dropped them into a big hollow tree. Serious-minded and sober men and women assure me that they have seen strange lights about this tree, and heard groans, and something like old-fashioned guncaps exploding all about. There are many other stories of ghostly visitors and spirit messages and supernatural occurrences of various kinds, but as they do not seem to differ essentially from those reported by spiritualists elsewhere, I have not troubled to record them.

Like most primitive folk, the Ozark natives attach considerable importance to dreams, but their dream interpretations are very similar to those current among the ignorant in other parts of the country. To dream of muddy water means trouble, to dream of snakes presages a battle with one's enemies, a dream of birth or death signifies a wedding, while a dream of marriage is a warning of approaching death, and so on. A dream related before breakfast, or one dreamed on Friday and told on Saturday, may always be expected to come true:

> "Friday night's dream, on Saturday told,
> Will always come true, no matter how old."

A dream of chickens is bad luck, to dream of a black boat means an early death, while the man who dreams repeatedly of fishes will attain great wealth. Whatever one dreams the first time he sleeps under a new quilt always comes true, and nearly every mountain man or woman is anxious to "dream out" a new quilt or coverlet.

Mountain men and women frequently carry buckeyes and turtlebones and amulets of various kinds to keep off evil spirits; they consult "seventh sons" and fortunetellers of different sorts, who employ cards and tea-leaves and coffee-grounds and the white spots on one's fingernails very much as similar gentry do elsewhere. There are some witches and wizards left in the Ozarks, too, but they are few and aged and uncommunicative, so that it is difficult to find out anything very definite about them. An acquaintance once told me very seriously that he thought his hogs were bewitched; it seems that they did not come as usual when he called them, but "jest sot on their tails an' squole!" A woman in a nearby village awoke one morning all tired out, with her hands and feet scratched and bruised, and told her family that she had been "rode for a horse" all night long by a witch. She named the witch, too—a half-mad old woman who lived several miles away—but nothing was ever done about it. There is a story also of two girls who lived alone, and were never seen to milk their cows, although they made large quantities of butter and cheese. Finally a neighbor peeped in at the window, and swore later that he saw them hang a dishrag on the pot-rack, and squeeze several gallons of milk out of it, while the cows stood contentedly chewing their cuds in the pasture, several hundred feet away! There are plenty of hillfolk who believe these tales, too, but they are nearly all elderly people—the younger generation is fast losing faith and interest in witchcraft. I know of one case in which a poor hill farmer, overwhelmed by a series of inexplicable and unpredictable misfortunes, conceived the idea that an old woman in the vicinity had bewitched him. In the old days he would have had recourse to a regular "witch-master", fully equipped with a silver-mounted rifle, silver bullets, little clay images and so on, but the last local witch-doctor had died some years previously, and he was forced to attend to the matter himself. He drew a crude picture of the alleged witch on a board, and emptied his revolver into the picture, the theory being that if the woman was really responsible for his troubles she would be killed or seriously injured. The woman appeared quite unaffected at the time of the shooting, but oddly enough she did suffer a very serious and unusual injury some three or four days later, and many people in the vicinity seem to regard this accident as evidence that she *was* a witch after all!

The great majority of the Ozark superstitions have to do with specific events which follow one another according to some mysterious hidden principle. There are some phenomena, however, which are believed to portend something exceedingly important, but of a rather vague and general nature. Very few of the mountain people would intentionally kill a spider, but there is no specific penalty for this offense, simply a general atmosphere of misfortune. In the same way, it is very bad luck to put the left shoe on before the right, or to put the left foot out of bed first in the morning, or to move cats or brooms from one house to another, or to take a ring from another person's finger, or to let anybody remove one's own ring, or to look back while walking, or to close a gate which one finds open. To come back into a house for anything which has been forgotten is a very bad omen, and the Ozarker never does this if it can possibly be avoided. In case of necessity, however, he can take the curse off in a measure by sitting down in a chair while he counts ten. The doors and windows must always be opened wide on New Year's Eve just before midnight—failure to attend to this would certainly bring bad luck in some serious but indefinite form. It is very bad luck to carry ashes out of the house on New Year's Day, too, and the woman who absentmindedly performs this task is sometimes shaken almost to the point of hysteria—although nobody knows of any definite or specific calamity which is supposed to result. A hen which makes any sound suggestive of crowing must be killed at once, lest it bring misfortune upon the entire household.

Many people will not eat such a fowl under any conditions, but sell it to the tourists, or even throw it to the hogs.

"A whistlin' woman an' a crowin' hen,

Is sure to come to some bad end."

What foul fate is supposed to follow a whistling woman nobody seems to know, but it is certainly a very serious one, and I have known little girls to be very severely punished for trying to whistle as their brothers do.

It is very bad luck to torment a lunatic or a feebleminded person, but many hillmen do it. To meet a cross-eyed man, particularly at the point where two foot-paths intersect, is a very bad omen; the only thing to be done in such a case is to cross one's fingers and count ten backward in an attempt to ward off disaster. To lay a knife on a bed, to carry an axe or a bridle into the house, to balance a chair on one leg, to whirl or spin a chair about, to laugh at anyone who has been unlucky, to wear an opal ring, to pick up a black or dark-colored button, to see the new moon through the treetops on the first night of its appearance, to move from one cabin to another in the dark of the moon—all of these actions are generally regarded as unfortunate or even dangerous.

If you happen to put on a garment inside out, by all means wear it that way for the rest of the day-it is very bad luck to remove such a garment immediately. Never begin a piece of work on Friday unless you are certain that it can be finished by Saturday night. The typical hillman is extraordinarily perturbed by any trifling piece of ill luck which occurs on his birthday, for he knows that he who is unlucky on this particular day is very likely to be unlucky for the entire year. Never, under any circumstances whatever, burn peach trees—dreadful results are almost certain to follow. I know a man and woman who cut down and burned some old peach trees, despite the protests and warnings of their neighbors. Sure enough, their baby became very sick a few days later. The neighbors helped them as best they could, but one and all refused to come into the house, or have anything further to do with the family if any more peach trees were burned.

There are many miscellaneous superstitions regarding animals and plants, some of which do not fall conveniently into any of the classes hitherto discussed. For example, there is the notion that cocks always crow exactly at midnight, and that their crowing at unusual hours heralds the approach of a stranger or an enemy. A dog's nose, the hillman thinks, should be black, and a red-nosed dog is always regarded with suspicion. If the family squirrel-dog follows a stranger, it means that the man is to be trusted. If a measuring-worm crawls over a person's clothing, he or she will soon get some new article of attire. When a hillman sees a spider in the middle of the path he knows that a letter is waiting for him at the post-office. Whoever hears the first dove coo in the spring will soon go on a long journey in the direction from which the sound came. There is a very general belief that black walnut trees are liable to damage by lightning, and it is a hardy hillman indeed who can be persuaded to stand under one during an electrical storm.

Various sorts of animals are believed to carry warnings. A woman in my neighborhood whipped her grown daughters unmercifully, until one day "th' redbirds come an' hanted her" by tapping on the window-pane, which gave her a terrible fright and caused her to mend her ways. Another of my mountaineer friends was greatly disturbed when a "rooster redbird" hovered about his door; he said that it was a warning of death, and, sure enough, one of his daughters died within a few weeks.

Snakes of all species are killed whenever possible, but are

nevertheless regarded with a sort of superstitious awe. When a snake gets into a cabin it means that the owner has a dangerous enemy in the neighborhood, and must be on his guard. The mountaineer always makes a special effort to kill the first snake he sees in the spring of the year, since failure to do this is likely to allow his enemies to ruin him before the snow flies again. Hillfolk who see me handling harmless snakes are usually horrified, and several old women have openly expressed the conviction that I am not only crazy, but probably in league with the devil! The old story of the hoopsnake which puts its tail in its mouth and rolls down the hill is believed by many, and everybody knows that the horn on this legendary serpent's tail is tipped with deadly poison. Blue racers are popularly supposed to chase people, the joint snake breaks in pieces and goes back together again, and no snake can possibly die till the sun goes down, no matter how badly it is injured—just as a turtle never lets go of anything until it hears a clap of thunder. No snake can cross a horse-hair rope, but if a single horsehair is placed in water in the summer time it ultimately turns into a snake.

Most hillmen are firmly convinced that snakes can "charm" birds and animals, and even human beings, simply by looking at them. Many people believe that before a cottonmouth moccasin takes a drink of water, it discharges its venom on a clean flat stone; having drunk, it sucks the poison into its fangs again. Dogs with dew-claws—all hounds are said to have dew-claws—are supposedly immune to snake poison. All snakes go blind when huckleberries are ripe. Poisonous snakes, when in the water, lie with the entire body floating on the surface while harmless snakes swim with only the head exposed. If a hillman sees a snake just as he is starting on a journey he is rather pleased than otherwise, as it means that he will be fortunate in his quest or business but he kills the snake nevertheless.

It is generally agreed that fish will not bite during a thunder-storm, and that catfish bite best when the roasting-ears are ripe, but there is a difference of opinion with reference to the signs of the zodiac; one school contending that the best time for fishing is when the sign is in the head, the other defending the thesis that fish bite when the sign is anywhere between the knees and the shoulders, but that the best fishing is in Virgo. It is very generally believed that if a fried eel is allowed to stand over night, it will be "blood-raw" again in the morning. Any hillman will tell you that an ordinary mud-turtle contains seven kinds of meat: pork, beef, mutton, venison, chicken, duck and fish. Despite this belief, the hill people as a class do not eat turtles, and my weakness for turtle soup horrified some of my neighbors.

Mr. Charles J. Finger tells me that his neighbors near Fayetteville, Arkansas, believe that the drops of resin found on pine boards somehow turn into bedbugs, and that the bite of the praying mantis or devil's-horse is deadly poison. A man assured me only the other day that a wren's bite is always fatal, and nearly everybody in the hills repeats the tale that the bite of a centipede makes the flesh fall off the bones, although many of us have seen people bitten by centipedes without any such effect. It is said that all hawks are blind in dog-days, and many farmers think that hawks call chickens to their doom by imitating the cry of a young chick in distress. Buzzards are supposed to seek out and vomit upon persons guilty of incest; a man near Siloam Springs, Arkansas, is generally believed to have seduced his two sisters, and it is said that he never ventures out into the open if a buzzard is anywhere in the vicinity. To kill a cat is very bad luck, but no misfortune results from mutilating these creatures, or from placing them where they will die by slow starvation.

A great many hillmen are convinced that the male opossum ejects his sperm into the nose of the female, which then blows the spermatic fluid into the vagina—a belief wholly without foundation, and which doubtless had its origin in the peculiar bifurcate form of the opossum's penis, and to the female's habit of nosing the vulva. There are several peculiar superstitions relating to the larva of the ant-lion, which lives in cone-shaped pits in the dirt under rock ledges. Every boy is told that if he finds one of these nests and cries,

> "Oh Johnny Doodlebug,
> Come up and I'll give you a
> bushel of corn!"

the insect will climb out and show itself immediately. Many of the old settlers believe that the cattle all kneel down and bellow at midnight on January 5th—the eve of "old Christmas"—in honor of the birth of Jesus, and there are men still living in the Ozarks who swear that they have actually witnessed this strange ceremony. A neighbor tells me that when he was a boy he watched repeatedly to see his father's oxen kneel, but was always disappointed. His parents told him, however, that the presence of a human observer broke the spell—the cattle must always salute the Savior in private. "But I jes' drawed a idy right thar," he added thoughtfully, "thet they warnt nothin' to it, nohow."

Many of the Ozark superstitions listed above are also known to the Southern Negroes, and have frequently been regarded as relics of some primitive African culture, but it is now fairly well established that they came originally from Europe, and have been preserved by the illiterate Negroes long after the more progressive whites have rejected and forgotten them. Negroes are not very common in the hill country, and the Ozarker has even less traffic with them than with the Indians from Oklahoma. Personally, I do not believe that either Negroes or Indians have made any important contributions to the Ozark folklore;

it seems to me that most of the hillman's peculiar folk-beliefs
came to him from the British Isles. The question of origins, however, must be left to specialists in these matters, who have the
whole literature of folklore at their fingertips. But the collecting
of these superstitions must be attended to at once, before the
entire body of Ozark folk-lore is driven into hiding by the laughter of the schoolmarms and tourists who are just beginning to
invade the hill country.

Because these beliefs are still so numerous, it might be
doubted that the old folk-lore is really disappearing very rapidly.
The fact is, however, that the decadence which doubtless began
in Europe has been retarded by the isolated situation of the
mountain people, and is now proceeding very rapidly indeed.
One has only to compare the young people with their grandparents, or the isolated settlements with the villages along the new
motor highways, to appreciate the present status of superstition
in the Ozark country. The decay of a great body of belief is
always a gradual process, however, and some of these survivals
of a ruder age will doubtless be with us for a long time to come.

CHAPTER VI.

The Passing of the Play-Party

T HE EARLY SETTLERS IN THE Ozark country had comparatively few social pleasures, and one of the most important was the play-party, a gathering at which young people of both sexes played what are called "party-games".

Most of the old-timers thought that dancing was immoral, and regarded the fiddle as the devil's own instrument. Less than a dozen years ago the people of my own village refused to allow a children's dancing-class in the town, and I myself heard one of our leading citizens declare that he would rather see his daughter dead than to have her dance, even in her own home. But the play-party, it appears, is a different matter altogether, and even the most fanatical religionists see no particular harm in it. The party-games are really dances, of course, but there is no orchestra; the players furnish their own simple music by singing lustily as they go through the intricate figures while the spectators clap their hands and stamp their feet as the spirit moves them.

The typical Ozark play-party is not arranged for any particular number of guests, and no special invitation is necessary; the news is simply "norated 'round" that there is to be a frolic over at so-and-so's place, and anybody is welcome who cares to attend.

Most of the parties at which I have disported myself drew people from a distance of five or six miles, which is a long ride over the rough mountain trails. Shortly after dark the guests begin to arrive; young people usually travel on horseback or afoot, while the old folk come in wagons, or occasionally in Ford cars. The girls generally make some effort to "dress up" for these affairs, but many of the young men are attired simply in heavy boots, hickory shirts, and overalls—which latter garments are known as "duckins".

The women usually go into the house immediately upon their arrival, but the cabins are too small to hold all the guests, so the menfolk wait their turns outside, where they stand about peering in at the doors and windows. At some play-parties no food is served, but often the dancers are regaled with watermelons or apples, and sometimes there is a plate of sandwiches or cold meat. The young men usually have a jug of whiskey out in the dark where the horses are tied, and drinks are free to anybody who wants them. There is a certain amount of clandestine love-making—which the hillman elegantly designates as "tom-cattin'"—and occasionally a party breaks up at dawn in a drunken riot, but on the whole I think there is less drunkenness and sexual irregularity than at most college dances.

Nowadays, when a man "swings his partner" he puts his arm around her waist in something approximating the ordinary ballroom position, but the old folk tell me that this was never done in their "day an' time". The proper thing then was to "swing" with all four hands held high, palms together. Sometimes, as one old man told me with a reminiscent twinkle, a very daring girl would pretend that she was about to permit the waist swing by holding out her left arm, but she always laughed and pulled her elbow down before the boy could put his arm around her.

The games usually commence inside the cabin, but if the

Sam McDaniels, Member of the Missouri Legislature

weather is fine the whole party often moves out to the cleared space in front of the house, so that most of the games are played by moonlight, or in the dim light which flickers out from the open door and windows. In the summer time, particularly, the date of a party is usually fixed with due reference to the almanac, so that the "doin's" may fall on a moonlit night.

Although I have read some books and papers about the party-games as played elsewhere, my reading has not altogether satisfied my thirst for information about the Ozark play-parties. Such questions as the age and origin of the games, the changes which they have undergone in their successive migrations, the

forces which have brought about these modifications, their obvious connection with balladry, their relation to the square dances
and to modern school children's games—all these are matters
of which I still know very little. I do know the songs and games
as they are sung and played in the Ozarks, however, and it is this
information that I shall try to record here, leaving all theoretical and scholarly considerations to specialists in these matters.

Perhaps the most popular of all the play-party games is the
one called "Skip to my Lou"—"lou" being an old dialect word
for sweetheart. In this game each boy chooses a girl to be his
partner, and then all the players form a large circle, while everybody sings:

While this is being sung, one couple steps into the ring and
chooses another boy, so that there are two men and one girl in
the center, who hold hands and dance about the circle with a
peculiar skip and double-shuffle step. The first boy and girl hold
their hands high, the odd boy steps under the arch thus formed,
and the first couple joins the circle again. The boy left alone

in the ring calls in another couple, then he and the girl make the arch and join the circle, leaving the new boy alone in the center. Then he chooses another couple, and so on. Meanwhile the song proceeds:

Little red wagon, painted blue,
Little red wagon, painted blue,
Little red wagon, painted blue,
   Skip t' my Lou my darlin'.

Dad's ol' hat got tore in two,
Dad's ol' hat got tore in two,
Dad's ol' hat got tore in two,
   Skip t' my Lou my darlin'.

Purty as a redbird, purtier too,
Purty as a redbird, purtier too,
Purty as a redbird, purtier too,
   Skip t' my Lou my darlin'.

Caint git a redbird, a bluebird 'll do,
Caint git a redbird, a bluebird 'll do,
Caint git a redbird, a bluebird 'll do,
   Skip t' my Lou my darlin'.

She is gone an' I'll go too,
She is gone an' I'll go too,
She is gone an' I'll go too,
   Skip t' my Lou my darlin'.

Git me another'n as purty as you,
Git me another'n as purty as you,

Git me another'n as purty as you,
    Skip t' my Lou my darlin'.

The "Waltz the Hall" song-game appears to be derived from "Skip to my Lou", although the hillmen themselves insist that it is a different game altogether. The players join hands and "ring up", with one couple in the center of the circle, while they all sing:

First   cou-ple out,   cou-ple on th' right,

Change them   pards   an'   waltz 'em out o' sight,

At this the first boy and girl call in another couple, change partners, and all four dance about until they hear the second verse:

When you're through   re - mem-ber my   call,

Change 'em a - gain   an'   waltz th'   hall.

Then each man takes his own partner again, and they "waltz the hall," that is, dance around the circle. The third stanza of the song has a line borrowed from "Skip to my Lou":

Like right an' left, of course you do,

Four hands up an' skip t' my Lou.

At "four hands up" both couples hold up their hands, form
a little circle of their own, and turn around once. Then all sing:

The final verse is almost exactly like the first:

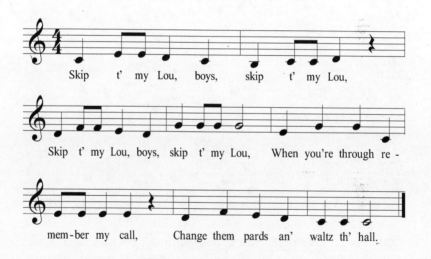

Skip t' my Lou, boys, skip t' my Lou,

Skip t' my Lou, boys, skip t' my Lou, When you're through re -

mem-ber my call, Change them pards an' waltz th' hall.

Next couple out, couple on th' right,
Change them pards an' waltz 'em out o' sight.

As these words are sung the original pair leads another
couple into the center, and the first boy and girl chosen resume
their places in the circle. And so it goes until everybody has

"waltzed the hall". Sometimes, just before the last verse is sung, everybody "goes right and left" or executes the "once and a half and a half all round" figure, familiar in the ordinary country dances.

The "Miller Boy" song is a very old one, many versions of which are still popular in England. In this game each boy takes his partner by her left hand, and they all form a double ring, with the girls on the outside. The odd man—the "Miller Boy"— stands alone in the center of the circle. The players march round and round, singing:

Hap-py is th' mil-ler boy that lives by th' mill, Th' mill turns round with a right good will, Hand on th' hop-per an' th' oth-er in th' sack, gals steps for-rerd an' th' men falls back.

As the ladies step forward the boys must get new partners— each man taking the girl directly behind him—and the "Miller Boy" attempts to snatch a girl for himself while the change is being made. If he succeeds, the man who loses his partner is the next "Miller Boy". A number of variations are sometimes intro- duced in order to make the "Miller Boy's" task more difficult. Sometimes they sing "men steps forrerd an' th' gals falls back," or occasionally "all turn round an' walk right back."

Another favorite game of the hillfolk is called "Old Quebec", which Carl Sandburg says was popular in Kentucky in the late 1840's, and describes as "a knapsack and marching tune with Mexican War references." As played in the Ozark country today, the game is similar to "The Miller Boy", but whenever the words "an' we'll turn back" are sung each couple does an about-face as quickly as possible. Two regularly appointed judges decide which couple is slowest in making the turn, and this couple is turned out of the circle. At the words "we'll open up th' ring" the circle is broken for a moment, and the boy and girl outside rush to get in before it can be closed against them.

We're march-in' down to ol' Que-bec, Whar th'
drums is loud-ly Beat-in', Th' 'Mer-i-can boys hev
won th' day, an' th' Brit-ish are re-treat-in'.

Th' war's all over an' we'll turn back
To th' place whar we first started,
We'll open up th' ring an' receive a couple in
To relieve th' broken-hearted.

My purty leetle pink, I used to think
I couldn't live well without you,

But I'll let you know before I go
Thet I don't keer much about you.

I'll put my knapsack on my back,
My rifle on my shoulder,
An' I'll march away to New Orleans
An' jine a band o' soldiers.

The "Weevily Wheat" game-song is a very old one, and the
Charlie referred to is probably the Bonnie Prince Charlie of the
Jacobite ballads, of whom the Scots sang so often, and loved so
much better than he deserved. Some scholars have regarded the
game as a degenerate form of an old Scotch weaving-play, the
first movements representing the shooting of the shuttle from
side to side, and the passage of the woof over and under the
threads of the warp; the last movements indicating the tighten-
ing of the threads, and the bringing together of the cloth. As
the fifth stanza indicates, this game is regarded with disfavor
by some of the hill people, because it is too much like dancing; I know several young girls who play the other games freely
enough, but always drop out when the "Weevily Wheat" song
is introduced. The players form in two parallel rows, with the
girls on one side and the boys on the other. The boy and girl
at the opposite ends of their respective lines swagger out to the
center and swing, then return to their places, to be followed by
the next couple. When all have swung, the whole party parades
about, swinging at intervals, after which the original lines are
re-formed and the whole performance repeated. Sometimes a
sort of Virginia Reel figure is introduced into the game.

Oh Charlie he's a fine young man,
Oh Charlie he's a dandy,
Charlie likes t' kiss th' gals
An' he kin do it handy!

Oh I don't want none o' your weev'-ly wheat, an' I

don't want none o' your bar-ley, But I want some flour in

half a hour, To bake a cake for Char-lie.

Th' higher up th' cherry tree
Th' sweeter grows th' cherry,
Th' more you hug and kiss a gal
Th' more she wants t' marry!

Yes, Charlie he's a fine young man,
Oh Charlie he's a dandy,
An' Charlie is th' very lad
Thet stole th' striped candy.

Grab her by th' lily-white hand
An' lead her like a pigeon,
Make her dance th' Weevily Wheat
An' lose all her religion!

Over th' river t' feed them sheep
On buckwheat cakes an' barley,
We don't keer whut th' ol' folks says—
Over th' river t' Charlie!

Unlike most of the play-party songs, "Old Dan Tucker" is comparatively recent and of known authorship; it was written by Dan D. Emmett, an early blackface comedian remembered chiefly as the author of "Dixie", and was popular in minstrel shows and vaudeville about 1841. In this game all the players choose partners and form a big circle, holding hands. An odd boy is called "Old Dan", and he stands alone in the center while the others dance around him.

At the words "first to the right", it is "Old Dan's" privilege to pull a girl out into the ring by her right hand, turn her around once, and thrust her back into her place again. When they sing "then to the left," he takes another girl out by the left hand, and swings her as before. At the words "then to the one that you love best," every boy swings his partner. It is at this moment that "Old Dan" tries desperately to grab a girl for himself, and if he succeeds the man who has lost his partner must be the next "Old Dan".

If "Old Dan" really wishes he can use one girl for all three movements of the game, and thus be sure of getting himself a partner, but this is not considered the sporting thing, and he does not do it often—usually not unless he loses his temper.

The following stanza is a sort of chorus, used to keep "Old Dan" in the ring as long as possible, since he has no opportunity to get a partner while it is being sung:

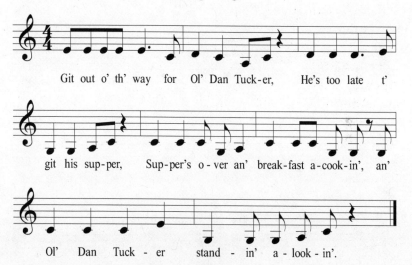

Git out o' th' way   for   Ol' Dan Tuck-er,   He's too late   t'

git his sup-per,   Sup-per's o-ver an' break-fast a-cook-in', an'

Ol'   Dan   Tuck - er   stand - in' a - look - in'.

Several other verses are used as fillers in this game:

Ol' Dan Tucker is a fine ol' man,
Washed his face in a fryin' pan,
Combed his head with a wagon wheel,
An' died with a toothache in his heel!

Ol' Dan Tucker down in town,
A-ridin' a goat an' leadin' a hound,
Th' hound give a howl an' th' goat give a jump,
An' throwed Ol' Dan a-straddle of a stump!

Ol' Dan Tucker he got drunk,

Fell in th' fire an' kicked out a chunk,

Fire coal got in Dan's ol' shoe,

Oh my golly how th' ashes flew!

The "Pig in the Parlor" game begins exactly like "Old Dan Tucker", except that the odd man in the center is called "The Pig" instead of "Old Dan". Everybody sings:

My paw an' maw was I-rish, My paw an' maw was I-rish, My paw an' maw was I-rish, And I am I-rish too.

Your right hand to your pardner,

Your left hand to your neighbor,

Your right hand to your pardner,

An' we'll all promenade.

As the ring is first formed, every boy has his partner at his right. At the words "your right hand to your pardner," he releases her left hand and takes her right. When they sing "your left hand to your neighbor," he drops his partner's hand, steps over to the next girl, takes her left hand and makes one turn around her—then rushes back to grasp his partner's right as the words "your right hand to your pardner" are heard for the second time. Then each boy takes his girl's left hand again, and all promenade—march around in a circle. The "Pig" usually manages to snatch a partner for himself while these complicated changes are being made, and the man who finds himself without a partner must be the next "Pig". When this occurs the game goes on exactly as before, except that the verse is changed to:

> We got a new pig in th' parlor,
> We got a new pig in th' parlor,
> We got a new pig in th' parlor,
> An' he is Irish too.

Several other verses, not set to any definite tune, are sometimes shouted out at unexpected moments in order to distract and confuse the "Pig". One of these runs about as follows:

> Pig in th' pen an' a three rail high,
> Bullet in th' gun an' th' pig must die!

The game called "Shoot the Buffalo" is popular in many parts of the Ozark country; in some sections there are two distinct ways of playing the game, one of which is known as "straight buffalo" and the other as "round buffalo". In my neighborhood the couples all form a ring and dance about the room singing at the top of their voices. When they come to the third line in each verse they change partners, and then promenade back to their original places in the circle. At some parties the first stanza is used as a refrain, being repeated before each of the succeeding verses.

> Rise ye up, my dearest dear,
> Present me to your paw,
> An' we'll all march together
> To th' state of Arkansaw.

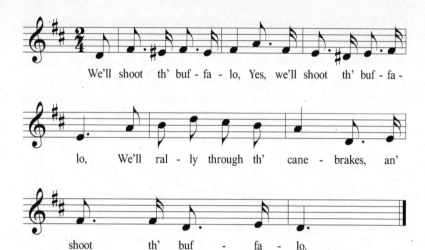

We'll shoot th' buf - fa - lo, Yes, we'll shoot th' buf - fa -

lo, We'll ral - ly through th' cane - brakes, an'

shoot th' buf - fa - lo.

Whar th' hawk shot th' buzzard
An' th' turkey stumped his toe,
We'll rally through th' cane-brakes
An' shoot th' buffalo.

I had a ol' saddle,
An' I hung it in th' loft,
Along come a cowboy
An' cut th' pockets off.

Yes, he cut th' pockets off,
He cut th' pockets off,
Along come a cowboy
An' cut th' pockets off.

Th' buffalo is dead,
Cause we shot him in th' head,
We'll rally through th' cane-brakes
An' shoot th' buffalo.

The following piece, which the Ozarkers know as "Four in the Middle", is a favorite in McDonald and Barry counties, in southwest Missouri. Each man chooses a partner, and all the players form a large circle, holding hands, with one couple in the center. They all sing slowly:

Cof - fee grows on white oak trees, Riv - ers flow with bran - dy O, Go choose some one t' roam with you, As sweet as 'lass - es can - dy O.

The boy and girl in the center each choose another partner from the big circle, so that there are two couples in the center instead of one. Then everybody sings the old "Skip to my Lou" tune:

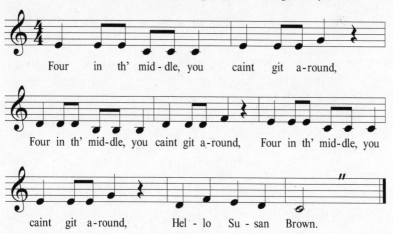

Four in th' mid - dle, you caint git a-round, Four in th' mid-dle, you caint git a-round, Four in th' mid-dle, you caint git a-round, Hel - lo Su - san Brown.

All this time the dancers "right and left," and then proceed
with several other verses:

> Big white house an' nobody livin' in it,
> Big white house an' nobody livin' in it,
> Big white house an' nobody livin' in it,
> Hello, Susan Brown.

> Hump-backed nigger caint jump Josie,
> Hump-backed nigger caint jump Josie,
> Hump-backed nigger caint jump Josie,
> Hello, Susan Brown.

> Git out o' th' ring if you caint jump Josie,
> Git out o' th' ring if you caint jump Josie,
> Git out o' th' ring if you caint jump Josie,
> Hello, Susan Brown.

As this last stanza is sung, the original couple dance out
of the center and join the big circle again, leaving the second
couple in the ring alone. The couple in the center then choose
another boy and girl, and the game goes on as before.

"Jingle at the Window" is a very popular Ozark play, which
was formerly well known in many other parts of the United
States. In this game the players choose partners and form a
double ring, with the girls in the inner circle, so that each boy
is opposite his partner. Then the boys march around in single
file, while the girls stand still, and everybody sings:

Jin-gle at th' win-der ti - de - o, Jin-gle at th' win-der ti - de - o, Jin-gle jin-gle jin - gle jin - gle jo, Jin - gle at th' win - der ti - de - o.

When the complete circle has been made, each boy returns to his partner and swings her around once, after which they begin another march, singing:

Pass one win - der ti - de - o, Pass one win - der ti - de - o, Jin - gle jin - gle jin - gle jo, Jin - gle at th' win - der ti - de - o.

But this time the boy passes his own partner and swings the next girl, until every boy has swung every girl in the party. The words of the song are changed with each repetition—"pass two windows," "pass three windows" and so on. When every boy has swung every girl the game begins again as before, except that this time the boys make up the inner circle, while the girls march around in single file.

The game known as "We'll All Go to Boston" is another old favorite, in which the boys and girls line up in two separate rows, facing each other. The couple at one end march forward between the lines, and then walk backward to their places again, while everybody sings the following verse, using the name of the girl who is marching:

Oh, oh, I-dy, I'll tell your gran'-maw, Oh, oh, I-dy, I'll tell your gran'-maw, Oh, oh, I-dy, I'll tell your gran'-maw, How you've been flirt - in'.

Then the same couple march forward again, but this time the boy stops at the head of the boys' line, while the girl leads all the girls in marching around the whole group of boys all singing:

> Come along, gals, let's go t' Boston,
> Come along, gals, let's go t' Boston,
> Come along, gals, let's go t' Boston,
> T' see thet couple married.

When the girls have returned to their places, the first boy leads all the others in marching around the girls' line, singing:

> Saddle up, boys, an' let's go with 'em,
> Saddle up, boys, an' let's go with 'em,
> Saddle up, boys, an' let's go with 'em,
> T' see thet couple married.

Then the next couple march down from the head of the lines and go through the same performance, and so on until everybody has "been to Boston". In some cases each verse is sung twice in succession, or even three times, in order to give plenty of time for the marching.

The "Ol' Brass Wagon" game is played not only in the Ozarks, but in country districts all through the South; it gets its name doubtless from the intricate crossing in the dance, which gives the whole party some fancied resemblance to the spokes of a wagon wheel. The game begins with the boys in one line and the girls in another. The first couple walk hand in hand down the lines, then swing at the words "you are th' one, my darling." With the next verse they separate, and the boy goes to the other end of the line and swings the girl at that end, while the girl is swinging a boy at the opposite end of the boys' line. Next comes a sort of "Virginia Reel" figure, then the original couple return

We'll all run a-way with th' ol' brass wag-on, We'll all run a-way with th' ol' brass wag-on, We'll all run a-way with th' ol' brass wag-on, You are th' one, my dar-lin'.

to their places. The next couple now walk down the line, and so on until all have swung.

> One wheel off an' t'other one a-draggin',
> One wheel off an' t'other one a-draggin',
> One wheel off an' t'other one a-draggin',
> You are th' one, my darlin'.

My first knowledge of "We'll All Go Down to Rowser's" came to me one moonlight night at a little village called Pack, in Southwest Missouri near the Oklahoma line. Like "Weevily Wheat" this game is not favored by the strict church-members—it is supposed to resemble the dance. The game is played very much like "Old Brass Wagon," but at the words "good lager beer" each boy and girl bow very low in an exaggerated, clownish fashion, and cut a similar caper at "corn whiskey clear". The girl often grasps her skirt at either side and spreads it out sidewise as she makes this bow. The tune is the same one used in the "Pig in the Parlor" game.

We'll all go down to Rowser's,
We'll all go down to Rowser's,
We'll all go down to Rowser's,
For there they have the beer.

Good lager beer, good lager beer,
Corn whiskey clear, corn whiskey clear,
We won't go home till mornin',
An' then we won't go home.

We'll dance all night,
Till broad daylight,
We won't go home till mornin',
An' then we won't go home.

We won't go home till mornin',
We won't go home till mornin',
We won't go home till mornin',
We won't go home at all.

The "Green Gravel" game is of Irish origin, and I have been told that it was originally connected with the Irish Catholic's contempt for the Masonic fraternity. The Ozark native knows nothing of this, however, and does not appear to associate "free meshin" with "free mason" at all. Professor W. W. Newell years ago reported a version in which "free masons" was changed to "free maidens", while "ashamed" became "arrayed". Dr. E. C. Perrow recorded several stanzas of a Mississippi variant in which it is the "fern nations" which are "ashamed to be seen". As the game is played at Fayetteville, Arkansas, the players all hold hands and dance about in a circle while they sing:

Green gra - vel, green gra - vel, th' grass is so green,

Free mesh - in, free mesh - in, a - shamed to be seen.

Oh Liz - zie, dear Liz - zie, your true love is dead,

I send you a let - ter to turn back your head.

When the last line is sung, Lizzie turns about and walks backward. Then the verse is repeated with another name instead of Lizzie, and so on until all the players are dancing backward.

Mr. Carl Van Doren, who heard a fragment of "Roxie Ann" in rural Illinois, thinks that it was brought out by early settlers from Kentucky, and may possibly be of Negro origin. The fragment given here was obtained from a woman who learned it near Pineville, Missouri, some thirty years ago, but she could not recall any more of the song, nor remember how the game was played.

> I'm goin' t' tell my Maw on you,
> I'm goin' t' tell my Paw,
> She's been a long time foolin', foolin',
> She's been a long time foolin' me.

Rox-ie Ann's a fool-in' gal, She fools me all th' while,

She's been a long time fool-in', fool-in',

She's been a long time fool-in' me.

The "Lead Her Up and Down" game, as played in the hills near Van Buren, Arkansas, is described as follows by Mrs. Isabel Spradley, who has made a careful study of the song-games of this region: "The boys form in one line and the girls in another, so that partners will be opposite each other. The boy on the lower end leads his partner up and down the rows, swinging her at the words 'won't you be my darlin',' and returning her to her original position. Then he goes to the other end of the line and swings the girl at that end, while his partner is swinging a boy at the opposite end of the boys' line. The partners swing again, then swing the next boy and girl, and so on until each boy and girl have been swung. The second couple then start swinging, and so the game continues. This is rather an exhausting game . . . if there are very many couples."

Wheel about, wheel about rows, Betsey Diner,
Wheel about, wheel about rows, Betsey Diner,
Wheel about, wheel about rows, Betsey Diner,
Won't you be my darlin'?

Lead   her   up   an' down   th' rows,   Bet - sey   Din - er,   Lead

her up an' down th' rows,   Bet-sey Din-er, Lead her up an' down th' rows,

Bet - sey   Din - er,   Won't you   be   my   dar - lin'?

All promenade th' rows, Betsey Diner,
All promenade th' rows, Betsey Diner,
All promenade th' rows, Betsey Diner,
Won't you be my darlin'?

In recent years the younger hill-people have come to regard the party-games as countrified and old-fashioned; many of them now go freely to the square dances, and some of the more progressive even favor the modern round dances introduced by the tourists and summer colonists. It is only in the more isolated and backward mountain settlements, where the current civilization has not yet penetrated, that the play-party is still in vogue, and even here the "frolics" are by no means so frequent nor so popular as they were a decade ago. The play-party is passing, and another ten years, in my judgment, will see its total extinction in the Ozark country.

CHAPTER VII.

Ozark Folk-Songs

IN PIONEER DAYS THE OZARK hillmen had religious scruples against dancing and card-playing, and singing was one of their principal forms of social entertainment. Men and women who sang well were always in demand, and enjoyed considerable prominence in the social life of the neighborhood. They had no written music, and most of them could not read anyhow, so they clung to the good old songs which their parents sang before them, and which had been perpetuated for generations by oral transmission.

Recently, however, the Ozark country has been commercialized as a Summer playground, and the younger hill people in particular are now more or less corrupted by contact with the tourists and realtors. Since the coming of schools, newspapers and phonographs the old songs and ballads are rapidly falling into disrepute; the younger generation knows little about them and cares less, while the older people have grown sensitive and sullen under the derision of the schoolmarms and other rural cognoscenti, and are more and more inclined to keep their memories to themselves.

It is still possible, however, for the diplomatic collector to obtain a considerable number of old songs in the more isolated sections of the Ozark highland, and it is a harvest well worth the reaping. Some of the oldest ballads came over from England with the seventeenth-century colonists, others are evidently later importations, still others had their origin in the mountains of Kentucky and Tennessee, and some are derived from comparatively modern songs which have somehow filtered into the hill country, to be gradually molded by the mountain singers into the traditional folk-song pattern. Whatever their origin, the Ozark singers have long ago lost all knowledge of the authorship and provenience of these pieces, and they are all true folk-songs in the modern sense of the term.

The collecting of this material is a delicate and difficult matter at best, and the man who simply rides up to a mountain cabin and asks somebody to sing old songs will never hear any songs worth recording. The successful collector must either be introduced and vouched for by someone whom the natives know and trust, or he must cultivate the hillman for himself, and lead up to the subject of balladry by slow and easy stages. The mountain man usually begins the conversation, and the stranger must always be prepared to give his name, his address, and all the details of his lineage and means of livelihood, after which he is usually permitted to talk on topics of general interest as freely as he likes. Meanwhile the hillfolk sit around and eye him narrowly, usually replying in a courteous but noncommittal fashion. After an hour or so of this, if he has convinced them that he is a serious minded and responsible person, not too "fine-haired" or "stuck-up", he may at least make known the object of his quest.

I usually begin by telling them frankly that I am getting up an old-fashioned songbook in order that our children may be able to sing the good old ballads, which are infinitely superior to the songs in vogue among the young folk today. Many people,

I aver, would be glad to buy a book with the real old-time songs in it, were such a book obtainable. The trouble is, however, that so many of the old ballad-singers have died recently—and here I name several local examples—that it is mighty hard to find anybody who can sing the old songs properly. At this point there is often a vigorous nodding of heads, because every singer knows that he sings the ballads correctly, and that all other versions are degenerate corruptions. "Now", I say to the most promising member of the group, "folks all tell me that you know more old songs than anybody else in these parts, and I have ridden a long way today to ask you to sing a few of the best ones, so that I can write them down and print them in my book."

Only in rare instances is there any immediate response to such a plea as this. Usually, after some meditation, the person addressed admits that perhaps he might have sung a little in his youth, but adds that he has long ago forgotten every word of the old songs. Very often he refers me to some other old singer, and volunteers minute directions as to the best route to the other singer's cabin. I always make a careful note of this information, but do not make any motion to leave; I rather try to lead the talk away from old songs for awhile, in order to let the singer consider the matter a bit, and get accustomed to the idea of singing for me.

After awhile, if nobody returns to the subject nearest my heart, I name over a few of the songs that I am most anxious to obtain. If this fails to get any response I whistle a bar or two, and then say suddenly: "By the way, I got a good one the other day from old man so-and-so," naming some local character known to my hearers, and then boldly begin to sing the ballad, but contrive to make some grievous error in the third or fourth stanza. This butchering of an old favorite is more than any genuine ballad-singer can endure, and he frequently bursts out with "Hell!

Thet aint it!" after which he is very likely to sing the entire song without any further persuasion. It is a peculiar fact that, the ice once broken, the singer will usually run through his whole repertoire without much more urging; if you can get him to sing one song, the entire stock is yours for the asking. The principal thing is to avoid a definite refusal early in the negotiations, for the hillman is a man of his word. If he once says that he will not sing, he feels in honor bound to refrain from singing, even though the original causes for his refusal may have long since been disposed of.

Another method of inducing the reluctant ridge-runner to sing is to lure him into your house and play some of the phonographic versions of the old songs, recorded by such singers as Vernon Dalhart, Al Craver, Riley Puckett, Carl T. Sprague, Harry McClintock, Kelly Harrell, Buell Kazee, Dock Boggs and Bradley Kincaid. Many of these songs are more or less modernized and "improved", and the hillman's ear is quick to detect the differences between the song as recorded and the genuine ballad that he learned from his "fore-parents". Very often he is moved to point out the defects of the phonographic version, and may then be induced to sing the song "like hit orter be sung". This approach is very successful with a certain type of diffident singer, and I have obtained several of my best songs from people who disclaimed all knowledge of them until I had broken the ice, as it were, with my phonograph records.

The faintest suggestion of criticism or amusement in these situations is absolutely fatal. I once played Al Craver's phonographic version of an old song called "The Three Drowned Sisters" to a group of tourists at an Ozark summer-resort; the city people all roared with laughter, but a mountain boy who happened to be present flushed angrily. It was exactly the type of song that his parents wept over at home, and he could see nothing humorous in the tragic fate of three young women. The old-time singer takes his art very seriously, and he knows perfectly well that people with "book larnin'" are apt to laugh at his songs—the very passages which bring tears to his old eyes seem to excite only cynical amusement in the sophisticated "furriner". The hillman may not understand just how this condition has come about, but he resents it very seriously, and the stranger who smiles at the wrong moment will get no more music from that particular singer.

It is a great mistake, ordinarily, to offer money to the hillfolk in connection with ballad-singing. One woman, the proprietress of a little crossroads hotel, told me of her encounter with a sports writer named Thompson, better known as "Ozark Ripley". Thompson heard her singing in the kitchen, and offered to "make it worth her while" to sing for him, so that he could write down some of the old songs. "But I jes' told thet feller," she remarked disdainfully, "thet I didn't want no truck 'ith no sich foolishness!" The same woman sang freely enough for me, however, and seemed pleased when I wrote the words of her songs in my notebook, but she absolutely refused to sing for my assistant who wanted to record the melodies. I discovered later that she had no conception of musical notation, but suspected that her voice might somehow be transferred from the music-paper to the radio, or to a phonograph record. "Hit shore would be fine, now wouldn't it, t' hear me a-singin' out o' one o' these hyar talkin'-machines, an' them fool boys down t' th' store a-laughin' 'bout it!" All my efforts to explain the situation were in vain, and she would have nothing more to do with us.

Too much emphasis can hardly be placed upon the importance of recording a song immediately, for if the singer once gets out of sight the opportunity is generally lost forever. He usually promises to come to your house and sing the song again,

or to have the "young-uns" write down the "ballet" for you, but
nearly always fails to do so. Old people, too, are exasperatingly
apt to die at unexpected and inopportune moments, and the
death of one of these ancient minstrels may mean the irrevo-
cable loss of songs which he alone can sing. I once travelled
nearly forty miles through the roughest kind of country to visit
a famous ballad-singer, only to learn that the old man had been
"horse-throwed" and fatally injured only a few days before.

Except for the religious and play-party pieces, the old songs
are nearly all solos. The work-song choruses chanted by Negro
laborers in the South are unknown in the hill country, as the
hillmen seldom work in gangs, and do not seem to care for
that sort of music, anyway. A man cannot very well sing while
engaged in such breath-taking labor as cutting down trees, but
when he is about some less strenuous task, such as hauling stove-
wood to town, or "bilin' down" molasses, the Ozarker very often
sings at the top of his voice. One of my neighbors used to wake
me on many a Summer morning, shouting out some lugubrious
old ballad as he rode his plow-horse down the trail to the corn
patch. A boy who "holp out" at the paternal still-house told me
that the only thing he disliked about this work was the necessity
for silence—his Pappy wouldn't let him sing!

In order fully to appreciate just how seriously the old songs
are taken by the hillfolk, one must note the reactions of the
audience as well as the behavior of the singer. I have seen tears
coursing down many a bronzed old cheek, and have more than
once heard sobs and something near to bellowings as the minstrel sang of some more or less pathetic incident, which may
have occurred in England three or four hundred years ago.
The old song of "Barbara Allen" which Samuel Pepys enjoyed in
1666 is still a moving tragedy in the Ozark hills, and women in
Missouri and Arkansas weep today for young Hugh of Lincoln,

murdered across the sea in 1255, whose story lives in the ballad of "The Jew's Garden".

On one memorable occasion I sat with several mountain men in a smoky little log kitchen, while a very old fellow quavered out the song known as "The Jealous Lover", one verse of which goes something like this:

Down on her knees afore him
She humbly begged for life,
But into thet snow-white bosom
He pierced th' fatal knife!"

At this point the old man stopped short with a kind of gasping sob, and then burst out in such a paroxysm of rage that I was startled quite out of my chair. "Oh Gawd!" he shrilled, "th' son-of-a-bitch! Dod rot sich a critter, anyway!" Our host, a hard-faced moonshiner with at least one killing to his credit, muttered some similar sentiment, and there were grunts of sympathetic approval from several of the other listeners. It would have been a hardy "furriner", indeed, who showed the slightest flicker of amusement at that moment.

Sometimes certain excitable members of the audience become so interested in the narrative that their shouted comments almost drown the singer's voice, and occasionally they even venture to join him in the singing of some particularly effective line or refrain. Very rarely someone so far forgets himself as to burst out with a different and presumably superior version, correcting the soloist at the top of his voice—an unpardonable affront, which cannot be overlooked by any self-respecting singer. This sort of thing has caused marked ill-feeling at several "singin's" in my neighborhood, and one rather serious drunken fight is said to have begun in a quarrel over the proper rendition of the "Jesse James" ballad.

A ballad is sometimes broken by long pauses at the end
of certain stanzas, so as to enable the singer to take a drink or
a chew of tobacco, to reply to his critics, or to introduce some
explanatory comment about the subject of his song. One old
man, when he concludes the eighth stanza of "Molly Vaughn"—

> Up stepped his ol' father, whose hair was quite gray,
> Sayin' son, dearest son, you must not run away!
> Stay in your own country till th' trial is at hand,
> An' you may be cl'ared by th' law o' th' land!'

always adds: "Th' ol' feller knowed whut he was a-doin'!"

Another senile ballad-singer of my acquaintance is so full
of sharp comments and bucolic wise-cracks that he talks almost
as much as he sings, and is very apt to lose track of the melody
altogether. The following is a fair sample of his version of the
old "Orange and Blue" song, with the spoken interpolations in
italics:

> I oft-times have wondered why women love men,
> *Mostly for whut they kin git out'n 'em!*
> But more times I wonder how men kin love them,
> *Now he's a-talkin' sense!*
> They're men's ruination an' sudden downfall,
> An' they cause men to labor behind th' stone wall.
> *They shore do, now!*

I have known two or three quiet, soft-spoken men who
always shout the old songs at the very top of their voices. One
old fellow leans back with closed eyes and sings in a peculiar
quavering falsetto until he reaches certain particularly moving
lines, when he opens his eyes and shouts in a very loud voice,
looking about as if expecting some commendation or comment
from his audience. I know one ballad-singer who accompanies

his music with an elaborate series of gestures and posturings, with winks and grimaces *ad lib*, but he is not highly regarded by his colleagues. The genuine mountain man never forgets that ballad-singing is a serious matter.

In general, however, there is a singular absence of affectation or self-consciousness about the Ozark minstrel's performance, and in applauding him one says simply "Thet shore is a good song", without any mention of the singer's personal talents or ability. The hillman insists that a song be sung "right"—meaning that he demands the exact words and the melody which he regards as authentic—but he seems to care very little whether the singer has a good voice or a bad one.

Many of the mountain minstrels do not care for instrumental music at all, but others prefer to be accompanied by a fiddle, guitar or harmonica. The old-time singers tell me that the accompaniments were formerly played on the "dulcimore", a home-made instrument which has been replaced by "store-boughten" fiddles and guitars. The only dulcimore I have ever seen was a crude, short-necked affair with three wire strings. Holding the instrument against his thigh, the musician presses one string at a time with the fingers of his left hand, while a piece of leather in his right is swept slowly across all three strings.

Many an old Ozark fiddler, even today, does not tuck his instrument under his chin, but nurses it dulcimore-fashion upon his lap; grasping the bow nearly in the middle, he plays with a movement very different from that of the conventional violinist. Whatever instrument is used, the accompaniment is rendered in a plaintive minor mode which is singularly adapted to the melancholy nature of the songs. There are not many cheerful numbers in the typical mountain singer's repertoire—he has a strange weakness for songs of death and doom, murder, cruel parents, unrequited love, unfaithful wives, girls gone wrong, jealous lovers and the like. The chief charm which these songs hold for the sophisticated auditor lies in their unconscious humor, and in a certain naive crudity, which is a welcome contrast to the labored realism of much of our modern literary verse.

One of the most interesting of the ballads sung by the Ozark singers is "The Turkey Shivaree", a degenerate version of a seventeenth-century English song called "The Golden Vanity". Some variants of this piece refer to a Captain Rolly, and Rose Wilder Lane and others have developed a theory that some of the Ozarkers are descended from the survivors of Sir Walter Raleigh's "lost colony", which disappeared from an island off North Carolina about 1590.

There was a ship sailed from th' North-ern Coun-try, Cry-in'

o'er th' low-lands low, There was a ship sailed from th'

North-ern Coun-try An' th' name that she went un-der was th'

Tur-key Shi-va-ree, Where she went sail-in' on th' low-lands lone-some

low, Where she went sail-in' on th' low-lands low.

They had not sailed more than weeks two or three
Cryin' o'er th' lowlands low,
They had not sailed more than weeks two or three
Till they come in sight o' th' Green Willow Tree
Where she lay anchored on th' lowlands lonesome low
Where she lay anchored on th' lowlands low.

Some was at hats an' some was at caps,
Cryin' o'er th' lowlands low,
Some was at hats an' some was at caps,
An' some was a-stoppin' of th' salt-water gaps,
Where she lay anchored on th' lowlands lonesome low,
Where she lay anchored on th' lowlands low.

I'll give you gold an' I'll give you fee,
Cryin' o'er th' lowlands low,
I'll give you gold an' I'll give you fee
An' my oldest daughter your wedded bride shall be'
If you'll sink 'em in th' lowlands lonesome low
If you'll sink 'em in th' lowlands low.

He bowed upon his breast an' off swum he,
Cryin' o'er th' lowlands low,
He bowed upon his breast an' off swum he
An' he come in sight o' th' Green Willow Tree
Where she lay anchored on th' lowlands lonesome low
Where she lay anchored on the lowlands low.

This laddie had a instrument just fit for th' use,
Cryin' o'er th' lowlands low,
This laddie had a instrument just fit for th' use

For to put agin th' cabin an' eleven holes to push,
An' sink 'em in th' lowlands lonesome low,
An' sink 'em in th' lowlands low.

He bowed upon his breast an' back swum he,
Cryin' o'er th' lowlands low,
He bowed upon his breast an' back swum he
Till he come in sight o' th' Turkey Shivaree,
Where she was sailin' on th' lowlands lonesome low,
Where she was sailin' on th' lowlands low.

Oh captain, oh captain, come take me on board,
Cryin' o'er th' lowlands low,
Oh captain, oh captain, come take me on board,
An' be unto me as good as your word,
For I sunk 'em in th' lowlands lonesome low,
For I sunk 'em in th' lowlands low!

Oh no, oh no, I caint take you on board,
Cryin' o'er th' lowlands low,
Oh no, oh no, I caint take you on board,
An' be unto you as good as my word,
Though you sunk 'em in th' lowlands lonesome low,
Though you sunk 'em in th' lowlands low.

Now if it war'nt for th' virtue o' your crew,
Cryin' o'er th' lowlands low,
Now if it war'nt for th' virtue o' your crew,
I'd do unto you as I done unto them,
I'd sink you in th' lowlands lonesome low,
I'd sink you in th' lowlands low!

He bowed upon his breast an' off swum he,

Cryin' o'er th' lowlands low,

He bowed upon his breast an' off swum he,

Bid an everlastin' 'dieu to th' Turkey Shivaree,

An' he left her sailin' on th' lowlands lonesome low,

An' he left her sailin' on th' lowlands low

Another of the old English ballads known to the mountain folk is "The Wife of Usher's Well", but the Ozarker calls it "The Three Little Babes", or sometimes "Lady Gay". There are several different versions, but the best one goes something like this:

A la-dy lived in th' West Coun-try An' she had chil-dren three, An' she sent 'em a-way to th' North Coun-try For to learn their gram-mar-ie.

They hadn't been gone but a month or two,

I'm sure it wasn't three,

Till death come an' spread all over th' land

An' swept her babes away.

It bein' close on to ol' Christmas time,
An' the nights bein' long an' cold,
She looked an' she seen her three little babes
Come a-runnin' down her mother's hall!

She made 'em up a bed in th' uppermost room,
Spread over with a clean white sheet;
Come, oh come, my three little babes
An' sleep in your mother's hall.

Rise you up, rise you up, says th' oldest one,
Oh mother, we caint sleep here;
For three long hours before daylight
We must jine our Savior dear!

A marble stone lays at our heads, mother,
An' cold clods lays at our feet;
An' th' tears that you will shed, mother,
Will wet our windin' sheet.

The English original of the following piece is pretty old; it was quoted by Beaumont and Fletcher in a play produced in London in 1611, and was probably an old song then. The name of the ballad is really "Lady Margaret", but the hill people have confused the title with a familiar proper name, and usually call the heroine "Lydia" or "Liddy Margaret". The text given here is only a fragment of what was once a very long ballad.

She throwed her ivy comb away,
An' she tore down her long yaller hair,
An' she fell right back: on her death-cold bed,
Set yander agin th' wall.

. . .

Lid - dy Mar - gret was a - stand-in' in her
own cham - ber room, A - comb-in' back her long yal - ler
hair, When she seen sweet Wil - lie an' his
new wed-ded bride, As they to th' church drawed nigh.

Where's Liddy Margaret, my own true love,
Oh where's she at, I say!
Is she in her own chamber room,
Or is she in th' hall?

She's neither in her own chamber room,
Neither is she in th' hall;
She's sealed up in her death-cold coffin
Set yander agin th' wall!

Th' first he kissed was her red rosy cheeks,
And th' next he kissed was her chin,
Th' next he kissed was them death-cold lips
That had so often kissed his'n.

Liddy Margaret was buried like it had a been today,
Sweet William was buried beside her,
An' out of her grave grew a red rose bush,
An' out of his'n a brier.

They grew to th' top o' th' ol' church tower,
Till they could not grow no higher,
They grew till they tied in a true love knot,
Th' rose bush an' th' brier.

The concluding stanzas of "Lady Margaret" are used also in the "Barbara Allen" song, which was formerly well known in many parts of the United States. "Barbara Allen", according to Albert J. Beveridge, was one of the songs which Abraham Lincoln sang as a boy in Indiana.

'Twas in th' ve-ry month of May, When th'
green buds they was swel-lin', Sweet Wil-liam on his
death-bed lay For love of Bar-bra Al-len.

He sent his servants into town,
An' there unto her dwellin',

Sayin' Mosso's sick, an' sent for you,
If your name is Barbra Allen.

So slowly, slowly she got up,
An' slowly she went to him,
She drawed th' curtains from Willie's pale face,
Sayin' young man, you are a-dyin'.

Oh yes, I'm sick, I'm very sick,
An' death is on me dwellin',
But never better will I be
Till I git Barbra Allen.

Don't you remember th' other night,
A-settin' in th' tavern,
A-drinkin' wine with th' ladies all,
An' you slighted Barbra Allen!

Oh yes, I remember th' other night
A-settin' in th' tavern,
A-drinkin' wine with th' ladies all,
But I never seen Barbra Allen.

So slowly, slowly she got up,
An' slowly she went from him;
She hadn't went but a mile or two
Till she heard th' death bell tollin'.

She looked to th' East an' she looked to th' West,
She seen th' chariots a-comin',
With two gray horses a-workin' in th' breast,
An' Willie's corpse behind 'em.

Oh mother, oh mother, go dig my grave,
An' dig it both long an' narrow,
Sweet William died for me today,
I'll die for him tomorrow.

They buried her in th' ol' church yard,
An' they buried him beside her,
An' out of his breast growed a red red rose,
An' out of her'n a brier.

They growed an' they growed to th' top o' th' church,
Till they could not grow no higher,
They linked an' they locked in a true love knot,
For all true lovers to admire.

Another old English ballad, called "Down by the Greenwood Side", is known to many old settlers in the Ozark country, but is very seldom heard nowadays. An old lady near Mena, Arkansas, sang the following version only after evicting a little girl who happened to be present, remarking that it was not a fit song for children to hear!

She leaned her back ag'in th' thorns,
All aloney;
An' there she had two purty sons born
Down by th' greenwood side.

She had a little knife both keen an' sharp,
All aloney;
An' she pierced them tender babies' heart,
Down by th' greenwood side.

She leaned her back a-gin th' wall,
All a-lone-y, She thought in her heart
her back would break, Down by th' green-wood side.

She washed her knife all in th' flood,
All aloney;
She turned th' river all to blood,
Down by th' greenwood side.

As she returned back home agin,
All aloney;
She seen three pretty babes playin' with a ball,
Down by th' greenwood side.

One was dressed in silks so fine,
All aloney;
T'others was naked as they was borned,
Down by th' greenwood side.

Oh babies, oh babies, if you was mine,
All aloney;

I'd take an' dress you in silks so fine,
Down by th' greenwood side.

Oh mother, oh mother, when we was yourn,
All aloney;
You dressed us in silks, not coarse nor fine,
Down by th' greenwood side.

You dressed us in our own heart's blood,
All aloney;
You turned th' river all to blood,
Down by th' greenwood side.

Seven year, seven year you shall burn in Hell,
All aloney;
Seven year you shall never enter Heaven,
Down by th' greenwood side.

A much more recent English song, still very popular among
the Ozark singers, is called "The Cuckoo" or "The Unconstant
Lover".

A-walkin' an' a-talkin'
An' a-walkin' was I,
If I am forsaken
I cannot tell why.

Oh meetin' is a pleasure,
An' partin' is a grief,
But a unconstant lover
Is worse than a thief!

Th' cuck-oo is a pur-ty bird, She sings as
she flies, She brings me good tid-in's,
An' tells me no lies.

A thief will but rob you
An' take all you have,
But a unconstant lover
Will put you in your grave.

He'll court you an' kiss you
And make your heart warm,
But soon as your back's turned
He'll laugh you to scorn.

Th' grave it will mould you
An' turn you to dust;
There's not one in twenty
That a young maid can trust.

Oh come all you purty maids,
Take warnin' by me,

Lew Kelley, the Singing-Teacher

An' never love a charmin' boy
That never will love thee.

If you do he will leave you
Just like mine left me,
To weep an' to mourn
Under a green willow tree.

Th' cuckoo is a purty bird,
She sings as she flies,
She brings me good tidin's
An' tells me no lies.

The following piece is pretty definitely dated by the mention of Jessie's "waterfall", since this particular coiffure was not in vogue later than 1860. After some difficulty I have identified it as a fragment of "Jessie, the Belle at the Bar", an English music-hall ditty, recently reprinted by Sigmund Spaeth in his book *Weep Some More, My Lady*. The word which the Ozarker renders "blow" was "swell" in the original, while the priceless line about the "modest harness-maker" fades to "quiet-looking Quaker" in the English version as given by Dr. Spaeth.

A tink-er an' a tail-or an' a dir-ty lit-tle sail-or An' a blow that used to talk a-bout his paw an' maw, A butch-er an' a bak-er an' a mod-est har-ness mak-er, A - court-in' pret-ty Jes-sie at th' Rail-way Bar.

When Jessie came my heart was all aflame,
To see her waterfall an' her bonnet trimmed so gay,
But on our weddin' day Miss Jessie run away
An' got married to th' man that sold th' Herald-Star.

The song which follows is known as "Johnny the Sailor" in
the Ozarks, but it was formerly common in English broadsides
under the names "Jack Tar" and "The Liverpool Landlady". The
lady who supplied this piece heard it sung by her grandmother
before the Civil War.

Oh John-ny been on sea, an' John-ny been on
shore, An' John-ny come to Lon-don, to where he'd been before, Wel-come home on shore, John-ny,
Wel-come home from sea, Last night my daugh-ter
Pol-ly lay a-dream-in' of thee.

Go fetch your daughter Polly
An' set her down by me,
By all that's melancholy
It's married we will be.
Oh what luck, my Johnny boy?
Very bad, says he,
I've lost my ship and cargo
On the ragin' sea!

My daughter Polly is absent, John,
An' won't return today,
But if she was here, John,
She no would let you stay.
John bein' drowsy
He hanged down his head,
An' called for a candle
To light him up to bed.

My beds are full of strangers,
Have been all the week,
An' for another lodging
You will have to seek.
Twenty shillings of the' new
An' thirty of th' old . . .
An' John pulled out his two
Hands full of gold!

The sight of th' money
Caused th' landlady to weep,
My green bed is empty,
An' there you shall sleep!

In come daughter Polly
With a smiling face,
She gave him a kiss
An' a fond embrace.

Before I had money
My lodging was to seek;
Before I'd sleep in your green bed
I'd sleep in th' street!
Now I have got money
I'll make the taverns whirl,
With a bottle of good brandy,
And on each knee a girl.

Songs of crime and criminals are popular among primitive people everywhere, and it is not surprising that many of the Ozark favorites are of this type. The hillman is an indomitable individualist first of all, with an open contempt for some generally accepted forms of legal restraint; he has always been accustomed to settle his personal difficulties in his own way, and frequently chooses to do it with firearms and cutlery. When a man felt himself seriously affronted, in the early days, he often sent a messenger to give the other party "fa'r warnin'", and some shooting affrays were arranged with a certain degree of formality—a rustic survival of the old duelling code. Many of our prominent citizens still carry revolvers, and a man who will "fight at th' drap of a hat" is regarded with a certain admiration even today, while he who relies upon the officers of the law to protect his life and property is looked down upon by his neighbors.

The mountain minstrel never ventures to glorify wickedness, however, and he seldom fails to point out that the way of the transgressor is hard indeed. In many cases a sort of homiletic epilogue is delivered from the scaffold by the criminal himself, or shouted out just after his execution by one of his sorrowful and moralizing relatives. With all this, there is no denying that even the most moral and religious of the hill people have a singular antipathy for the restraints of the regularly constituted authority, and they still feel a certain sympathy and admiration for anybody who has the courage to defy the vague power of the law.

The hillman has a particular weakness for the light-hearted rascality of bank-robbers and the like—a reaction which comes easily to a man who has no money and who does not believe much in banks. I have observed however, that this friendly tolerance does not extend to horse-thieves or petty grafters whose operations do affect the mountaineer's personal fortunes. It must be remembered that the genuine outlaws with whom the hillman is acquainted do not come into the Ozarks on business bent, but merely to recuperate and "lay low" for a time—they do their robbing elsewhere. In any case the native has nothing to fear from these gentry, for the simple reason that he has nothing worth stealing. Not only this, but a successful bank-robber on a vacation is singularly open-handed—very much more generous than the tourists and summer-resort people that the Ozarkers have come to know.

There are many old people in the Ozarks who knew the James and Younger boys very well indeed, and stories of their gallant deeds and unparalleled generosity are still current in many of our best hill country families. Of Frank James in particular it is said that he never left a mountain cabin without placing a gold-piece on the "fireboard" to pay for his night's lodging, and some of his colleagues in derring-do were equally liberal. It is no wonder that the poverty-stricken hillfolk welcomed such men, concealed them when concealment was necessary, and helped them in every possible way.

There are no James's or Youngers in the Ozarks now, of course, but something of the same attitude still persists, and real outlaws are not altogether lacking even today. I remember a quiet, hard-faced young fellow whom one of my friends introduced as his "cousin from out West", but it was not until several years later, when I became much more intimately acquainted with the family, that I learned his true identity. The fact that this man was a notorious criminal was kept from me at the time only because I was still regarded as a "furriner", and I discovered later that at least a dozen people in the neighborhood knew all about him. It is said that this man really did "rob th' rich fellers an' holp out th' pore folks" in true Robin Hood fashion; at any rate, he is still remembered affectionately by those who knew him in the hills, and is regarded as something of a hero by many of my neighbors.

There is no ballad about this man as yet, but one has only to talk with any of the local gossips to hear thrilling stories of his courage, generosity, kindness to women and children, and loyalty to those whom he regarded as his friends. Doubtless there is a grain of truth in every one of these stories, but the touch of the troubadour is upon them all. Such characters as Jesse James and Cole Younger have already become semi-mythological heroes, and the material of the songs and stories about them is even now more legendary than historical.

There are perhaps a dozen versions and variants of the "Jesse James" ballad in the Ozarks; the one which follows tells the story in a very few words, and was sung for me by a man near Sulphur Springs, Arkansas. The "Mister Howard" mentioned was merely a *nom de guerre* used by Jesse when he lived on Lafayette Street in St. Joseph, Missouri, where he was shot down by Robert Ford in April, 1882.

Jes - se James he was a man That was knowed thru all th' land, For Jes - se he was bold an' bad an' brave, But th' dir - ty lit - tle cow - ard that mur - dered Mis - ter How - ard, has went an' laid pore Jes - se in his grave.

Hit was on a Friday night

An' th' moon a-shinin' bright,

An' Bob Ford had been hidin' in a cave;

He had ate of Jesse's bread,

He had slep' in Jesse's bed,

But he went an' laid pore Jesse in his grave.

The adventures of Cole Younger, who was a captain of Confederate cavalry, rode with Quantrell's guerillas, and later robbed banks with the James brothers, are told in a long ballad called "Cole Younger the Highwayman", which begins:

Cole Younger died at Lee's Summit, Missouri, in 1916. I saw him about 1904, and have interviewed several persons who knew him well, but it appears that the major portion of the "Cole Younger" ballad has already gone beyond recall; many hill people recall snatches and fragments of it, but I have never found anybody who could sing the entire song.

The story of Sam Bass, another famous outlaw, killed in Texas in 1878, has been preserved in considerable detail. The song which follows is known not only in the Ozarks, but in many other parts of the South and Southwest.

Young Sam he dealt in race stock,
One called th' Denton Mare,
He matched her in scrub races
An' tuck her to th' Fair,
Sam always coin-ed money
An' spent it jest as free,
He always drunk good liquor
Wherever he might be.

Sam he left th' Collins ranch
In th' merry month of May,
With a herd of Texas cattle,
Th' Black Hills for to see.
Sold out in Custer City
An' all went on a spree—
A harder set of cowboys
You seldom ever see.

On their way back to Texas
They robbed th' U. P. train,

Sam Bass was borned in In - di - an - a, That was his nat - ive home, An' at th' age of sev - en - teen Young Sam be - gan to roam, He first come out to Tex - as A team - ster for to be, A kin - der heart - ed fel - ler You sel - dom ev - er see.

They busted up in couples
An' started on again;
Joe Collins an' his partner
Was overtaken soon,
An' with all their hard-earnt money
They had to meet their doom.

Sam Bass come back to Texas
All right side up with care,

Rid into th' town of Denton
With all his friends to share;
Sam's time was short in Texas,
Three robberies did he do,
He took an' robbed th' passengers
An' mail an' express too.

Sam had four brave companions,
Four brave an' darin' lads,
There was Richardson an' Jackson,
Joe Collins an' ol' Dad;
As brave an' darin' cowboys
As Texas ever knew,
They whupped th' Texas Rangers
An' run th' boys in blue.

Sam had another companion
Called Arkansaw for short,
He was shot by a Texas Ranger
By th' name of Thomas Floyd.
Tom he's a big six-footer
An' thinks he's mighty fly,
But I can tell you his racket—
He's a deadbeat on th' sly.

Jim Murphy was arrested
An' then released on bail,
He jumped his bond at Taylor
An' took the train for Trail;
Ol' Major Jones had posted Jim,
An' that was all a sell,

It was all a plan to capture Sam
Before th' comin' Fall.

Sam met his fate at Round Rock
On July twenty-first,
They pierced pore Sam with rifle balls
An' emptied out his purse.
Sand within th' valley,
Pepper in th' quay,
An' Jackson in th' bushes
A-tryin' to git away.

Jim Murphy borrowed gold from Sam
Their robberies to pay,
Th' only way he seen to win
Was to give pore Sam away;
He sold out Sam an' Barnes
An' left their friends to mourn,
Oh whut a scorchin' he will git
When Gabriel blows his horn!

"McFee's Confession" is generally believed to be the record of a murder which was committed "back East some'rs", and was well known in the Ozarks before the Civil War. There are several versions, but the following is probably the most popular.

My woman she was good to me,
As any woman needs to be,
An' she'd be a-livin' without no doubt
If I had not met Miss Hattie Stout.

'Twas on a balmy summer night,
Ever'thing was still, th' stars was bright,

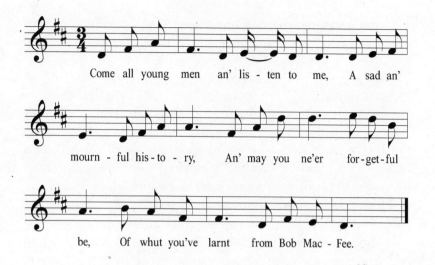

Come all young men an' lis-ten to me, A sad an'
mourn-ful his-to-ry, An' may you ne'er for-get-ful
be, Of whut you've larnt from Bob Mac-Fee.

My wife was a-layin' on th' bed
When I approach-ed her an' said:

"Dear wife, here's medicine I've brought,
For you this day that I have bought,
Of them wild fits it will cure you,
Oh take it, dear, oh darlin' do."

Ten thousand pounds I'd freely give
To fetch her back with me to live,
To bring her back again to life,
My dear, my darlin' murdered wife.

Her body lies beneath th' sod,
Her soul I trust is with its God,
An' soon into eternity
My guilty soul must also flee.

Young men, young men, be warned by me,

Keep away from all bad company,

An' walk in ways of righteousness,

An' God your souls will surely bless.

Another popular murder song is called "The Death of Naomi Wise", and is a great favorite with many of the old-time singers. Mr. Bascom Lamar Lunsford says that Naomi was drowned in 1808, and that he himself has visited her grave near Deep River, North Carolina; Professor H. M. Belden, of the University of Missouri, contends that she lived in Virginia; Miss Myrtle Lain showed me a copy of the song obtained from one of her neighbors at Linn Creek, Missouri, who says that the original Naomi was murdered at Adams Spring, not far from Springfield, Missouri. There are many different versions of the song, but the following is the best one I have heard in the Ozark country.

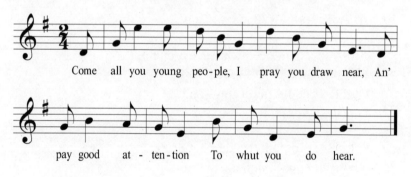

Come all you young peo-ple, I pray you draw near, An'

pay good at-ten-tion To whut you do hear.

I'll sing you a ditty

Of pore Oma Wise,

How she was deluded

By Lewis's lies

When he first come to see her

Fine stories he'd tell,

How when they got married
He'd use her so well.

He told her to meet him
At Adams's Spring,
Some money he'd bring her,
An' other fine things.

He brought her no money,
But flatterin' th' case,
He says we'll git married
An' it aint no disgrace.

Jump up behind me,
We'll ride down through town,
An' then we'll be married,
In union be bound.

She jumped up behind him
An' away they did go,
They went to Deep River
Where th' waters overflow.

Little Oma, little Oma,
I'll tell you my mind,
My mind is for to drownd you
An' leave you behind!

Oh pity, oh pity,
Oh pity, she cried,
Oh let me go a-mournin'
An' not be your bride.

No pity, no pity,
No pity, he cried,
My mind is for to drownd you
An' leave you behind.

He slipped up behind her
An' choked her down,
An' throwed her in th' water
Just below th' mill dam.

He jumped on his geldin',
Rode off at great speed;
Sayin' now I'll see pleasure,
From Oma I'm freed.

Th' screams of pore Oma
They follered him nigh,
Oh I'm a pore rebel
Not fittin' to die.

In come Oma's mother
An' these words did say:
"George Lewis drownded Oma,
An' he's now run away."

In prison, in prison,
In prison he's bound;
He's made his confession
An' wrote it all down.

Genuine Negro folk-songs are not very common in the hill
country. A few Negro slaves were brought into the Ozarks before
the Civil War, but the vast majority of the early settlers came

from the poverty-ridden mountain districts of the Southern
Appalachians, and had never made any considerable contact
with either slaves or slave-owners. There are comparatively few
Negroes in the Ozarks today, and large numbers of people in the
more isolated sections have never even seen a Negro. A friend of
mine who used to go into the White River country for the bass
fishing told me that the natives came from miles around to see
his colored cook, and children stood about his camp for hours
on end, gazing at the black man in open-mouthed amazement.

The Ozark singers may know a few fragments of real Negro
songs, inherited from pioneers who learned them from Negroes
in Kentucky or Tennessee, but I suspect that most of them are
mere echoes from the old-time "nigger-minstrels" which have
somehow drifted into the Ozarks in comparatively recent years.

It appears that the nation-wide craze for "nigger" music
began about 1830, when such songs as "Zip Coon," "Jump Jim
Crow" and "Ole Virginny Nebber Tire" suddenly became popular on the vaudeville stage. The very earliest of these jingles
were probably of Negro origin, but there is no evidence that any
of the really important singers were Negroes, and at any rate,
spurious songs soon replaced the genuine article, just as burnt
cork came to be substituted for natural cutaneous pigmenta-
tion. Certainly the principal performers, such as Dan Emmett,
Charles White, T. G. Booth, "Jim Crow" Rice and Henry H. Paul
were white men, and there is no question that they wrote many
of their song-hits themselves. Charles White once offered a cash
prize of fifty dollars to anybody who could prove that he was not
the author of some forty "nigger" songs, including several which
were claimed by other celebrated minstrels of the day.

There are practically no theaters in the Ozark hill country even now, but the old-fashioned medicine-shows are still
common; most of them feature a long-haired doctor with his

marvellous Indian herb remedy, and two or three black-face singers and banjo-pickers. It is said that the Weaver Brothers, well known hill-billy comedians, once travelled with a "med-show" troupe in the wilds of Northwestern Arkansas. In the early days it appears that these medicine-shows were even more numerous than they are at present, and it may well be that they are in a measure responsible for the persistence of these "nig-ger-minstrel" songs.

One of these old minstrel pieces is called "Went to the River," and is representative of a group of "swappin' songs," many of which have Negro or pseudo-Negro references.

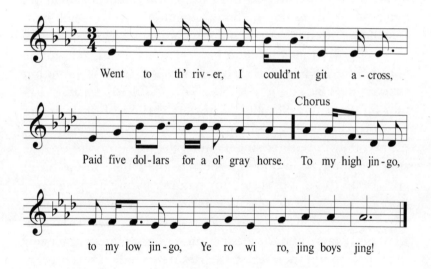

Went to th' riv-er, I could'nt git a - cross,

Paid five dol-lars for a ol' gray horse. To my high jin-go,

to my low jin-go, Ye ro wi ro, jing boys jing!

Plunged him in an' I found he couldn't swim,
Paid five dollars for to git him out agin!

Sold my horse an' I bought me a cow,
Went out to milk but I never knowed how!

Sold my cow an' I bought me a calf,
Never made a bargain but whut I lost half!

Sold my calf an' I bought me a goose,
Aint thet a purty thing to set on a roost?

Sold my goose an' I bought me a hen,
Aint thet a purty thing to put in a pen?

Sold my hen an' I bought me a louse,
Jumped in my head an' he made hisse'f a house!

The "Jawbone Song" probably derives from an old minstrel piece, but it contains genuine Negro elements nevertheless. The slaves frequently used the jawbone of a horse or mule as a musical instrument, played by drawing a bit of metal across the teeth. Several country dance melodies are still known vaguely as "jawbone tunes."

I laid thet jaw bone on th' fence,

An' I aint never seen thet jaw bone since.

Wah jaw bone to my jangle lang,

An' A wah jaw bone to my jangle lang!

Some of the Ozark singers know the piece which follows as "Mister Booger," while others call it "The old Wagoner's Song." The refrain is borrowed from the chorus of an ante-bellum Negro reel called "Johnny Booker," a great favorite with General J. E. B. Stuart, the famous Confederate cavalry leader who always kept a banjo-player with him in the field. There have been many versions and variants, and it is said that some of them were popular with the medicine-show comedians as late as 1900.

I hitched my team to drive to Wright's shop, An'

there I hol-lered for th' driv-er to stop, So

walk a John-ny Boo - ger to he'p that nig-ger, An'

do Mis-ter Boo-ger to he'p him a - long.

Says I to him, kin you mend my yoke?
He stepped to th' bellus an' he blowed up smoke,
So walk a Johnny Booger to he'p that nigger,
An' do Mister Booger to he'p him along.

An' I driv from there to Anthony's mill,
An' there I got stalled a-goin' up hill,
So I put my shoulder agin th' wheel
An' on th' ground I placed both heels.

Wal there I shoved an' there I strained,
But all my work it proved in vain,
So I set right down an' begun for to cry,
When along come a wagoner a-passin' by.

Says I to him, caint you-all he'p me?
He onhitched his horses with a one, two, three,
An' while I was a-wipin' th' fallin' tears,
He hitched them horses on afore my steers.

Wal, its now I've ended my ol' song,
I'll start to Arkansaw a-rackin' along,
So walk a Johnny Booger to he'p that nigger,
An' do Mister Booger to he'p him along!

Most of the early settlers in the Ozarks were hard-drinking southerners, and one of the first things they did in the new country was to establish suitable distilleries. Liquor was good and plentiful and cheap; it was sold everywhere, and used freely by everybody who cared for it. The late seventies saw a marked increase in the religious element in the hill country, however, and many of the itinerant evangelists began to preach temperance and even total abstinence. Then came several temperance societies, such as the "Blue Ribbon Club", the "Murphys", the "Good Templars", the "Sons of Temperance" and finally the "Woman's Christian Temperance Union". These people held frequent meetings in the churches and schoolhouses, pledged themselves never to touch intoxicants, wore conspicuous badges and distributed temperance tracts. Some of the more fanatical even went with song and exhortation to the homes of the local drunkards, and women followed these unfortunates about the streets, crying up the numerous advantages of religion, sobriety and so on. As one old man told me, "some of them women went plum hawg-wild 'bout this hyar temp'rance—jest made a plumb dam' fool out o' theirself!"

During this period of temperance agitation many songs dealing with temperance and temperance legislation were introduced. They were sung in the churches, in street parades, at the meetings of the temperance organizations, and even by children in the public schools. Although I have been unable to identify many of these songs, or to find any reference to them in the literature of the subject, I have no doubt that they all go back to print, and probably appeared in the temperance song-books of the time, or in the leaflets distributed by the various temperance societies.

Such songs as Henry Clay Work's "Father, Dear Father, Come Home With Me Now" and the English piece called "The Drunkard's Dream" are too well known even in these intemperate days to be worth reprinting, but there are many others which seem to have been lost along with the rest of the old-time temperance movement. The lugubrious ballad of "The Drunkard's Doom," however, is still remembered by elderly people in various parts of the American hinterland; Carl Sandburg printed seven stanzas of an Ohio version in his American Songbag, with a very effective harmonization by H. L. Mencken.

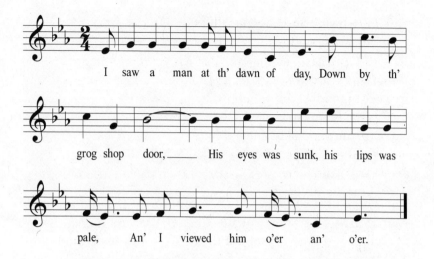

I saw a man at th' dawn of day, Down by th'
grog shop door,___ His eyes was sunk, his lips was
pale, An' I viewed him o'er an' o'er.

His oldest son stood by his side,
An' weepin', murmerin' said:
"Father, mother is sick at home
An' sister cries for bread."

Th' drunkard rose an' staggered in
As he oft had done before,
An' to th' landlord falterin' says:
"Oh give me one glass more!"

He tuck th' glass in his tremblin' hand
An' drunk th' bachanal foul,
He drunk while wife an' childern starved
An' his childern has cried for bread!

"Oh Gawd forgive my husband dear,"
Th' dyin' woman said,
"Although he's been unkind to me
An' his childern has cried for bread."

In just one year I passed that way
Th' hearse stood by th' door,
I ask th' cause, an' they told me
That th' drunkard was no more.

I seen th' funeral a-passin' by,
No wife nor childern there,
For they had gone on long before
An' left this world of care.

"The Curse of Rum" song is another of the old favorites
—little girls in starched white dresses used to sing it in the
churches, and even in front of the court-house at election time.
And the grown folk listened in all seriousness, it is said.

Oh dear, I'm so tired an' lone-some, I won-der why
mam-ma don't come, She told me to shut up my blue eyes,
An' 'fore I wake up she'd come home.

I think I'll go down and meet papa,
I reckon he stopped at th' store,
It's a pretty big store full of bottles,
I wisht he wouldn't go there no more.

Sometimes he is sick when he comes home
An' stumbles an' falls on th' stair,
An' one time he run in th' parlor
An' kicked at my pore little chair!

An' I 'member how papa was angry,
His face was so red an' so wild,
An' I 'member he struck at pore mamma
A-smilin' so meek an' so mild.

But I reckon I better go find him,
Perhaps he'll come home with me soon,
An' then it won't be dark an' lonesome
A-waitin' for mamma to come.

Out into th' night went th' baby
Her little heart beatin' with fright,
Till her tired feet reached th' gin-palace
All radiant with music an' light.

Th' little hand pushed th' door open
Though her touch was as light as a breath,
Th' little feet entered th' portal
That leads but to ruin an' death.

"Oh papa," she cried as she reached him,
An' her voice rippled out sweet an clear,
"I thought if I come here I'd find you,
I knowed you was sure to be here!"

A moment th' bleared eyes gazed wildly
Down into th' face sweet an' fair,

An then as th' demon possessed him
He grabbed at the back of a chair.

One moment—one second—'twas over,
Th' work of th' fiend was complete,
An' his pore little innocent baby
Lay quiverin' an' crushed at his feet!

Then swift as th' light come his reason
An' showed him th' deed he had done,
With a groan that th' devil might pity
He knelt by her quiverin' form.

He pressed her pale face to his bosom,
He lifted th' fair golden head,
A moment th' baby lips quivered
Then pore little Phoebe was dead.

Then in come th' law so majestic
An' says with his life he must pay,
That only a fiend or a madman
Would murder a child that-a-way.

But th' man that had sold him th' pizen
That made him a demon of hell—
Why, he must be loved an' respected
Because he was licensed to sell!

He may rob you of friends an' of money,
Send you down to perdition an' woe,
But so long as he pays for th' license,
Th' law must protect him, you know.

Gawd pity th' women an' children
Who live under th' juggernaut rum!
Gawd hasten th' day when agin it
Neither heart, voice nor pen shall be dumb!

The early temperance workers had a trick of setting their propaganda to music already popular—a method used in later years by the Salvation Army, the Industrial Workers of the World, and various other organizations of well-meaning persons who labored zealously but ineffectively for their own particular brands of economic and social reform. It was with singular appropriateness, however, and a humorous appreciation of values quite unusual in such people, that they sang this "Whiskey Seller" song to the familiar air of "The Little Brown Jug."

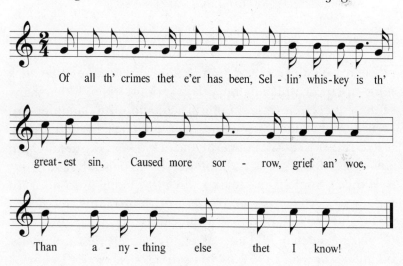

Of all th' crimes thet e'er has been, Sel - lin' whis-key is th'
great-est sin, Caused more sor - row, grief an' woe,
Than a - ny - thing else thet I know!

Th' ol' distiller an' th' whiskey seller
Has ruint many a clever feller,
Caused more sorrow, grief an' woe
Than anything else thet I know!

You rob th' strong man of his stren'th,
An' throw him in th' mud full len'th,
Leave him there for to curse an' roll
An' don't care nothin' for th' pore man's soul!

You rob th' statesman of his brains
An' fill his head with aches an' pains,
He's often in th' gullies found
A-feelin' upwards for th' ground!

You rob th' childern of their bread,
An' they are hungry sent to bed,
Hit causes them such bitter cries
An' makes tears flow from th' mother's eyes!

Except for the general choruses heard at play-parties, where
the unaccustomed levity may be attributed to the combined
influence of whiskey and womenfolk, the Ozarker's favorite
songs are those which he regards as serious. It is true that many
of these pieces move the sophisticated auditor to laughter, but
their humor is unconscious and unintentional. The adult male
ballad-singer is mostly concerned with love and death and high
adventure, and regards all "foolishment" as beneath his dignity.
And this, I think, is the reason why most hillmen do not care
for our modern songs—simply because there is little violence in
them, and few serious or tragic narratives.

As one old man told me: "Most all o' these hyar funny songs
is kinder silly like, an' I wouldn't sing no sich even if I knowed
any—which I don't, nohow." And another aged singer of the
traditional ballads said: "My mammy she sung me t' sleep 'ith
them kind o' songs when I was a leetle feller, an' my woman she
sings some of 'em yit, but I never pay her no mind. They aint
no sense in full-growed menfolks a-messin' with th' like o' that."

I have heard a few humorous and nonsense songs shouted out
by drunken hillmen at dances and frolics and fish-fries, but as
a general thing such follies are left to the women and children.

Years ago in Arkansas I used to visit a farmer who had somehow obtained an old parlor organ and set it up in his shanty—
the pride and show-place of the entire settlement. Nearly every
evening his three strapping barefoot girls gathered around this
instrument and sang at the top of their voices—kept it up for
hours on end. They did not know many of the old ballads, but
had a great store of religious and sentimental songs. They sang
a number of nonsense and nursery pieces, too—some of these
in a strange, wild, but singularly pleasing fashion.

One of the best of the frivolous songs is "The Courtin' Cage".
The general idea of this song, and many of its lines and phrases,
occur also in an old song called "The Spanish Lady," but the
first stanza is not mentioned in any of the folk-song literature
that has come to my attention. I should like very much to know
just what a "courting cage" is, but have never yet found anybody
who can tell me.

Ma-dam, I have a court-in' cage, It stands in yon-der town, An' my es-tate I'll give to you If it be ten thous-and pound, If it be ten thous-and pound.

I know you have a courtin' cage
That stands in yonder town,
An' your estate I do not want
If it be ten thousand pound,
If it be ten thousand pound.

Madam, I have a very fine house
Just newly erectified,
An' you may have it at your command
Whenever you'll be my bride,
Whenever you'll be my bride.

I know you have a very fine house,
Likewise a very fine yard,
But who would stay at home with me
When you're off a-playin' cards?
When you're off a-playin' cards?

Madam, I do not do that way,
I do not think it right,
If you'll consent to marry me
I'll stay at home ever' night,
I'll stay at home ever' night.

Well sir, I know what that's done for,
It's just to take me in,
Do you reckon I am fool enough
To marry a barrel o' gin?
To marry a barrel o' gin?

Madam, I have a very fine horse,
He paces like th' tide,

A Singer of Ancient Ballads

An' you may have him at your command
Whenever you'll be my bride,
Whenever you'll be my bride.

I know you have a very fine horse,
He stands in yonder barn,
His master likes a glass o' wine,
I fear th' horse might l'arn,
I fear th' horse might l'arn !

Madam, I have a very fine farm,
Full sixty acres wide,

An' you may have it at your command,
Whenever you'll be my bride,
Whenever you'll be my bride.

I know you have a very fine farm,
A pasture at th' foot,
If you git me you'll turn me out,
You know a hog will root,
You know a hog will root.

Madam, I think you're a sassy jade,
An' too dang hard to please,
When you git old an' chill with cold
I swear I hope you'll freeze,
I swear I hope you'll freeze!

Your sassy wishes I disregard,
You caint do me no harm!
When I git old an' chill with cold
It won't be you that'll keep me warm,
It won't be you that'll keep me warm!

Here is another old song dealing with matrimonial ventures,
which I heard near Jane, Missouri, only a few miles from the
Arkansas line. In Arkansas, of course, it is sung with some slight
but significant changes in the text.

They will lead you out in them black-jack hills
There so much against your will,
Leave you there for to perish on th' place,
An' that's th' way of th' Arkansaw race!

When they go to meetin' th' clothes they wear
Is a ol' brown coat all tore an' bare,

Come all you Mis-sou-ri gals an' lis-ten to my noise,

Mind how you mar-ry them Ar-kan-saw boys, For

if you do your por-tion it will be, Cold

john-ny cake an' ven-i-son is all you will see!

A ol' white hat without no crown,
An' ol' blue duckins th' whole year round!

"The Boys Around Here" is regarded as a "comical" song
by the people who sing it, but some of the verses are not without bitter and cynical reflections. The text which follows is only
a fragment of a much longer piece-perhaps twenty-five stanzas
altogether.

On Saturday night they'll primp an' they'll comb,
Put on their best clothes an' then they'll leave home,
They'll whip an' they'll slash an' still that won't do,
They must have a brass watch an' a big pistol, too.
An' oh me, but they think they are some!

Th' boys a-round here, they'll primp an' they'll plan, They'll hear a word said an' tell it a-gain, Add some more to it, that is if they can, There's scarce-ly a boy but thinks he's a man. An' oh me, but they think they are some!

They'll set by a gal for a good little while,
An' primp up their mouth for a laugh or a smile,
They'll put one arm around her like a goose with one eye,
An' look round to see if th' ol' woman's nigh.
An' oh me, but they think they are some!

The hillfolk sing many other frivolous ballads and non-sense-songs, of course, but this chapter must end on a melancholy note, in the typical Ozark tradition. The piece which follows is called "Little Birdie," or "The Dark Hollow."

Little birdie, little birdie,
Come sing me a song,
I want t' live in a dark holler
Whar th' sun kin never shine!

Pur - ty wom - an, pur - ty wom - an, Jest
see whut you' ve done, You caused me to
love you, Now your hus - band has come!

I'd ruther be a sailor
Way out on th' sea,
Than t' be a married man
With a baby on my knee.

Little birdie, little birdie,
Whut makes you act so quare?
You've no cause for t' worry,
No sorrow for t' bear.

So much for the folk-songs still current in the Ozark country.
Some of the people who have studied the hillman and his ways
have been fascinated by these songs and ballads, while others
see no merit or amusement in them. Valuable or not, however,
the songs of a people certainly cast a singular light upon the life
and culture of that people, and no study of the Ozark hillfolk
can possibly be complete without a brief consideration of the
Ozark folk-songs.

CHAPTER VIII.

Ways That Are Dark

WHEN THE OZARK COUNTRY WAS first settled everybody drank whiskey as a matter of course, and nearly every substantial farmer had a little still of his own. People lived so far apart in those days, and the mountain trails were so very bad that the farmer had great difficulty in hauling anything anywhere, and the best way to get his corn to market was to carry it there in jugs. There was no sale for fruit then, either, and no way to transport any perishable crop, so that many hillmen thought it best to turn their surplus fruit into brandy. Liquor was sold freely everywhere, and was so cheap that many of the general stores had a jug of whiskey beside the water-bucket on the counter, free to anybody who cared to drink it. The old-timers tell me that pure corn whiskey sold for twenty-five cents a gallon, and excellent brandy was almost as cheap. These prices were standard too, and liquor served as a convenient medium of exchange in places where coin and currency were almost unknown to many people.

Except for a temporary war measure of 1812, there had never been any specific tax on liquor in the United States since 1791, when Alexander Hamilton almost caused a civil war by trying to collect an excise of eleven cents per gallon, but during the Civil War the government levied a tax of one dollar and fifty cents per gallon, which was later increased to two dollars! And this at a time when corn was selling for about thirty-five cents a bushel, and apples and peaches at ten cents a bushel, delivered at the still! The hill people could not pay such a tax, and it appears that the revenue officers were so busy elsewhere that they did not bother such sparsely settled regions as the Ozarks for a long time. In 1868 Congress reduced the tax to fifty cents per gallon, which was raised to seventy cents in 1872, and to ninety cents in 1875. At about this time, too, the "revenuers" began to drift into the Ozark country, and a few of the natives set up comparatively large legal distilleries, but great numbers simply moved their little stills back into the mountains and made their own whiskey exactly as their fathers and grandfathers had done before them. They fought the revenuers on occasion, of course, but revenuers were few and far between in those days, and the local officers showed little interest in collecting the federal tax on whiskey. The hillman felt then, exactly as he does now, that a man who raises corn has a right to use it in any manner that seems good in his eyes, and that the "Guv'ment" in far-off Washington has nothing to do with the matter.

From 1862 on I doubt if a day passed without some illicit liquor being made or sold in the Ozark country, and the business picked up a little in 1894, when Congress raised the tax from ninety cents to one dollar and ten cents per gallon, but on the whole it appears that the profits were small, and comparatively little of the Ozark moonshine went beyond the local market. With the passage of the Eighteenth Amendment and the Volstead Act the whole situation changed. Just before the United States entered the World War moonshine whiskey could be purchased in the Ozarks, in ten-gallon lots, for about one dollar and fifty cents per gallon—only forty cents more than the federal tax on whiskey made under Government supervision. For a year or so after Prohibition the hill country was practically dry, and what little liquor we had was very expensive; I have known ordinary corn whiskey to retail for twenty dollars per quart in Fayetteville, Arkansas. Even today a similar product brings from five dollars to fifteen dollars a gallon in the woods, and our new motor highways permit the moonshiner to take it down to the summer hotels, where the thirsty tourist and his lady will often pay as much as five or six dollars a quart.

Such prices as these allow the illicit distiller to make enormous profits, and have tempted many men into the moonshining game who would never have considered such a thing in pre-prohibition days. It is mighty hard for a man to work from daylight to dark, hoeing corn which sells for seventy-five cents a bushel, or cutting stove-wood at one dollar and fifty cents a cord, when he knows that a few weeks of distilling will keep his whole family in comparative luxury all winter.

There are certainly more moonshiners in the Ozarks now than ever before in the history of the country. Some years ago I lived in a mountain village of about four hundred souls, and it is my opinion that fully twenty-five per cent of the population derived a part of their living from the manufacture and sale of moonshine whiskey. I was personally acquainted with perhaps twenty moonshiners who lived in or near this community, and my native friends told me of at least twenty-five more. The local sheriff and his two deputies destroyed an average of one still a week the year round, and I recall one occasion when they captured seven stills in one day, all of them in a single little "holler" some ten miles from the village.

The Ozark moonshiner as I know him is not at all the bloodthirsty mountaineer of fiction and the stage, stalking about with rifle ready to shoot down any stranger seen near his still-house, but at the same time it is best for "furriners" to avoid knowing too much about the moonshining business. Twice I have been politely but none the less firmly directed away from certain secluded "hollers," and once I stumbled upon a still going full blast in broad daylight; in this latter case I lost no time in getting away from the place, knowing that several pairs of eyes must have been watching me from nearby thickets. Once known and trusted, however, anybody who is interested in the matter will have no great difficulty in seeing plenty of stills; they are mostly small affairs, and are shifted about so often that their temporary location is not particularly significant. Several times I have refused invitations to visit stills or caches of liquor, feeling that if the owner should happen to be robbed or raided soon afterward I might somehow be held responsible.

The most conspicuous thing about a moonshiner's outfit is not the still itself, but a group of barrels in which the "mash" is made. In the old days the distiller kept shelled corn in a warm place until it sprouted—a process which turns most of the starch into sugar. This sprouted corn was then ground into meal, and mixed with warm water to make what was called "sweet mash." Nowadays most moonshiners just fill the barrel about one-fourth full of ordinary corn meal chop, add fifty pounds of sugar and a little yeast, and then fill the barrel up with water. If the operator is a stickler for cleanliness, he ties a piece of burlap over the top, to keep out the birds and insects. In a few days this mixture ferments and produces a whitish liquid known as beer. It has a tart but not unpleasant taste, and evidently contains a considerable amount of alcohol; I have known men and women to become quite intoxicated after drinking a few gourdfulls of beer out of the mash-barrels.

The cooker or "biler" is a homemade copper tank, with a

removable lid and a copper pipe projecting from the upper part. It is set upon two or three piles of stone in such a way that a fire may be built underneath, and is often constructed with a double bottom to prevent the contents from burning. The next unit of the moonshiner's apparatus is a comparatively recent invention called the doubler—a tight keg partly full of water, with two holes in the top of it. The pipe from the boiler enters one of these holes and reaches nearly to the bottom of the keg; the short copper pipe which issues from the other hole does not touch the water at all, and runs directly to the worm or condenser. The old-fashioned worm is simply a copper tube coiled into a trough of cold water. The best stills nowadays do not use a worm at all, but a double-walled copper cylinder which serves as a condenser; the pipe from the doubler enters at the top, and the liquor runs out through another pipe at the bottom. The whole condenser fits loosely into a barrel, and is surrounded by cold water diverted from a spring or branch.

When the mash is ripe the moonshiner prepares to "run a batch" by straining the beer through a cloth and pouring it into his boiler. Next he builds his fire, and for good and sufficient reasons he makes as little smoke as possible. It is said that this result is achieved by using peeled hickory sticks; however this may be, it is certainly true that some of these fellows can build quite a fire with practically no smoke—a fire that all the power and majesty of the United States Government have so far failed to smother. When the beer in the cooker begins to get hot the alcoholic content turns into steam and passes out through the pipe into the water in the doubler; when the water in the doubler is heated sufficiently the alcohol is again converted into vapor, and passes over into the worm or condenser. At times the boiling water in the doubler makes a peculiar hollow thumping sound—hence the doubler is frequently known as the thump-keg. When the hot alcoholic vapor passes into the cold worm or condenser it is converted into a liquid again, and flows out of the pipe at the bottom of the condenser. Sometimes it runs directly into the jugs or kegs in which it is to be carried away, but the best operators put it through a carbon filter, even if this is nothing more than a big funnel with some pieces of charcoal in it.

Before the invention of the thump-keg the liquor as it first came from the still contained an excess of water and had a rank taste; this was called the "first run" or the "singlings" and was not considered fit to drink. When the "singlings" are distilled again, at a somewhat lower temperature, a better grade of liquor is produced, known as "double-run" or "doublings," and it is this that the old-time moonshiner used and sold. Nowadays, by means of the thump-keg or doubler, the distiller is able to produce a fairly satisfactory whiskey at one distillation, thus expediting the process and lessening his chances of being captured at the still.

The mountain moonshiner has no thermometer and no instrument for measuring the alcoholic content of his distillate; he judges it solely by the taste and by the "bead," which is his name for the bubbles which arise when the liquor is shaken in a bottle. Making whiskey under such conditions calls for considerable technical knowledge, and it is really remarkable that the average moonshiner succeeds as well as he does. It is certainly no job for an amateur. I know one poor farmer who invested his savings in a cheap little still, dumped a fermented mess of water and corn-chop into the boiler, and built a rousing fire underneath. Pretty soon the burnt corn-chop stopped up the pipes somehow, and the whole thing exploded with a terrific report. "I war a-settin' thar a-suckin' of my pipe," the amateur distiller said later, "an' all of a suddint I seen th' biler was swole plumb to a strut, an' pooched out like a cat full o' kittens! An' th' next thing I knowed th' hull dang contraption blowed up louder'n th' crack o' doom, an' th'owed bilin' corn-mush all over Snake County! Hit's Gawd's own marcy I warnt scalded plumb t' death, an' I shore taken it as a warnin'!"

As it comes from the still, corn whiskey is a colorless, transparent liquid—"water white, simon pure an' crystal clear," as one bootlegger described his wares to me. It has a bad odor and a worse taste, and is in my opinion quite unfit for human consumption. However, it must be admitted that the hillmen drink it in considerable quantities with every symptom of satisfaction, and apparently suffer no serious after-effects. Some moonshiners soften the taste a bit by putting in shreds of hickory bark, and a few have been known to color new whiskey by adding burnt sugar and the like, but most of them sell their product in its raw condition. Some of the local wise men improve their liquor by shaking it up with powdered charcoal, but it is mighty sorry whiskey at best. However, if this raw moonshine is placed in a new charred keg and left to age six months or more, it acquires color and flavor from the wood, and seems to be about as good as most of the cheap Bourbon whiskey of pre-Prohibition days. It is, I think, better than much of the whiskey retailed as bonded goods in New York and Chicago today.

It is necessary that the oak in which the liquor is aged be charred while it is green, since it is the combination of charcoal and sap which imparts the proper taste and color. The "store-boughten" kegs and barrels are best, but they can be used only for one batch of whiskey, and it is a lot of trouble to get these kegs brought in from the railroad towns in which they are sold. Most hillmen char a lot of white-oak chips and put them in the kegs which have been used once, and they seem to work almost as well as new kegs. The liquor from these second-hand kegs comes out black and opaque, because of the presence of fine particles of charcoal from the chips, and must be filtered in order to restore the clear reddish color. Whiskey ages best when it is kept warm, and it is said that a temperature of about 90° F. is best. In the summer months a barrel hidden in a haystack seems to age very well, and in the cold weather it is said that a large manure-pile is the best place for it. I once noticed a hillman pouring water on a great heap of horse-manure, and a daughter of the house told me later that her pappy always did this in dry weather, as it is thought to generate heat in the interior of the dunghill, thus expediting the proper ageing of the whiskey.

The old-time distillers were content to make two gallons of whiskey out of one bushel of sprouted corn, but nowadays, by the addition of sugar, the moonshiner gets from five to eight gallons from each barrel of mash. In recent years some scoundrels have learned to increase their product by diluting it with water, after which it is necessary to add lye, pepper, carbide, soda or tobacco to give it the proper "bite," with a little soap or glycerine to insure plenty of "bead."

One day, after a moonshiner had told me of the high prices which he had obtained for his whiskey, I asked, "Henry, how is it that you fellows don't all get rich?" He chewed his cigar—my cigar—for a moment and replied: "Wal, if a feller could make it hisse'f, an' sell it away off some'ers, he *would* git rich, shore 'nough. But soon's ever I git a batch run off, hyar comes all my kinfolks in on me, an' all their friends, an' all my woman's kinfolks, an' all their friends. A feller caint turn down his kinfolks, an' so they all drinks an' buys on credit, an' never pays nothin', an' purty soon hyar I am busted! Or else somebody'll git mad an' go tellin' folks whut a stingy ol' devil I am, an' th' sheriff 'll git wind of it, an' come a-chargin' out hyar with his choppin'-axe. . . . Makin' whiskey is th' hardest work a feller ever done, an' there aint no money in it nohow. No sir, they *shore* aint!"

On several occasions, being assured that there was no likeli-hood of any moonshiners being captured, I have accompanied the local officers on raids into the hills. We usually rode out in motor cars as far as possible, walking the rest of the way up the bed of a mountain stream—the stills are of necessity located near running water. The officers separated so as to approach the place from several directions, walking as quietly as possible; one of them told me that "them fellers kin hear a acorn drap a mile off." Once the boiler was still warm as we came up, but no moonshiners were in sight, and it very seldom happens that anyone is caught in raids of this type.

It is easy for the moonshiner to post a guard on a hilltop overlooking the roads to signal the officers' approach long before they can get close enough to be dangerous. I met one of these fellows once, sitting out on a high ridge with a repeating shotgun across his knees. Asked if he would really fire on an officer who appeared suddenly, he said with a slow smile: "Naw, I don't aim t' fight no sheriffs—not for no two dollars a day. Jim he jest told me, if I seen anybody comin', t' begin shootin' at squirrels; he told me how many times t' shoot, too, an' jest how t' space them shots." In this boy's cabin, however, I saw a new box of twelve-gauge "hulls," with six cartridges missing—the six that were in his pump-gun. They were buckshot shells, too, and altogether unsuitable for squirrel shooting.

Every Ozark family has a "blowin'-horn"—a sort of trum-pet, made by scraping and polishing a cow's horn until it is almost transparent. This instrument is used primarily as a hunt-ing-horn, and the mountain man can blow a blast which calls his fox-hounds for miles. The women use it as a dinner-horn, or to summon their menfolk from the fields in case of need. It is also used in communicating with the neighbors several miles away, and by varying the length and number of toots, and doubtless also by more subtle differences in tone and inflection, the hill people are able to transmit rather complicated messages—just how complicated I do not know, as I have never been able to master the code. I am convinced, however, that some of them can tell each other that there are riders on the trails, whether the party is large or small, and whether they are strangers or natives, besides certain general information about their location and the direction in which they are moving. When a party of revenuers ride into the hills, the women in the roadside cabins notify their friends farther back, and soon "blowin'-horns" are heard faintly tooting all over the country, and the moonshiners know all about the situation long before they can be reached by the raiders.

When the officers really want to catch a moonshiner they usually arrest him on the road as he takes his liquor to market, or when he is delivering it to tourists at some summer resort or hotel. When a moonshiner is captured at his still it usually means that the officers have gone into the hills the evening before and "bushed up" all night, surprising their quarry as he comes to work in the morning. Not many of the mountain stills are operated at night, since it is impossible for the guards to watch the trails properly; another disadvantage is that most of the outfits are situated in the open, or under overhanging bluffs, and the fire under the boiler can be seen at a considerable distance.

A few large stills are set up in caves, or in rude still-houses hidden in the underbrush, and these can be operated at night, but the typical Ozark moonshiner uses a small outfit which is easily shifted from one place to another. He knows perfectly well that there are only a few suitable caves with running water in any given locality, and that the officers know where they are as well as he does. If he works very long in one place he is certain to leave a trail as he "totes" his raw materials in and his whiskey out, and it is truly astonishing how easily a hill-bred sheriff can track a man over rocks and through rough country where scarcely a mark is visible to the untrained eye.

In my innocence I once remarked to an officer that it should be easy to find these stills in the Winter, as soon as the foliage had disappeared. "Hit shore would be, now," he replied, "only they aint no stills workin' then. They allus buries 'em in th' ground come Fall." Upon my demanding to know why there was no distilling in the winter-time, he explained patiently that the moonshiner working out-of-doors has no way to keep the mash at the temperature required for proper fermentation. "Haint you ever noticed, Doc," he asked "that you allus git th' best whiskey 'long 'bout March? Well, that's cause it's ben aged ever sence hot weather. An' likewise you git th' worst liquor 'long in th' summer, 'cause last year's stuff is all drinked up, an' you're a-gittin' new whiskey." As a matter of fact, however, a certain amount of moonshine *is* made in the winter, but it is necessary to bury the mash barrels with manure packed around them, and to put an unusually large amount of lye into the mash. I know one man who was so anxious to run off a batch for Christmas that he literally sat up with his mash for four days and nights, boiling some of the stuff in a great kettle and pouring a little hot mash into the barrels at regular intervals.

My moonshiner friends tell me that the federal agents who come into the Ozark region are quite incorruptible, but that some of the local officers have been known to sell protection for cash, or to "lay off'n" certain influential distillers in return for political favors. However, I have never seen any evidence of such obvious and wholesale corruption as seems to exist in almost every large city, and my opinion is that many sheriffs do not attempt to enforce the prohibitory law simply because they are not personally in sympathy with it, and because they

A Moonshine Still in Operation

feel that the majority of their fellow-citizens are not in sympathy with it, either. I once heard an officer say of a man he had just locked up for moonshining, "Ed he don't think makin' whiskey is no more wrong than walkin' down a corn-row." And then he added, reflectively, "I reckon it *aint* whut you might call wrong, nuther—it's jest agin th' law!"

Another sheriff, asked if he ever felt himself in danger of being murdered by moonshiners, said scornfully, "Hell no! Them fellers aint got nothin' agin me. I give ever'body a fair chance to git away. I'm sheriff, an' they's a law agin moonshi-nin', an' it's my duty to make 'em quit it, an' bust up all the stills I can. But I don't aim to kill nobody, or put nobody in jail, neither. . . . They all got sense enough to run when they see me a-comin'. Yes, I shoot sometimes, but I don't never hit nobody, an' th' boys all know it."

I remember one case of an aged hillman who was acquitted of a moonshining charge. Two or three days later he rode into town, hunted up the sheriff and demanded his still. "Listen hyar now, Jim," he said, "I've knowed you ever sence you was knee-high to a toad-frog, an' you bein' sheriff don't cut no ice 'ith me. My gran'pap he fetched thet 'ar worm from Tennessee, an' hit's mine, an' I aim to hev it, too!" The officer humorously reminded the old man that he had denied all knowledge of distilling at his trial, and remarked that if the worm was really his, he must be guilty of perjury. "Dang it all, I aint guilty of nothin'!" the old man roared. "You heared th' jury turn me loose, didn't ye? You give me my worm, an' be dang quick about it, or I'll hev th' law on ye!" Just how it was managed I do not know, but the old gentleman got his still back somehow, and it is hanging in a tree in his dooryard today.

In recent years there have been several cases of moonshiners working "in cahoots" with the officers by betraying their competitors, but this usually occurs when the hillman has become entangled with some "furrin" bootlegger who retails the stuff to tourists at the summer resorts. A good many of these outsiders have entered the field of late—hotel clerks, barbers, waiters, filling-station attendants, dancehall managers, professional golfers and the like—all outsiders who spend their summers at the Ozark resorts. A few permanent residents pick up a bit of extra money by delivering liquor, also; I know one preacher, three country doctors, two school teachers and several rural mail-carriers who are said to eke out their scanty incomes in this manner.

The tourist accustomed to the bars and speakeasies of the city will be astonished at his inability to buy a drink of liquor in the hill-country; it is only in a few of the hotels and summer resorts that liquor is sold in this manner. The native moonshiner may "set 'em up" to a prospective customer, but he seldom sells less than a quart, and often flatly refuses to sell less than a gallon. Another strange thing is that the hillmen have very few bottles, and an ordinary pocket flask is something of a novelty. Most of the Ozark whiskey is sold in Mason fruit-jars, or in stone jugs, or in kegs. The hillmen who sell liquor about the tourist camps and resorts usually have no liquor on their persons. When a tourist wants to buy a quart or a gallon the bootlegger gets into the customer's car, and directs him to drive down the road a little way, where the required amount of whiskey is produced from behind a stone by the roadside, or lifted out from under a culvert. Many Ozark moonshiners drink their own liquor on occasion, and there are plenty of drunkards in every settlement, of course, but as a class the hill people do not habitually drink to excess. I am quite certain that they are more temperate than the tourists who visit the Ozarks in the Summer time, and I do not believe that they drink as much as most of the people I know in New York and Chicago.

So much for moonshining and bootlegging in the Ozarks. It is a subject that does not interest me particularly, since liquor seems to be made and sold everywhere nowadays, and the Ozark methods of production and distribution probably do not differ greatly from those practiced in other sparsely settled parts of the United States. I have observed, however, that almost every "furriner" who visits us of late displays an almost morbid curiosity about this matter, and it would never do to write a book about the Ozark country without some mention of moonshine and moonshiners.

CHAPTER IX.

Shooting for Beef

T HE OLD-TIME OZARKER WAS A rifleman first of all— his life very often depended upon his ability to shoot accurately—and even today the old muzzle-loader hangs over the "fire board" in many a mountain cabin. These "rifleguns" are all of the same general type; long heavy barrels, comparatively small caliber, double-set triggers, full length stocks. They are nearly all fitted with percussion locks now, but many of them were originally flintlocks. Students of such matters tell us that weapons of this type were the first accurate firearms ever made, and the real ancestors of all modern rifles. The rifle as an instrument of precision is purely an American product, developed by the forebears of the men who use them in the Ozark hills today.

Firearms with spirally grooved barrels were made in Central Europe as early as 1500, but they were short, big-bored flintlocks, not a whit more accurate than a first-class smoothbore. These guns were brought to America in considerable numbers, and even manufactured in Pennsylvania about 1700, but they were never satisfactory, and some of the pioneers discarded them in favor of bows and arrows taken from the Indians. Rifles of the

European type were notoriously inaccurate, they consumed vast quantities of powder and lead, they made too much noise, and were very slow in loading, since the unlubricated ball had to be driven into the barrel by blows of a hammer on an iron ramrod.

The American gunsmiths set about the manufacture of a better weapon, and by 1760, or thereabouts, they had evolved the first consistently accurate firearm ever built—the first rifle in the history of the world which could be trusted to repeat its initial performance. The barrel was made very long for the sake of accuracy, and very heavy because the bulk of metal reduces the report. The pioneer reasoned that the louder the report of his piece, the more likely it was to attract the attention of distant Indians, which was not at all what he desired. The caliber was reduced as far as possible, too, because powder and lead are expensive and heavy to carry. One of the greatest improvements, however, was the invention of patching—the practice of wrapping the bullet in a piece of greased cloth or leather. These patched bullets did not need to be driven into the barrel with a hammer, but were seated easily with a light wooden ramrod, and this new ease in loading permitted a rapidity of fire hitherto undreamed of. Not only this, but some of the pioneer gunsmiths experimented with different kinds of grooves or lands, and worked out some notion of the relation between twist and accuracy, until by the time of the Revolutionary War there were rifles in the American colonies which were almost as accurate, at short range, as any of our modern sporting rifles.

In 1775 a Virginia rifleman gave an exhibition shoot at Lancaster, Pennsylvania, where he put eight consecutive bullets into a two-inch bullseye at sixty yards, shooting without a rest. This is very good shooting even today, and it is easy to see how it must have impressed the British, who had never even seen a gun which could be depended upon to hit a barn-door at sixty paces. A Hessian officer recorded solemnly in his diary a note about the "American riflemen who can hit a man's head at 200 yards," while General Howe at Boston spoke feelingly of the "terrible guns of the rebels," and sent a captured rifle back to England to show his superiors what he had to contend with. General Ferguson once tried to disperse some mountaineers who had met peaceably for a shooting-match, with the result that some eight or nine hundred of them attacked him at Kings Mountain and defeated more than twenty-five hundred trained soldiers—and the battle lasted only an hour or so.

Nearly every Ozark family has one of these old rifles today, and it differs hardly at all from the weapons used against Ferguson at Kings Mountain, except that the flintlock mechanism has been replaced by a percussion lock. The one I have is nearly six feet long, and weighs fourteen pounds. It shoots a round ball of about 35 caliber, and it is said that a pound of lead will make between ninety and a hundred of these bullets. Nearly all of these old rifles are heavy and badly balanced, according to our modern way of thinking, but when it comes to accuracy they are equal or superior to any ordinary modern hunting weapon at ranges up to one hundred yards. Alvin York, who has used these same rifles in the Tennessee mountains, says that they are the most accurate guns in the world—and Sergeant York ought to know something about it. I have seen the Ozark mountain target-shooters beat men with Winchesters and modern military rifles at sixty and one hundred yards, although there is no doubt that the muzzle-loaders would be hopelessly outclassed at the longer ranges.

The Ozark gunsmith usually bought his lock ready made, but the rest of the rifle was a product of his own skillful craftsmanship. When one considers the complicated machinery used in the making of an ordinary modern rifle-barrel, it seems almost miraculous that these mountain gunsmiths, with a few crude homemade tools, were able to bore and rifle their barrels as well as they did. The first step was to drill a hole lengthwise through a bar of soft iron—a delicate job in itself—but the real work began with the cutting of the twists or grooves inside the barrel. I have never seen this done, but an old gunsmith showed me the tools used for the purpose, and explained the process to me as best he could.

The grooves or "rifles" in the barrel are cut one at a time with a little hand-made saw soldered to the end of a long rod, but the course of the saw is directed by a spiral cylinder of wood, as long as the barrel and about two inches in diameter—all cut out by hand. The furrows in the wooden guide correspond exactly with the grooves to be cut in the barrel. The actual cutting is done by working the wooden cylinder back and forth by hand, the barrel being clamped in a vise, and the movements of the cylinder are somehow regulated by the socalled head-block, a contrivance of wood and leather, the operation of which I have never been able completely to understand. The fact that these old fellows, with their crude homemade machinery, are able to do such delicate work as boring rifle-barrels is a never ending source of astonishment to me, and some reflections on the evolution of firearms in general increase the respect I have always had for the mountain craftsman's ability.

I know of one Missouri blacksmith who lacked the skill to groove a rifle-barrel, but who made light smoothbores of such superior quality that a whole neighborhood used them for many years. They could not compete with the best match rifles, of course, but they were accurate enough for ordinary hunting, and cheaper than the rifles made by the regular gunsmiths. Another Ozark craftsman made several freak weapons called "double groove" rifles, having only two very deep grooves on

opposite sides of the barrel. The bullet was not round, but cast
with a sort of butterfly-wing projection on each side, and in loading was inserted so that these projections fitted into the two
opposite grooves. I have seen one of these old barrels, but the
working parts of the gun were damaged beyond repair, and the
bullet-mold was missing. It is said that the "double groove" guns
were quite as accurate as the ordinary turkey rifle, and were
supposed to have a greater killing power because of the "wings"
on each side of the bullet.

The butt plate, trigger guard and other mountings of many
old rifles were made of wrought iron, but most of those now
in use have brass fittings; sometimes these were made at home
from the bar metal, but in later years many were purchased in
the rough, to be fitted to each particular arm by the gunsmith.
The front sight was usually made from a silver coin, but I have
seen a few old rifles with gold front sights, and there was usually
a silver or gold name-plate attached to the stock. The stock itself
was made of maple or black walnut, and a great deal of care was
devoted to shaping its slender, graceful lines. A receptacle with
a hinged metal cover was usually set into the right side of the
stock, and this is called the "taller box", but most of the Ozark
riflemen use it for percussion caps rather than tallow. Even the
ramrod was very carefully made, of selected and seasoned hickory, and fitted snugly into its place beneath the barrel.

The powder is carried in a cow's horn, polished and scraped
so thin that one can tell how much powder it contains simply by
holding it up to the light. The horn is usually worn under the left
arm, supported by a leather strap over the opposite shoulder,
and a leather bullet-pouch is often attached to the same strap,
dangling just below the powder horn. The bullet-pouch originally contained not only bullets but a mold to make them, also a
piece of cloth for patching, and a lump of tallow for lubricating

the patches. There is often a sharp wire set in a wooden handle, too—this is the picker used for cleaning out the touch-hole when necessary. Sometimes the pouch contains a screw arrangement to be fastened to the ramrod, used in drawing charges which have failed to explode. Most Ozark riflemen today, however, leave their bullet-molds at home on the mantel-piece, and many do not use the pouch at all, preferring to carry bullets and prepared patches loose in the pockets of their overalls.

The molding of bullets is a task for evenings and rainy days at home. The lead is melted in a ladle heated on the coals in the fireplace, and poured into the hand-made iron mold, which is then snapped open and the bullet dropped out into the ashes to cool. The bullet does not fall perfect from the mold, however; there is always a little neck to be cut off, and often a ridge entirely around the ball, where the edges of the mold do not fit together very tightly. Any irregularities are carefully trimmed up with a jack-knife, and great care is taken that the finished bullet is as nearly perfect as possible.

In testing a rifle, the hillman sometimes leaves a bullet untrimmed, just as it falls from the mold, and loads it so that the little neck or "tit" of the bullet will point straight to the rear. Then he fires into a block of green wood, and if the bullet turns so that the neck is inclined to one side, it means that the barrel is not properly rifled, and the gun will never be entirely satisfactory as a match weapon.

The best patches are simply round pieces of slightly worn linen cloth, lightly greased with tallow; some riflemen have metal dies to cut the patches with, and carry a bunch of ready-made patches in the bullet-pouch. Others prefer to carry their patching all in one piece, and lay this cloth over the muzzle before inserting the bullet. Then, when the bullet is pressed down just below the muzzle, they cut off the surplus patching with a hunting-knife. When the hunter is required to load in a great hurry he simply wets the bullet in his mouth and rams it home without any patching at all. The wet powder next the ball is sufficient to hold it in place until the piece is fired. Somewhere about his person, either in the bullet-pouch or tied to the powder horn, the rifleman carries a powder measure, usually made from the tip of a deer's antler. The old rule for determining the proper charge was to place a bullet in the palm of the hand and pour out just enough powder to cover it. The load so measured seemed a bit heavy for my rifle, so I cut my charger down a little. This measuring of the proper powder charge is a matter of individual taste among the Ozark experts; I remember one old hunter who poured out enormous charges, apparently without any attempt at uniformity. The strange thing about it was that he seemed to shoot as well as any of his more methodical competitors!

Even as recently as Civil War times some hillmen made their own powder by mixing saltpeter, which they obtained by boiling the bat-manure found in caves, with crude sulphur and home-made charcoal. They smelted their own lead sometimes, too, by breaking the ore up into small pieces and firing it with cedar sticks inside a hollow stump. When the fire burned down next day the hillman had only to rake the little drops of smelted lead out of the ashes.

The Ozark rifles were originally hunting arms, of course, but at present most of the younger generation hunt with cheap breech-loading shotguns, and use the old "rifle-guns" for target shooting only. In the old days the shooting-matches were taken very seriously, and when the news of one of these affairs was "norated round" people came over the hills for miles—not only the sharpshooters, but numbers of spectators who wanted to bet on the results of the contest. We still have shooting-matches occasionally, but most of the famous old marksmen are dead now, and shooting is not nearly so important in the social life of the settlements as it used to be.

Some of the matches nowadays are shot for cash prizes, but the ordinary shoots are usually for prizes of fresh meat. A live steer is led out and tied to a tree, and each contestant pays for his shot according to the value of the animal. The target is made by cutting a diamond-shaped hole in a piece of paper, which is then fastened to a charred board, so that the shooter fires at a black bullseye on a white background. The usual distance is somewhere between forty and sixty yards, and the shooting is always offhand. The two best shots get the hind-quarters, the two next best win the fore-quarters, while the fifth is given the hide and tallow. Sometimes it happens that a single family wins all five prizes, and drives the "critter" home on the hoof! Occasionally a notoriously good shot is barred from the match, so as to give the other boys a chance, and sometimes the use of a particular rifle is forbidden for the same reason. I remember one man who owned a very fine rifle which he called "Ol' Jake", a piece so incredibly accurate and lucky that nobody would pay good money to shoot against it. The result was that this rifle was barred at all the neighborhood shoots, although its owner was at liberty to enter, provided he used another weapon.

Besides the regular shooting-match, it often happens that a turkey-shoot is held at the same time, and here the target is the head of the turkey, the bird being tied in such a way that the body is protected by a log. These turkey-matches are usually shot at thirty yards, offhand, and the winner must put his bullet squarely through the bird's head—it is always understood beforehand that "bill shots" do not count. On other occasions the turkey or goose is staked out on a hillside about 150 yards away, and here the shooter fires at the whole body-the first man who draws blood above the knee-joint gets the fowl.

There are no womenfolk in attendance at the shooting-matches, but the promoters usually arrange a barbecue, or provide a lunch of some kind. There is not much drinking among the riflemen themselves, but the spectators usually come provided with jugs of corn whiskey, and the whole affair frequently ends in a drunken riot. One cause of trouble is the tendency of certain shooters to "rattle" their opponents by some more or less subtle method. No mountain man would think of tampering with an opponent's rifle or ammunition, and any obvious heckling at the firing-line would never be tolerated for a moment, but there are still many sly and underhanded means of shaking a shooter's nerve, particularly hillmen who are dyspeptic and high-strung. I remember one old man who threw down his rifle in a rage, shouting, "He threwed me off, Gawd damn it! Ol' Jeff Whatley threwed me off, a-clickin' of his Gawd damn' tongue agin!"

This tendency to drinking and fighting, together with the fact that they were frequently held on Sunday, caused the old shooting-matches to be frowned upon by the religious element. Some even went so far as to opine that shooting for beef was no better than gambling, and the fact that the boys did play cards sometimes after the match was over did not help matters any. The introduction of modern firearms, the rapidly diminishing supply of game, the growing popularity of other and less picturesque forms of social entertainment—all of these factors combined with the disapproval of the religious people to bring the old-time shooting-match into disrepute, and it is now practically a thing of the past, except in a few of the wildest and most isolated sections of the Ozarks.

CHAPTER X.

Jumpers, Giggers and Noodlers

F OR MANY YEARS IT WAS my unspoken conviction that Missouri grows the biggest liars in the world. It appears that something in the Missouri atmosphere renders people so notoriously untruthful that they cannot even believe one another; their incredulity has become proverbial, and the simple statement "I'm from Missouri" has come to be recognized everywhere as a refusal to credit one's veracity, and a demand for positive and objective proof.

Of late, however, I have discovered that some of the most improbable of the Missouri stories are absolutely true; I have seen things myself in the Missouri Ozarks which I should never have credited from any spoken or written testimony. Some of these tales cannot be printed in this book, nor in any other book at this time, but others may safely be told. One of these latter concerns the old story that black bass are so abundant and vigorous in the Ozarks that the fishermen don't use any tackle—just row along the shore and string the bass as fast as they jump into the boat!

My own acquaintance with this matter began a good many years ago, when Bill Haney and I were fishing in the James River, somewhere below Galena, Missouri. The river was muddy—altogether too muddy for any sort of bass fishing—and it looked to me as if we should have to live on bacon and beans until the water cleared up. "What! Not have no fish t' eat? Shucks!" said Bill, and with that he clambered into his boat and drifted off down toward the mouth of Flat Creek. An hour later he was back again with two nice big-mouth bass, which we cooked and ate in silence. Of course I was curious to know how he managed to catch those fish, and I thought about it at intervals all the next day, but he volunteered no explanation, and I wouldn't have asked him for the best launch on Lake Taneycomo. That's the kind of a fellow Bill Haney was.

Later on, I did mention the incident to a native Ozarker named Fitzhugh, and he laughed uproariously at my ignorance. "W'y, he goosed them fish, o' course—jumpin' 'em, some calls it. Whenever'n th' river gits good an' muddy like, them 'ar line-sides lays in th' weeds, an' if you-all runs in 'twixt them an' deep water hit skeers hell out'n 'em, an' they most ginerly allus jumps right spang in th' boat, an' caint git out noways! Bill he goosed them 'ar fish, 'cause bass caint be ketched no other way when th' river's muddy. Hit's agin th' law nowadays, an' thet's why he snuck off thataway, an' never let on how he ketched 'em."

I thanked Fitzhugh and went grinning on my way, marvelling at the imaginative powers of the hill people. The idea that there could possibly be any truth in his ridiculous explanation never once entered my mind, and I was perhaps just a little offended that this poor unlettered hill-billy should have so underestimated my intelligence. I do not claim any particular authority in these matters, but I have fished a little in my day, and besides . . . Why, any fool knows that bass don't jump into one's boat!

Later on I told the story to my old friend Clarence Sharp,

who knows more about the habits of bass than anyone else in this section, and I was utterly flabbergasted when he confirmed Fitzhugh's yarn. "Sure you can jump bass, if the water's murky enough; I've often seen it done on the White River in Arkansas. The rivermen in that country go out at night with a lantern in the boat, set just high enough to throw a shadow about four feet from the gunwale. Then they move slowly along a weedy shore, with the stern of the boat hugging the bank, and the bow swung out at a forty-five degree angle. In trying to escape, the bass usually break water just at the edge of the shadow; many of them clear the boat by seven or eight feet, but others fall into it, and mighty few of them are able to flop out again. They catch a lot of fish that way in the Ozarks, but it's against the law, and there's no sport in that kind of fishing, anyway."

"Do you mean to tell me," I asked him, "that you have actually seen all this—bass jumping into people's boats?" Sharp raised a belligerent eyebrow. "Didn't I just tell you?" he said. "Why, I've seen fifty fish jumped in a single evening, and God only knows how many missed the boat. What's so unreasonable about it? You've seen bass leap over the top of a seine, haven't you? Well, they jump over a boat the same way." He changed the subject. But I changed it right back again. "Can you tell me why," I asked, "these bass don't swim under the boat instead of jumping over it?" "How should I know why fish do this or that? Probably a good many do go under the boat, but a lot of them jump over, and quite a number fall in, too. I've seen it, I tell you, with my own eyes." And he refused to discuss the matter any further.

From this time forward I was really convinced, because I know that Sharp never jokes about serious matters such as bass fishing. Nevertheless, the thing kept coming to my mind at intervals, and finally I wrote to Keith McCanse, Missouri State Fish

Commissioner, and asked him about the bass-jumping story. And this is what he wrote: "In reply to your letter . . . will say that the story of bass jumping into boats in the Ozark region is absolutely true. I have had this happen on a great many occasions, and there is no doubt but what bass actually do jump into the boat in Lake Taneycomo and the Ozark streams under certain conditions. This will happen when the waters are muddy and murky, and the bass thinks he is cornered. In order to get away from being caught between the boat and the bank he will begin to jump, often landing in the boat. . . . The practice of catching fish in this manner is illegal. . . . Drop into the hardware store at Pittsburg, Kansas, sometime, and see Jack Lindburg; he will verify the fish jumping story."

A few days later I did see Lindburg, who told me at once that the practice of jumping bass is well known to everybody who has fished much in the Ozark waters. "I have never," said he, "intentionally jumped a fish in my life, but I have often seen bass jump into and over boats, particularly at night, when a lantern is carried by trot-line and bank-line fishermen. The so-called hickory shad often jump at lights, too, and I suppose one could fill a boat with them if he wanted to. But," he added, "the practice of jumping fish is unsportsmanlike and illegal, it spoils a lot of good fishing water, and no decent fisherman will have anything to do with it."

Very recently, at one of the Ozark resorts which shall be nameless here, I heard that certain local young men were addicted to this sort of fishing, and I deliberately cultivated them in order to learn more about this business. Finally one of these worthies tipped me off that the water was just right for jumping, and shortly before dusk I sat down near their secluded boat landing, where I could see exactly what happened. And this is what I saw: First, the boys nailed four sticks upright on one side of the boat, and stretched a minnow-seine across them. To each upright they fastened apiece of trace-chain about five feet long, which hung down into the water—supposedly to prevent the bass from swimming under the boat. A lantern was set on a box in the middle of the boat, just 'high enough so that the shadow of the gunwale fell on the water about four feet distant. Shortly after nightfall they started out, and I followed in another boat, unwilling to be too intimately associated with lawbreakers, but very anxious to see what was going on. They pushed the boat along close to the weedy shore, with the side of the boat to which the net was fastened toward the river, and the bow pointed out at an angle of about forty-five degrees. As the boat moved slowly along, the boy in the stern slapped the weed patches with a long cane fishpole.

And by all the gods, believe it or not, the bass actually did begin to jump! Some of them appeared to jump at least six feet high! They didn't all leave the water just at the edge of the shadow, as I had been told they would; they didn't all jump into the boat, or even in that direction, but they certainly did jump—plenty of them. Some leaped clear over the boat, minnow-seine and all, but quite a number struck the seine and fell back into the boat and once in they seemed quite unable to jump out again. I do not know how many fish those young rascals caught that night, but they must have strung at least a dozen fine bass while I looked on. And I didn't stay long, either, but went thoughtfully and sadly back to the hotel alone.

Well, I saw what I came to see, but one evening's observation was quite enough. Had I not seen the thing for myself I should never have realized the deadly effectiveness of jumping as a method of killing game fish. I have reason to believe that it is still practiced extensively by the natives in certain parts of the Ozark country, and occasionally resorted to by outsiders who

should know better. The old-time rivermen are all agreed however that the practice is less common than it was ten years ago,
and are confident that a growing appreciation of the ethics of
sportsmanship will soon eliminate jumping altogether. Let us
hope that this optimism is justified, for the wonderful fishing
waters of the Ozarks will certainly be seriously depleted unless
this unsportsmanlike method of killing bass goes out of fashion.

The practice of gigging, also popular among the Ozark fishermen, is another matter altogether. For many years, long before
I took up my permanent residence in the Ozark country, I used
to come every year to fish in the mountain streams, which still
afford some of the best bass fishing in the United States. But on
every trip, no matter how many fish we caught, some member of
the party always complained that the fishing was getting worse
every year, usually adding that this lamentable condition was
due to the thrice-damned giggers. A gigger is a native Ozarker
who kills fish with a spear known as a gig. And I, in my ignorance, used to denounce the gigger as loudly as anybody, and
I cursed also the legislators of Missouri and Arkansas because
they refused to pass laws to prohibit the nefarious practice. For
several years past, however, I have spent most of my time in the
Ozark foothills, and have become acquainted with the natives,
and learned more about this gigging business. Not that I have
turned gigger myself—God forbid!—but I have satisfied myself
that the practice is not a serious menace to the game fish in my
section of the Ozarks, and am further prepared to concede that
gigging, as practiced here, has even some claim to be regarded
as a sportsmanlike method of taking fish.

A few giggers creep along the borders of deep pools, and
strike their fish from the bank, but the vast majority prefer to
use boats. The Ozark "skifts" are all homemade, of rough native
lumber from the sawmills. They are long and narrow, often with

both ends alike. They can be used in very shallow water, usually drawing only about four inches, and have no rowlocks, being propelled by poles or paddles. The choice of a gig is a very important matter, because they are all handmade by the local blacksmith—the "store-boughten" fish spears are quite worthless, and would not survive a single "lick" on our hard limestone river beds. The best gig I ever saw was made of a discarded plowshare; the blacksmith worked at the thing nearly all day, and then sold it for two dollars. Two dollars is a lot of money in our poverty-ridden hill country, however—perhaps equivalent to about fifteen dollars in New York. That is one of the reasons why I prefer to live in the Ozarks.

Most of the better gigs have three barbed tines, about five inches long, but I have seen crude home-made affairs with five and even six prongs. The quality and temper of the metal is of great importance, as the gig strikes the hard rocks with terrific force; if the steel is too soft it bends, and if too hard it breaks. It is essential that the tines be straight and the proper distance apart—so essential that when one of them is bent the gigger must land and build a fire to heat the thing, and will not proceed until his gig is properly straightened and tempered. The points must be filed at frequent intervals, too; a gig which is almost needle-sharp at the beginning of a day's fishing will be hopelessly dulled and blunted by dinnertime. It is necessary also to "set th' beards" with a hammer and cold-chisel occasionally.

The shank of the gig proper is hammered into a sort of tube or socket which fits over the end of the pole; the best gigpoles are of pine, about fourteen feet long, and an inch and three-quarters in diameter. Most poles are made by ripping a straight two-by-four and dressing it down with a plane, but one gigger of my acquaintance drives fifty miles to the lead-mines near Joplin, where he buys the machine-made powder-sticks

used in tamping shots. These make beautiful gig-poles. Fasten
the gig firmly on one end, fit a stout iron ferrule on the other,
and the thing is ready for use. The pole is usually oiled to keep
it from warping, and the gig must be always kept in a dry place
when not in use, out of the direct sunlight. In actual fishing, the
first thing the gigger does is to wet his gig-pole, so that it will
slide easily through his fingers, but it must not be allowed to lie
in the water for any great length of time. It is essential that the
pole does not warp—no man can kill fish with a crooked gig.

Gigging cannot be done at all unless the water is perfectly
clear, and even our crystal Ozark streams are a bit dingy for several days following a big rain. If the water is too deep one can't
see the fish, and if it is too shallow the fish become so "skeery"
that the gigger can't get near enough to strike them. It is no use
to fish in the rapids or "riffles", because the visibility is always
poor; the best places for gigging are quiet pools from four to
six feet deep. The good gigger always likes a pool containing
gravel, too, because it does not damage his gig; a single blow on
a hard rock bottom often bends a gig so badly that it is useless
until heated and hammered into shape again.

A windy day is unsatisfactory because the wind ruffles up
the surface so that the gigger cannot see into the water very
well, and a dark day is bad because the general illumination is
reduced, but a sky full of fleecy white clouds is worst of all. "Hit's
them dang clouds fools a feller—they shore do make shadders
look like suckers!" In general, the best gigging is done between
ten o'clock in the morning and three in the afternoon, before
the river is darkened by the shadows of the wooded hills.

Before I actually saw the thing for myself, I did not regard
gigging as a sport at all, but simply as a means of catching fish,
comparable perhaps to seining or fishing with trotlines. I pic-
tured the gigger as drifting idly along in his boat, looking into

the water ahead of him, and I supposed that when he saw a fish resting on the bottom he just stuck his spear into it and pulled it into the boat—about as exciting as picking up cigarette butts in Central Park.

Actual gigging, however, is not at all like picking up cigarette butts—it is more like shooting quail on the wing with a small-bore shotgun, or catching hummingbirds in a butterfly net. The fisherman stands up in the front end of the boat, which he propels by pushing against the bottom of the stream with his gig-pole. Fish flash by on either side, and the gigger strikes out at them as best he can. Usually he misses, of course—the best gigger I have ever seen scores ten or twelve misses for every fish he kills. The gigger must not only make allowance for the refraction of the water, but he must "lead" the fish according to the speed and direction of its flight. He must be able to estimate distance, too, since many of the fish struck at by amateur giggers are clearly out of reach. The average gig-pole is about fourteen feet long, and very few fish are taken less than ten or twelve feet from the boat.

Even after a fish is struck, the matter of landing it is not nearly so simple as one might suppose; an expert gigger always hoists the fish carefully and steadily until it is clear of the water before swinging it toward the boat. An experienced man will land large fish even if they are very insecurely hooked, while a tyro will almost invariably lose them in such cases. When a fish is once in the boat, the gigger thrusts his gig backward over the middle seat and pulls the barbs free with a sudden jerk, while the fish falls into the bottom of the boat. Most fish are instantly killed or so badly injured that there is no danger of their escaping, but when an eel is taken the gigger holds it fast against the bottom of the boat, and does not remove it from the gig until he has killed or disabled it with a blow from a short club which he carries for the purpose.

A few of the hill people to the southwest of us use a much shorter and lighter spear with a single slender prong, the handle being fastened to the wrist with a long cord. These spears are seldom more than five or six feet long, and are called "pitchin'-gigs". It is said that they are modelled after the fishspears used by the Osage Indians. The short gigs are thrown or pitched, and are even more difficult to handle than those of the ordinary type, which are contemptuously called "churn-gigs" by the devotees of the shorter weapon. The pitchin'-gig with its light, slender handle enters the water almost without a sound or a splash, and it is really a pleasure to watch an expert pitch-gigger kill fish with it. Men of this type are few and far between, however, and ninety-nine Ozarkers out of a hundred are content to use the long-handled, three-tined gig that I have described above.

In order to gig successfully at night, a powerful light is necessary. Every old-time gigger has a fire-jack—a sort of iron basket made by the local blacksmith—fastened in the center of his boat. In this he builds a fire of pine knots, which burn for a long time with a clear, steady light—the best gigging light known. The pine-knot fire is too hot for comfort in the summer time, however, and pine knots are hard to find near the streams at present, so that many of the village boys are now using discarded auto casings instead. These make a brilliant light, but burn so rapidly that the fire must be constantly replenished, besides filling the fire-jack with a thick, evil-smelling, tarry mess which is difficult to get rid of. More modern giggers use gasoline lamps and torches of various kinds, with a piece of tin fastened over the top to shield the gigger's eyes.

Suckers, bass and trout are the only fish encountered by the daylight gigger, but the man who fares forth at night sees other species also: catfish, eels, perch and goggle-eyes. It appears that many fish are somewhat less active at night, and therefore easier to kill, but this applies only to those which have been approached quietly and have not yet taken alarm. Once disturbed, they seem to be even wilder than they are in the daytime, and make for the shadows with astounding celerity. A pitch-dark night is necessary for successful gigging—it is quite impossible to see the fish clearly on moonlight nights. A little breeze which ruffles the surface is disturbing at night, too, and worst of all, in the summer time, are the myriads of insects which are attracted to the light. Most men, barring those who have a weakness for eels and catfish, prefer to do their gigging in broad daylight.

Every gigger sees plenty of bass and a few rainbow trout, but it is my opinion that very few of these fish are gigged, at least in the section of the Ozarks with which I am most familiar. The truth is that game fish are too fast for any but the most expert giggers. I have seen a few bass killed, and the boys who do their gigging at night sometimes get a goggle-eye or two, but at least ninety-five per cent of the fish gigged in the Ozark streams are suckers—fish that are of no use to the angler. Another thing: most native Ozarkers actually prefer suckers to either bass or trout, and will regularly pass up game fish in order to strike at a big redhorse or hogmolly! This is not because of the fish laws, for it is not illegal to gig game fish in either Missouri or Arkansas; it is not from any idea of sportsmanship, either, for the hillfolk make no distinction between game fish and any other sort. It is simply that the Ozarker kills his fish primarily for the table, and he honestly believes that a sucker in good condition is the finest pan-fish that swims.

There are several different varieties of suckers in the Ozark streams—redhorse, white sucker, hogmolly, oil sucker, buffalo, carp—and all of them are taken and eaten on occasion, but the redhorse and the white sucker are the commonest and the best. Both of these fish are slender, graceful, golden-colored creatures, with large pinkish fins; they look very much alike to me, but a native fisherman can distinguish them at a glance, even in several feet of water. The redhorse has a slightly thicker body, a bigger mouth and a blunter nose than the white sucker, and is said to be somewhat less bony, but I have my doubts about this latter point. The hogmolly or hog sucker is a peculiarly mottled fish, with a very large head and a round, tapering body; it is somewhat more sluggish than the redhorse and the white sucker, and the natives regard it as rather less palatable, but I have never been able to detect any great difference in this regard.

Fish of the sucker type, even when caught in nets, do not live very long, and they cannot be kept very well on strings or in live-boxes. Once dead, such fish deteriorate very rapidly, so that they must be cleaned at once, and either cooked immediately or frozen. Some summer giggers carry a tub of ice right in the boat, so that they can dress and ice their catch as they go along. In the winter time, of course, this is not necessary, and the fish are simply strung on a stick and trailed in the icy water. Once frozen a sucker keeps indefinitely, but it must be cooked immediately when it thaws out. Some hillmen contend that one can keep suckers fresh for several days simply by wrapping them up in walnut leaves, but I suspect that this is only another superstition.

The sucker's scales are large and very loosely attached, so that one can almost scale a fish of this type with one's finger-nails. The Ozark fisherman makes short work of this; he scales and guts a sucker in the twinkling of an eye, and it requires only a few more strokes to lop off the head, tail and fins. Very large redhorse are usually skinned like eels or catfish, but it is thought best to scale the smaller fish. There is no denying that all suckers, particularly in the smaller sizes common in the Ozark streams, are literally full of tiny bones, and some of the "furriners" prefer to eliminate these by putting the whole fish through a food-chopper; the resulting mess is seasoned, made into patties and fried like sausage. This method disposes of the bones well enough, and is very satisfactory for those who are content to eat fish-cakes, but the really fine flavor of the sucker is completely lost; the man who is satisfied with fish-balls might as well make them out of catfish or canned mackerel.

The real Ozarker scorns all such "fotch-on" contrivances as food-choppers, and he would not eat a fish-ball on a bet. His "woman" splits the fish lengthwise, and then "rings" it; that is, she takes a very sharp knife and makes a series of lateral cuts nearly through each piece, just as close together as possible, never more than a quarter of an inch apart. Then she rolls the fish in cornmeal, working the meal well into the cuts, and fries it as one would a doughnut, by dropping into a deep kettle of boiling lard. A sucker's bones are very fine and cartilaginous; the "ringing" cuts them up into short sections, and the boiling grease either softens them or dissolves them altogether. At any rate, the fish is not noticeably bony after it is cooked, and when one finishes with a properly cooked sucker there is little left but the spinal column and the long white ribs. But enough of this dissertation on cookery.

The Missouri law now permits gigging between July first and January thirty-first, with a creel limit of fifty pounds of fish per day, but prohibits the sale or shipment of gigged fish. The Arkansas statutes prohibit the gigging of game fish from March first to June thirtieth, and the creel limits for game fish apply the same as to hook-and-line fishing, but suckers may be gigged the year round. In recent years an increasingly powerful group of sportsmen has advocated the passage of laws which would prohibit gigging altogether, in both Missouri and Arkansas. It seems to me that such legislation is quite unnecessary. As I have said, there are not very many streams in which fish can be gigged, and not very many days in the year when weather conditions permit gigging. There are only a few men in any given locality who are skillful enough to gig many fish, and ninety-five per cent of those which they do kill are suckers, of no value to the sportsman anyway.

Infinitely more dangerous to the game fish in the Ozark streams is the practice known as "grabbing" or "snagging". The grabber equips himself with a long cane pole, with half-a-dozen big treble hooks fastened a foot or so apart on his line, and a heavy sinker at either end of the row of grabhooks. Perched on an overhanging rock, or a leaning tree trunk above a shallow pool, he allows this outfit to lie extended on the bottom, and as a fish moves leisurely across the line, a sudden jerk nearly always fastens one of the big hooks in its body. In the Spring the suckers spawn or "shoal", assembling in vast numbers to deposit their eggs in the shallow water. At this time the hillmen do a great deal of grabbing, and I have known three men to catch more than a hundred suckers in an hour's time. One has only to drag his tackle through the swarms of spawning fish—sometimes two or three are taken at one haul. If the water is a little dingy the grabber's chances are even better than when it is clear, since he does not need to see the fish, once the school is located. Shoaling lasts only a few days, fortunately, else the suckers would be seriously decimated.

Unlike the gigger, the devotee of the grabhooks is not content with suckers, but kills a great many bass also, particularly during the spawning season. Bass deposit their eggs in shallow eddies, and both sexes remain at the nest until the eggs hatch, driving off crawfish and other marauders which would despoil the nest if it were left unguarded. Once a nest is located, these parent bass are easy prey for the grabber, and very few of them escape the big hooks. Grabbing is illegal in both Missouri and

A Gigger Turns His Back

Arkansas, and the fishwardens and sportsmen do what they can
to prevent it, at least during the time when bass are spawning, but
it seems to me that their labors have met with but small success.

In the summer time many an Ozark boy does not bother
with boats or gigs or grabhooks, but gets right down into the
water and "noodles" his fish-pulls them out from under the
rocks with his bare hands, or with a short gaff known as a "noodlin' hook". Some of these hooks are made of steel by the local
blacksmiths, but the average noodler prefers to make his own

by lashing a bigfishhook to a wooden handle. One cuts a green
stick about three feet long and three-fourths of an inch thick;
ironwood is best because it sinks readily, but sycamore will do in
a pinch. The larger end of the stick is flattened on one side and
a groove cut for the shank of the hook, also a notch to hold the
heavy cord with which it is lashed on. It is also best to mark the
handle on one side, so that the operator can tell which way the
hook is pointed, merely by feeling the grip.

Thus equipped, the noodler finds a good place, preferably
one where there is a ledge of rock or a lot of large loose stones, in
shallow water near a deep hole. He then strips and gets into the
water, feeling about under the rocks with his hook. He very often
dives to reach a submerged cavern, but the best noodling is done
in water where one can work with one's head above the surface.
An experienced noodler can tell by the "feel" or the "lay o' th'
gravels" whether or not large fish are using a particular hole.

The fish under these rocks are mostly catfish: flatheads, rock
cats, channel cats or blue cats. Big catfish seem to spend much
of their time in these holes, particularly in the summer months.
It is said that they spawn in such places—whether or not this is
true I do not know. They are sometimes found in cavities from
which they could not possibly escape—the entrance has to be
enlarged before the noodler can get them out. I have seen a
seven-pound flathead dug out of a rock cavern with an entrance
less than three inches in diameter; it must have moved into the
hole when quite small and grown up in confinement, living on
crawfish and minnows which ventured in at the entrance. Bass
are found under rocks sometimes, but they do not go into these
small cavities, and usually rush out the moment they are disturbed. Noodlers do not take many bass. They get a few perch
and goggleeyes, usually in sloughs and bayous, under brush and
in hollow logs. Eels are noodled occasionally, but fish of the

sucker family not at all—suckers do not seem to enter these cavities among the rocks.

The noodler works very slowly and carefully, and his brown body seems strangely distorted as he walks along the ledges in the clear water—looks as if he were doubled up like a jack-knife. When he feels a fish against his stick he can tell what kind of a fish it is by the "feel," and by the way the creature behaves. If a bass, it rushes out immediately past any and all obstacles, sometimes upsetting the noodler crouched before its lair. A cat-fish seems reluctant to leave the place at first, and does a lot of "chugging" or flapping up and down against the rock, which makes an astonishingly loud noise.

When a big fish is located, the noodler tries to plug all exits to the place except one, by placing rocks in front of the openings. If two men are working together, one often stops holes with his hands or feet, while the other thrusts his hand or noodlin'-hook into the main entrance. I know of one such case, where the noodler thrust his hook clear across the cavity and sank it in his partner's foot with a tremendous jerk, thinking he had hooked a large fish. A terrible wound it made, too, necessitating a twenty-mile ride to a country doctor, and much cursing and recrimination. I recall another scarcely less exciting occasion when a noodler thrust his hook under a slanting rock in such a manner that it appeared above the surface, behind the rock. A practical joker slipped down behind the ledge, out of the noodler's sight, and pulled at the gaff with all his strength. Thinking his hook still in the water, the noodler yelled to his comrades, "Gawd-a-mighty, fellers, run hyar! They's a cat en-under this hyar rock'll weigh a hunderd pound! He like t' pulled th' hook out o' my hand!" Nor would he believe otherwise until he climbed out on the bank and saw for himself that the apparently promising cavity was really shallow and open at the rear.

Very frequently fish are lost in the landing. Very often, too, a catfish escapes through some opening which has been overlooked, or even bursts out at the main entrance, rushes past the noodler and escapes. The noodlers themselves cannot see where an escaped fish goes, partly because their activities have "riled up" the water nearby, but a watcher on the bank above can often follow it with his eyes, and direct the noodlers to its new refuge. It is odd that each fish seems to be somehow attracted to one particular hole, and will almost invariably return to it, even if severely wounded. This condition seems to hold true the year round, and is evidently not dependent upon the spawning or breeding season. Once the noodlers have spotted the lair of a big catfish its doom is usually sealed; if they do not get the fish at the first attempt they return for it later. There are only a few places in any given neighborhood where noodlers can work to advantage, and they take fish year after year from a few well known holes. Noodling is illegal and unsportsmanlike, of course, but since the noodler seldom takes game fish the "furrin" anglers have made no great outcry against him, and there seems to have been very little effort to prevent the practice in the Ozark streams.

Some hillmen catch fish in traps, designed exactly like the little glass minnow traps used by anglers everywhere, but much larger, and made usually of hickory withes or coarse wire netting. Most of these traps must be hidden beneath overhanging willows or under brush to escape the prying eye of the fishwarden, but I have seen traps made of hollow logs lying on the bottom in plain sight, which could not be recognized as traps at all, save by a very close scrutiny. The traps are baited with corn for perch and goggle-eye, while the man who wants eels or catfish generally puts a skinned rabbit or some sort of decaying animal matter into the trap. I have found several of these traps in the

Ozark streams, and some of them were literally crammed with perch, goggle-eye, crawfish and drowned water-snakes, but I do not believe that many bass or trout are taken in this manner. The Ozarker sometimes shoots large fish with a high-powered rifle, if he can get such a weapon, but this method is never very popular because the ammunition is too expensive. I have a nine millimeter Luger-pistol, with a long barrel and a detachable stock, which several of my neighbors have been very anxious to "swap me out'n", but I have refused to part with it because of my fear that it might be used in killing big bass and rainbows.

A few farmers who live near the Oklahoma border are said to make an occasional use of the old Indian method of poisoning fish. Many years ago the Cherokees used to come down every Autumn to the Illinois River below Siloam Springs, Arkansas, and dig great quantities of buckeye roots. Then a group of squaws sat down in a shallow riffle and pounded these roots in rude stone mortars, so that the active principle was released into the water. It is said that all of the fish in the river, for several miles below the camp, were so crazed by the poison that they fell easy prey to the men who waited with nets and spears to take them. Old-timers who witnessed these forays tell me that the Indians caught literally tons of fish, which were smoked over great furnaces like barbecue pits, and packed away for winter use. Today, however, the poisoning of fish is done on a very small scale, and is not sufficiently popular to be a serious menace to the game fish.

The mountain fishermen do not use seines or trammel-nets to any great extent, and they are violently opposed to killing fish with dynamite; several giggers and grabbers of my acquaintance claim that dynamiting ruins the fishing for everybody, and that a pool which has been dynamited remains empty of fish for five or six months. Most of the dynamiting, at least in the streams with which I am most familiar, is done by newcomers or outsiders, and several of these gentry have been "turned in" by natives and heavily fined.

The truth is that most of the sportsmen who come into the Ozarks from other parts of the United States, and most of the legislators from the non-mountainous parts of Missouri and Arkansas, understand neither the fishing conditions in the Ozark country nor the peculiar characteristics of the hillman. The conservation measures which they advocate and the laws which they enact do not fit the local situation; they excite only derision in the mountain people and they are almost impossible of enforcement. The zealous and well-meaning gentlemen who are trying to conserve the fishing in the Ozarks had best devote their attention to the dynamiters, jumpers and grabbers, for these are the fellows who are really killing the game fish. And as long as the native gigger is content to eat suckers, and the native noodler is satisfied with eels and catfish, leaving the bass and trout for the anglers from the city, the "furrin" sportsmen will do well to let the giggers and noodlers alone.

CHAPTER XI.

Fools' Gold

T HE OZARK MOUNTAIN COUNTRY HAS always had a curious fascination for treasure-seekers. In fact, it was the search for gold which first brought the white race into the region. De Soto and his band of adventurers came up the Mississippi in 1540, searching for Indian villages said to be paved with precious metals. At about the same time Coronado, lured on by tales of the mythical "golden cities of Cibola" to be looted, marched overland from the Southwest. Early in the eighteenth century came intrepid French explorers such as M. de la Motte Cadillac, who visited the Ozarks about 1715, looking for the fabled mountains of pure gold, and "rivers with diamonds coming down their flow." And there were many others later on, but they all failed to find anything worth carrying off.

The fact is that gold has never been found in the Ozarks, and that silver occurs only in small quantities, as a by-product of the lead mines in southern Missouri. The reputable geologists of the present day are agreed that it is most unlikely that either gold or silver, in commercially important quantities, will ever be found m this region. The scientists who have studied the remains of Indians and prehistoric cavemen have found no indications of treasure, and there is no historical evidence that the French and Spanish explorers ever buried anything here save their dead comrades and their hopes of conquest. The native Ozarker, however, knows little and cares less what the scientists and historians may think about the matter, and some of the most persistent of all the hill-country legends are concerned with lost gold-mines, fabulously rich deposits of silver, and buried treasure generally. These old tales are still told and still believed, and wild-eyed treasure-seekers in ragged overalls and hickory shirts still wield their picks and shovels in the Ozarks.

Only a few weeks ago I visited what is known as the Bear Holler mine, in McDonald County, Missouri, near the Arkansas line. A great amount of dirt and stone has been moved at this place, a cave opened and a shaft sunk, and a primitive pump set up to remove water from the workings. Nine men are employed at the excavation, living in a small brush shelter and a dilapidated tent. They get no wages for their labor, and must provide their own food; several have mortgaged their little farms in order to carry on the work, and they can expect no money at all until they find the treasure, which is to be shared among the whole company. Charley Nidiffer, a veteran treasure-hunter who seemed to be in charge, told me the story of the enterprise.

In 1837 a company of thirty Spaniards had been mining and smelting silver and gold in the vicinity. Loading twenty-five burros with precious metal, they started on a trip to Mexico, but were attacked by hostile Indians and three of their number slain. They buried their dead and concealed the treasure in the mine, which they sealed up and flooded before making a final desperate effort to escape from the Indians. Most of them were killed in the running fight which followed, and only one of the entire company ever found his way back to his friends in Mexico. In 1879 an old Mexican woman, dying in Pierce City,

Missouri, told the story of the hidden mine to a man named Van
Wormer, and gave him a faded buckskin map and some written
directions about the location of the cache. Van Wormer came
to Bear Holler in 1882, and found the place easily enough.
He saw the "seven mule-shoe marks and a 68" cut into a tree;
there was "LE 67" carved on another, and a great "44" on an old
elm just in front of the walled-up entrance—all just as the old
Mexican woman had said. There were the three graves, too, and
when one of these was opened it contained buckles and other
metal equipment said to be of Spanish or Mexican design. Van
Wormer opened up the mine without difficulty, but it was full
of water, and no good pumps were available in those days. He
sunk a shaft in an effort to find the hidden vault "eighteen feet
long and six feet wide, full of silver, with one bushel of gold", but
finally wearied of the whole thing and returned to Pierce City.

After the death of the elder Van Wormer, his son came into
possession of the old map, and formed a company to dig out
the mine. He came to Bear Holler in 1927 and set up a pump
and a steam engine, but after a few months of fruitless toil his
men deserted him, and he abandoned the whole enterprise in
disgust. In the Autumn of 1929 he turned the whole thing over
to Nidiffer, who is now managing the excavation. Nidiffer would
not permit me to enter the mine, but said that he had penetrated to a depth of two hundred and eighty feet, and found an
artificial lake dammed up with rocks and filled with cedar logs.
To the right of this lake, he opines, is the concealed entrance to
the famous treasure vault, but it is still covered with water and
has not yet been precisely located.

In evaluating all this it is well to remember that neither
Charley Nidiffer nor any of his men have actually *seen* Van
Wormer's old chart, nor the hieroglyphics on the trees, nor
even the Spanish buckles from the grave which Van Wormer,

Senior, discovered in 1882. They have faith, however, which passeth all understanding and is said to move mountains; they have dreams and visions, too, and have consulted various seers and fortune-tellers, and all feel that the actual recovery of the treasure is merely a matter of a few months. When and if the Bear Holler treasure is finally recovered, I shall certainly make Nidiffer a public apology for the title of this chapter. I shall, as Charley himself might express it, "acknowledge th' corn", and those who know the Ozarks will agree with me that Bear Holler is a singularly appropriate spot for such acknowledgments.

My old friend Pete Woolsey, now the proprietor of a restaurant in Bentonville, Arkansas, was also a gold-seeker in his youth, but he was infinitely less credulous than the Bear Holler treasure-hunters. In 1902 Pete was a youngster near what is now Monte Ne, Arkansas, when a dark-skinned gentleman known as "Mexican Charlie" appeared, seeking a cave with a semi-circular cistern at the entrance, which was sealed up with stone and mortar. Charlie's story was that a long time ago, as a group of Spanish miners were taking a great treasure South on burros, an Indian attack forced them to conceal the treasure in a cave. Charlie's great-grandfather was one of the survivors of this expedition, and the story, together with the usual buckskin map, had been handed down to Charlie. Some of the local squirrel-hunters soon located "Half Cistern Cave" near Eden Bluff, and Woolsey and several other local men agreed to dig for a share in Mexican Charlie's gold.

Charlie would not allow any of them to examine his map, but he copied portions of it on paper, and described in advance just what would be found inside the cave: several human skeletons, primitive straw hats, hair ropes, coarse matting, bushels of arrowheads and many bear skulls. In one place, said he, there were two rows of animal bones, and two human thigh-bones set up on end, also a "petrified eagle" stalagmite, and a large rock cut into the shape of a half-moon. The boys had to use a twenty-foot ladder to reach the walled-up entrance to the cave, and had considerable difficulty in breaking into it. Once inside, they began digging under Mexican Charlie's direction, and found almost every one of the landmarks he had described. Woolsey says that there is no doubt that some kind of primitive people—not modern Indians—had lived and worked in the cave, and that Mexican Charlie knew a great deal about it.

No treasure was found, however, and as the boys had very little money for food and clothing they grumbled a good deal, and took to quarreling among themselves. One of them—he is still living in Arkansas, and I suppress his name—suggested that they kill Charlie and take his map for their own purposes, but Woolsey and the others would not agree to this. After about six weeks they all quit work in disgust, and Mexican Charlie disappeared a few days later. Some people in the vicinity still believe that Charlie found the treasure and carried it away with him, but Woolsey is inclined to the opinion that the whole quest was a failure for everybody concerned.

Down on Big Mulberry Creek, in Franklin County, Arkansas, bands of optimistic hillmen are still searching for Spanish treasure, as their forefathers have done for several generations past. The story is that nine Spanish galleons, laden with gold and silver from the mines of Mexico and South America, sailed out of the harbor at Vera Cruz, bound for Spain. Pursued by a squadron of French and English privateers, the treasure-ships put into port at New Orleans and claimed the protection of the authorities. While anchored thus at the mouth of the Mississippi the Spaniards heard wild tales of rich Indian villages up the great river. Their lust for gold still unsatisfied, they loaded the treasure into small boats and followed these rumors up the Mississippi to

the mouth of the Arkansas, and up the Arkansas to Big Mulberry
Creek. Here, it is said, they found the Osages tunneling into the
limestone ledges in search of gold. Capturing the mines and
enslaving the Indians was not difficult, but after this was accomplished it was discovered that the amount of gold recovered was
so small as to be scarcely worth bothering with.

The neighboring tribes were rising against the invaders,
too and then came word of the Louisiana Purchase; it was'
said that United States troops were moving into St. Louis and
New Orleans. In view of all these circumstances, the Spaniards
thought best to bury most of their treasure in a deep shaft, kill
the Indian miners who knew where it was hidden, and return
to Mexico until conditions became a bit more settled. Hostile
Indians, accidents, fevers and other troubles practically extermi-
nated the company, and only two or three of the original sixty
ever reached Mexico. From these survivors, however, the tale
spread all over America, and there are men in Franklin County
today who fully expect to find the "Lost Louisiana" treasure
within a month or so.

Dr. L. G. Hill, of Mulberry, Arkansas, gave up his practice
and spent most of his savings in the search for the Franklin
County treasure; he died in 1925, and his grandson is still carrying on the work. Young Bill is said to have in his possession a
book called *The History of the Lost Louisiana Treasure Mine,* which
gives him a great advantage over the other gold-hunters. One
George Martin of Fort Smith, Arkansas, gave nineteen years of
his life to digging for this treasure, and many Franklin County
farmers still devote most of their spare time to the fruitless quest.

Another version of the "Lost Louisiana" story relates that
the treasure was buried near a large "ebb-and-flow" spring. One
would imagine that this would be sufficient to locate it, since
there are only seventeen of these "ebb-and-flow" springs in the

world. However, the difficulty is that six of the seventeen are in the Ozarks, and three of them in Shannon County, Missouri. The largest, however, is located near the town of Birch Tree, Missouri, and it is here that most of the seekers after this particular hoard of Spanish gold have congregated. The treasure-hunters whom I met at Birch Tree had been anything but successful, and if any gold has ever been found in the vicinity I have yet to hear of it.

Just east of Reeds Spring, in Stone County, Missouri, is the "Old Spanish Cave", discovered in 1892 by a group of treasure-hunters provided with the usual Mexican map. No treasure was ever discovered, however, as far as the local sleuths have been able to find out. The cave now belongs to a man named Frank Mease, who has put in electric lights and gets fifty cents per person for showing tourists certain old diggings and other evidences of early occupation.

Another famous "Spanish Treasure Cave" is located about three miles southeast of Sulphur Springs, Arkansas, just off the highway between Sulphur Springs and Gravette. Not many of the natives are able to find this place offhand, although everybody has "hearn tell" of it. There are two entrances, one closed by a heavy oak door chained from within, and the other by an iron door fastened with a large padlock. There is an old log house nearby, said to have been occupied by treasure-seekers of other years, and a long iron track which formerly extended into the cavern. The story is that an old Mexican came to Sulphur Springs in 1895, with a map showing the location of the cave and the treasure concealed in it. He told a local man that he had found a duplicate of this map carved on a tree, and when he disappeared some three months later many people believed that he carried a large amount of gold away with him. About the time of the Spanish-American War one G. W. Dunbar bought the cave and sold an interest in the treasure to "Doc" Knight. These fellows certainly did a tremendous amount of work; engineers who have inspected the dump say that the excavation alone would cost at least twenty thousand dollars today. Dunbar literally worked himself to death—died of miner's consumption, according to the oldtimers. What became of "Doc" Knight I was unable to find out, but there is no record that either of them ever found a dollar's worth of gold in the cave, or anywhere else.

Near Melborne, in Izard County, Arkansas, is a cavern which is reputed to contain vast stores of Spanish gold. A large spring gushes out of the entrance of this cave, and the natives claim that the spring once brought forth a metal vase bearing inscriptions in a language which nobody in the neighborhood could read, and which was thought to be Spanish. Some Spanish coins, too, are said to have been found in the water nearby. The strange vase has disappeared, however, and the coins likewise, so that the location is not now taken very seriously by the professional treasure-seekers.

Marvel Cave, in Stone County, Missouri, is said to have been prospected in the seventeenth century by Don Jose Valerio, who owned the land for twenty miles on both sides of White River, under a grant from the King of Spain. Valeria's men were looking for silver, not gold; silver at that time being worth about twenty times its present value, according to the native tradition. Several old ladders have been found in Marvel Cave recently, made of pine logs hewn on one side, and fastened together with very large hand-forged spikes. The local wise-acres call them "Spanish" ladders, but nothing is known of their origin. An old soldier hinted to me that they were probably built by deserters or refugees who lived in the cavern during the Civil War. This cave is said to have been worked by Indian miners, as well as the usual Spaniards. In 1883 an aged Delaware squaw told Mr.

Trueman Powell that her father had brought her there as a little girl, so that she could tend the light while he dug out silver for use in making ornaments. There have been many excavations here by prospectors and treasure-seekers, but nobody has ever found anything of value, so far as is known.

In Franklin County, Missouri, along the Meramec River, in the Meramec State Park, an old man with a formidable set of whiskers is devoting his life to a search for Spanish gold. His name is James Henry Woodruff, and he was formerly a tie-hacker— chopped out railroad ties for a living. The story is that a Spanish pirate named Antonio came up the Meramec with a great treasure, and was robbed by a band of French miners who had been working the lead and copper mines in Franklin County under a concession from Louis XV. The Frenchmen carried away what they could, and hid the rest in "a cavern beside the waters". They sealed up the cavern and marked the place with crosses and signs on adjacent cliffs. One of these Frenchmen died in 1848, and just before he died he told the story, but his English was poor and nobody was able to find the map which he said was hidden in his cabin. Woodruff discovered the map many years later, however, and has been searching for the treasure ever since. On certain days in the year he goes out at sunset and stands on a hilltop; just as the sun is setting he starts toward it, counting paces as he goes. After a certain number of paces he drives a stake in the ground, and from this point he takes other bearings, too complicated for the hidden watchers to follow. Woodruff himself says: "I have found out how to work this here map now, an' I kin find th' gold whenever I git ready." But he doesn't seem to be quite ready. For one thing, the land belongs to the State now, and it is said that Jim thinks the secret-service men are watching him, and that the moment he unearths the treasure it will be claimed by the State authorities. At any rate, he just sits before his cabin and smokes his pipe, and dreams his golden dreams.

A variation of the usual Spanish treasure yarn is told of Rock-House Cave, near Cassville, Missouri. The story here is that it was the Indians who sealed up the treasure in the cave, so that the attacking Spaniards should not find it. Many Indian "tracers" from Oklahoma are said to have visited Cassville in the search for this cache. The treasure-hunting rights to Rock-House cavern have recently been purchased by one William G. Carlin, who has documents and maps by means of which he expects to locate gold and other valuables in the near future.

At the mouth of Rush Creek, in Marion County, Arkansas, is a cavern called Dated Cave, said to be so named because the Spaniards carved the date 1540 on the wall. The same Spaniards, fearful of an Indian attack, concealed a great quantity of gold, silver and jewels in the cave, and did not return, according to the story. George and Jake Baughman, who are now living in Boone County, Arkansas, explored this cave as boys; they found no treasure, but there was a primitive smithy at the entrance, with horse-shoes and other iron work lying about—all very old and rusty. While the Baughman boys were in the depths of the cavern they heard a loud noise; rushing out, they found that the cliff over the shop had fallen in, hiding forever all evidences of human activity there!

Many people have dug for treasure near what is called the Old Spanish Camp Ground just southeast of Springfield, Missouri, where a strange serpent-shaped blaze on an old tree is supposed to indicate the location of a vast store of buried gold. The old-timers are not agreed as to whether the hidden wealth belonged to the Spaniards or to the Indians, but they all insist that the place is guarded by a goblin of some sort—probably the ghost of some unfortunate who was buried with the ill-gotten treasure. About fifty years ago a dying man named Allsopp gave a map of this place to a Mr. Lisenby, who lived near Springfield. Lisenby sought the treasure for some time, and one day rushed home in great excitement, shouting that he had found a great pile of gold, but fell to the floor unconscious and died without telling his secret. The Reverend S. P. Newberry, of Springfield, always claimed that he had seen this map of Lisenby's, and also another almost identical map belonging to a Choctaw Indian named Griffin. Some years after Lisenby's death, one Barney Johnson sank a shaft near the marked tree, and died there from some unknown cause, his body being found lying beside the excavation. There have been several other treasure-seekers here in recent years, and numerous piles of rocks and earth may still be seen at the haunted camp ground. Old residents of Springfield also remember the story of the Spanish treasure said to be concealed near the St. De Chantal Academy, where many prospect holes were sunk in a hillside, and the gold-seekers who used to work in Preacher's Cave, located just west of the town.

Many years ago one Fred McWrightman, an elderly lumberman living near Iron River, Michigan, met a hobo who told the following tale: Once upon a time, during the Civil War, a deserter from the Federal Army hid himself in a cave on White River, near the present site of the Rockaway Beach resort, Taney County, Missouri. He found a great pile of gold nuggets in the cavern, and drew a rude map of the locality, which later came into the possession of an innkeeper—name and place of residence not known. . . . Somehow the Iron River hobo obtained the map, and for some unknown reason he gave it to McWrightman. In 1928 McWrightman and his wife Sarah and his grown son came to Taney County in a dilapidated Ford car, and spent the last of their money for twenty acres of hill land near Rockaway Beach. Almost destitute now, they built a log hut—dragged the

logs themselves, since they had no horses—and began a frenzied search for the hidden gold. Suspicious, they did most of
their treasure-hunting at night, with a great show of stealth and
secrecy. After several months of this the son gave up his share
in the enterprise, and made his way back to Michigan as best he
could. A little later the old folks sold the cabin to a tailor named
Pat Carroll, from Hannibal, Missouri, and left in their flivver for
parts unknown. The McWrightmans said disgustedly that they
couldn't even find the cave, much less any treasure, but there
are people in Taney County today who insist that they must have
carried away a great fortune in gold nuggets.

In Boone County, Arkansas, there is a persistent legend to
the effect that the Indians who formerly inhabited the region
shod their horses with silver, which they mined and smelted
in a cave somewhere in the vicinity. Indians have been seen in
recent years, riding through the hills at night with bulging sacks
fastened to their saddles, and it is believed that some Oklahoma
Indians know of the place, and are still taking silver from the old
mine. It is said that years ago several Indians took a white man
named Burton into the lost cavern, but blindfolded him so that
he could not find it again. The fact that Burton mysteriously
disappeared soon afterward made this tale seem the more rea-
sonable, in the hillmen's opinion. A few years ago an old man
from this neighborhood told me that in his youth he actually saw
a silver horseshoe, which must have been made by the Indians.

Gourd Creek cave, in Phelps County, Missouri, is supposed
to contain one hundred thousand dollars in gold, cached there
by an Indian squaw after all of her friends and relatives had been
slain by enemies in search of the family treasure. Just how the
Indians obtained all this money has never been explained, but
many people have dug up the floor of the cavern in the effort
to find it. Only a few years ago two young men spent several

weeks in the vicinity, but found nothing but a few bones and arrowheads in the ashes of ancient fires.

Another famous Indian treasure cavern is located some eighteen miles south of Lebanon, Missouri, on a farm home-steaded by Jacob Smittle in 1840. It is now owned by Mr. A. D. Smittle, the pioneer's grandson, who guides tourists through the cavern, and has made a nice bit of money out of it. More than three thousand tourists visited Smittle Cave in 1929. The legend is that an Indian medicine-man once lived in the cave, and claimed to be able to produce rain, fair weather, health, good hunting and other blessings at will, collecting tribute from his fellows and storing his wealth in a hidden room of the cave. Finally he disappeared, and it was believed that he had left the country, leaving his treasure concealed in the cavern. Years later two local white men made a careful search for the medicine-man's hoard, and just when they thought they had found it, a great fire burst up through the floor of the passage in which they stood and they were forced to flee! Many persons now believe that the medicine-man's spirit still lingers there, to drive away treasure-seekers. Mr. Smittle himself is an old-fashioned hillman, born near the cavern; it is said that he has never ridden on a railroad train nor travelled farther than Springfield. He says he has found some Indian arrowheads and other flint implements in the cavern, but takes no interest in the medicine-man yarn, nor in any similar "foolishment." The only treasure that he is concerned with, he says, is the money he collects from tourists at the entrance of Smittle Cave.

In 1880 "Doc" Benna, an old California prospector, began digging for gold in McDonald County, Missouri. After some five years of solitary toil he interested two local men in what he called his "big strike", and an assayer declared that the ore taken out was rich in gold and silver. Finally a rich Indian named Mathias

Splitlog took over the project, and built something of a town near the mine, a village still known as Splitlog Settlement. He even promoted a company which built and equipped a railroad from Splitlog to Joplin which was later taken over by the K. C. P. & G. Meanwhile the rich ore was found to be quite worthless, "Doc" Benna's bubble burst, and Mathias Splitlog died a pauper about 1897, somewhere in the Indian Territory.

Old-timers will recall the great gold-rush near Monette, Missouri, where it was claimed that the ordinary red sandstone ran seventy ounces of gold to the ton. Thousands of acres of cheap land in the vicinity were leased by stock-selling corporations. The assayers at the Missouri School of Mines reported that the ore samples were worthless, whereupon the promoters declared that this particular variety of gold could be detected only by a special secret sort of analysis, unknown to the ordinary chemists of the schools. The whole undertaking blew up finally, and no gold was ever smelted simply because, as the School of Mines people pointed out, there wasn't any gold there.

Some years ago the papers were full of the rich silver ore discovered in the hills near Seligman, Missouri. The backers of this enterprise provided their own assayer, a woman who had set up an old cookstove in the woods near the shaft. She simply mixed the pulverized ore with lard in a long-handled spoon, and held it over the flame. As soon as the grease was burned away she turned the residue out on a board, displaying a little button of white metal. A local wag crushed a brick made at Coffeyville, Kansas, together with a piece of an old grindstone, and presented it to her for analysis. It was found to be rich in silver! To a chemist who criticised her methods of analysis the old woman said in a moment of exasperation, "Do you think I'm saltin' it? It would take all th' tinfoil in th' state to salt that much ore!" Inquiry soon located the proprietor of a crossroads store who admitted selling great quantities of tinfoil to the promoters of the silver-mine. The "silver" was nothing but tinfoil which the woman "assayer" had hidden in the grease!

In 1923 Professor M. H. Thornberry, of the Missouri State School of Mines, received a cautious letter from a man in one of the hill counties, describing his discovery of a sealed-up mine and smelting plant formerly operated by "cave-dwellers". He enclosed some samples of ore, too, of which he wrote:

> You will understand that if the secrets of the rocks I am sending you today were to be known to the people around here my life would not be safe for a day. Be very careful so nothing leaks out before I get ready to open up. There is enough blood sticking to this gold without spilling any more. I will explain history to you later. Remember Virginia City of Klondike!

Analysis showed no gold nor other precious metal in the samples, however, and nothing more has been heard from this particular gold-miner.

Near Kingston, Arkansas, an enthusiastic gold-hunter, after a search of more than thirty years, discovered a vein of gleaming "gold ore" one hundred and thirty-four feet long and about thirty feet wide, which he claims runs about nine dollars to the ton. Otto Ernest Rayburn, editor of *Ozark Life*, sent a sample to an assayer at Denver, who reported "gold and silver in small quantities." Dr. Albert W. Giles, professor of geology at the University of Arkansas, writes me that there is no gold in the Ozark region, but the amateur miner was still at work late in 1929.

The only treasures which have actually been found in the Ozarks, as far as I am able to learn, were not mines or Spanish gold at all, but private hoards of coin and currency buried in comparatively recent years. Down on War Eagle Creek, near Huntsville, Arkansas, Jim Hawkins built the first grist-mill ever known in that vicinity. He operated a distillery also, and made money and saved it. After old Jim's death his daughter Mattie took charge of the mill, and when she died recently the good neighbors started to clean up the old place a bit, as it was soon to be occupied by a young Hawkins and his bride. Intending to rebuild the dilapidated fireplace, they began to remove the hearth-stones. Under the central rock was a wire loop, buried in fine ashes. Fastened to this was an old iron-bound box, and when this chest was broken open it was found to contain eleven thousand dollars in gold coin and greenbacks. Further search uncovered several smaller caches about the place, and the whole treasure amounted to more than nineteen thousand dollars— the savings of two life-times, representing more than a century of uninterrupted toil.

When I lived near Pineville, Missouri, two men asked permission to dig for treasure on the hillside just above my cabin, and others dug without permission, supposedly for gold buried there during the Civil War. Whether they found it or not I never knew, but I do know that people in the vicinity still dig for the twenty-six hundred dollars which Asberry Carter buried somewhere near the place in 1862. Carter was shot by an Indian in 1863 and died before he could tell his friends where the money was hidden. Many searches have been made, people have brought maps and charts and measurements, but none of the money has ever been found, so far as is known. Another buried treasure near Pineville is that of Henry Schell, killed by some raiding Yankee scouts. After the war his two sons hunted for it all over the place, and finally found about two hundred and fifty dollars buried in an old log stable. The rest of Schell's money— the amount is not precisely known—has never been unearthed.

About a mile from my cabin people were still digging for gold buried years ago by "Greasy Jack" Reynolds, who died in Pineville about 1900. Reynolds was a bewhiskered, eccentric little man who was believed to have obtained a large sum of money from his father, a former governor of Missouri. He was never known to spend any money, nor to deposit any in the local bank, so the hillfolk reasoned that he must have buried it somewhere. No money was ever found on the Reynolds place, so far as I know, but the legend still persists in the neighborhood.

Such minor treasure-tales as these may be heard in every Ozark community. Even today many hillmen are prejudiced against banks, preferring to hide their scanty cash in the caves and "rock-houses" as their fathers did before them. . . . One of my neighbors, on leaving home, always ties his money up in a dirty pot-rag and throws it on the ground just in front of his beehives! And so it is that treasure-hunters are still at work everywhere, but failures are many and successes few, and the Ozark caverns still yawn cynically at them both.

CHAPTER XII.

The Coming of the "Furriners"

THE FIRST CITY PEOPLE TO invade the Ozark country were sportsmen—deer-hunters and fishermen who came down from Kansas City and St. Louis in the eighties. These fellows were quite willing to rough it with the natives, they were generous with those whom they employed as guides and boatmen, and were deservedly popular everywhere. Of late years, however, hundreds of tourist camps and summer hotels have sprung up along the new highways, and the people who stop at these places are "furriners" of an altogether different type. The old-time hillman is impressed not a whit by the fine clothes and big motor-cars of the invaders; for he knows perfectly well that nearly all tourists are salaried people—"nothin' but hired hands"—while he himself is a landed gentleman despite his rags, and "don't take no order from nobody". Like most rustics the Ozarker regards all cities as sink-holes of iniquity, and believes that all city-dwellers are grossly immoral. The behavior of the modern tourists, particularly the women, shocks him profoundly, and he feels that the coming of civilization is by no means an unmixed blessing.

The realtors who are booming the Ozarks as a summer

playground talk a great deal about how the tourists help the poor hillfolk by bringing money into the country, but the truth is that the hill farmer sees very little of this money; most of it goes to the resort-keepers, the bootleggers, and the merchants in the Ozark villages. These gentry cry up the tourist trade, naturally, but the tourist brings nothing but trouble to the real hillbilly. Tourists fish in his streams and hunt on his land without permission, they trample down his scanty crops, use his fence-rails for fuel, leave his gates open, and even steal his fruit and roasting-ears. They take advantage of the mountain man's hospitality, pay him nothing, corrupt his children, and ridicule his picturesque customs and traditions almost to his face.

The hillman is inordinately sensitive to ridicule, and the humorous contempt of the "city feller" is hard enough for him to bear, but the serious reactions of critics from more progressive parts of the country are irritating almost beyond endurance. Mr. H. L. Mencken, who lives in Baltimore, once wrote:

> Several years ago I enjoyed the somewhat depressing pleasure of making a tour of the country lying along the border between Arkansas and Oklahoma. . . . Such shabby and flea-bitten villages I had never seen before, or such dreadful people. Some of the former were so barbaric that they did not even have regular streets. The houses, such as they were, were plumped down anywhere, at any angle. As for inhabitants, it is a sober fact that I saw women by the roadside, with children between their knees, picking lice like mother monkeys in a zoo. . . . There were few fences. When one appeared it was far gone in decay and there was always a sign on it, painted crudely, with the e's backward: 'Prepare to Meet Thy God.'"

Mencken is bad enough, but we have had many harsher critics. A motion picture actor named Gardner James once spent four weeks in the Ozarks, and the *Motion Picture Classic* quotes him as follows:

> "It's incredible, but we have here in America people living in a lower state of culture than the savages we dispossessed. . . . Unless you have seen them, you cannot possibly grasp the full degree of filth and squalor into which they have sunk. . . . They're savages, that's all! They even look like an entirely different race—not at all like the types we're used to calling Americans. They don't live as we do, they don't think as we do, they don't seem even to feel as we do—they're just not as the rest of us in this country are. . . . They seem to me a decidedly lower grade of human than the American Indian, the Polynesian, or the best native tribes of Africa. . . . It's quite the ordinary thing to see a family of five living on a yearly income of one hundred and twenty five dollars or one hundred and fifty dollars. . . . They live almost exclusively on pork, tough chickens, and hominy grits. . . . They cannot even afford medical aid in cases of childbirth. . . . They are not even as cleanly as most animals are. . . . I didn't see a single person who seemed in the normal state of health of the average city dweller. . . . The majority had skin trouble, all were malarial, and all showed unmistakable signs of malnutrition. . . . They move just like a slow-motion picture. . . . That is the country of which Harold Bell Wright draws such beautiful pen pictures; that is 'God's country'—but to me it was like nothing else so much as a good, stiff dose of physic!"

Those who know the Ozark people will understand just about what Mr. James saw and heard during his brief stay in the hill country, and will realize that he may be telling what he believes to be the truth. And yet the truth is that Mr. James doesn't know what he is talking about. . . . I once lived in Hollywood for several weeks, and my impressions of the motion-picture folk are probably as near the truth as Gardner James' opinions of the Ozark hill people, and not very much more flattering. . . . Still, I do not feel competent to write authoritatively about the motion-picture industry.

The typical hillman has never heard of Gardner James, of course, but he has encountered plenty of city people who share Mr. James' feelings, and he cordially detests them all. In recent years he has grown more or less conscious of his backwardness, so that even a conservative and truthful description of the Ozark situation is often very offensive to him. The backwoodsman has no patience with mere exposition, and any dispassionate statement of fact seems to disturb and baffle him. He thinks that a thing is either good or bad; if good, it should be lauded to the skies, if bad, it should be vehemently denounced; he feels, furthermore, that the value of this point of view is evident to everybody, and that there is no other attitude for an honest man to take! It is easy to see how he has arrived at this singular position, since the ordinary hillman reads nothing at all, and hears no speakers except preachers, politicians and auctioneers, none of whom is primarily concerned with the mere presentation of fact.

The tourist who visits a few backwoods cabins often imagines that he understands the hillman perfectly, regarding him as a simple child of nature, whose inmost thoughts and motivations may be read at a glance. Nothing could be farther from the truth. The hillfolk are simple in that they live close to the essential facts of life and they ask intimate and personal questions in a childish fashion, but they are secretive and sensitive and suspicious beyond anything that the average city dweller can imagine. The mountaineer is accustomed to go about his affairs in a singularly sly and circuitous fashion, concealing his real thoughts and desires behind a mask—often a mask of childish vacuity. Any straightforward statement, any proceeding directly to the heart of a matter, seems to astonish and offend him. It is almost impossible for an old-time Ozarker to enter into the simplest business agreement without a long series of debates and hypothetical questions and false starts. Try to buy something from one of them, and it is only with the greatest difficulty that you can get him to put a definite price on it; accept his offer at once and he is terribly "sot back", sure that he could have easily obtained at least twice the amount mentioned, and feeling somehow insulted besides!

Another thing which has prejudiced the hill people against outsiders is the fact that so many of them feel called upon to save the hillman's soul, or show him how to build a new-fangled privy, or advise his wife about the proper feeding of her children. The Ozarker is fiercely proud of his own accomplishments and his independence. He despises all uplifters, and contemptuously rejects anything suggestive of "help". The hillman will "borry" anything you have, and he may return it in an utterly dilapidated condition without any apology, but you cannot give him anything unless it is presented with the utmost tact. I have known a mountain man to refuse things that he sorely needed, simply because he smelled something of patronage in the offer, something degrading to his high spirit, insulting to his assumption of equality and independence. He will accept help if it is offered in a neighborly fashion, and will repay it with some goods or service of his own, but he will have nothing that smacks of charity.

Most of the self-appointed missionaries and reformers who come to the Ozarks seem to be altogether ignorant of the local situation, and temperamentally unfit for work in this field. It is easy for the engineer or the physician from the city to tell the hillfolk what to do about housing conditions and sanitation, but one has a better understanding of these matters after he has lived in the hill country for a while. The man who has cut and hauled

wood to heat a large house can easily see why the hill-billy crowds
his family into a small one; the man who tries to dig a well in a
hard limestone country understands why the natives are satisfied
with surface water; the man who carries water uphill to his cabin,
and heats it in a kettle in front of his fireplace, knows why the
Ozarkers do not bathe much in the Winter time. A more intimate acquaintance with the hillfolk explains much of their grotesque social behavior, too, and many customs which are strange
to the outsider appear so only because he does not understand
the environment which produced them. Doubtless the hillman
who comes to the city sees some peculiar things, also. . . .

One of the Ozarker's outstanding characteristics is his clan-
nishness—his deep feeling of attachment for his kinsmen. I used
to enjoy bombarding my ultra-conservative hill country friends
with anti-moral, anti-patriotic and anti-religious epigrams, but
even the wildest and most blasphemous of my borrowings from
atheistic and anarchistic writers did not shock them as deeply as
a thoughtless remark to the effect that my relatives were thrust
upon me, but I choose my own friends. The idea that a man
should turn from his "blood kin" and seek his intimates among
outsiders strikes the hillman as horrible and unnatural.

Because of the Ozarker's almost fanatical loyalty to his kinfolk, nearly every isolated mountain settlement has gradually
come to be dominated by certain families and clans. In general
this influence is beneficial rather than otherwise, but there have
been cases in which these hill-billy leaders ruled by force in such
a brutal fashion that whole neighborhoods were utterly terror-
ized, and men and women practically enslaved. Rose Wilder
Lane touched upon this condition in her novel *Cindy*, and there
have been many other more or less cautious references to it in
the Ozark literature.

In Stone County, Arkansas, the investigation of an alleged

murder in 1929 incidentally uncovered one of these hill-billy dictatorships. Mr. C. H. Nelson, of Mountain View, Arkansas, was quoted in the newspapers as saying that peonage had existed in Stone County for nearly forty years; that certain families regarded themselves as the aristocrats of the mountains, and made and administered their own laws, insofar as they applied to the proper disciplining of the subjugated hill people. It appears that these "barons" forced their serfs to work, and paid them nothing more than food and lodging; they took hillmen's wives and daughters at their pleasure, and brought them back when they had tired of them; they flogged men, women and children for petty offenses; it is charged that they mutilated a "furrin" farmhand and later burned him to death, simply because he insisted upon marrying a hill girl for whom the barons had other plans.

Mr. W. G. Secrist, who investigated peonage in the Ozarks for the Kansas City *Journal-Post*, said of the citizens of Mountain View: "Inured to the privations and suffering of the illiterate hill folk as a result of their treatment at the hands of their more fortunate neighbors, it required a murder as brutal as the burning alive last March of Connie Franklin, thirty-year-old farmhand, to bring home to the townspeople the real gravity of the situation. While their apathetic attitude toward the mistreatment of the mountain people . . . was not due to any lack of sympathy, they had become so accustomed to tales of floggings, mistreatment of women and girls and the enslavement of men and boys until to them it had descended in the scale of importance to the point where it was viewed as regrettable, but unavoidable."

Whatever may be said of the Connie Franklin case, there is little doubt that the Stone County tales of peonage and other outrages have some foundation in fact. I visited the place in question and talked with the natives several years before the alleged murder. I heard stories of men forced to cut wood and grub sprouts for weeks at a time, and knocked down by their masters at the mere mention of payment. One woman's children, according to local gossip, were taken from her and farmed out as servants to first one and then another of the clan chieftains, with no compensation other than their food and lodging. A group of mountain bravos, it is said, pulled two young women out of their beds and flogged them for no reason at all, "jest t' see 'em a-dancin' round in their shirt-tails". . . . It appears that similar conditions obtain or have obtained in at least two other places beside the Mountain View neighborhood.

Wild rumors of other abuses are still whispered in various quarters, and I believe that some of them are true, but it must be understood that these are isolated and exceptional cases, and in no way representative of the Ozark country as a whole. The typical Ozark hillman can never be enslaved by anybody. He is almost insanely jealous of his independence and his personal liberty, and will fight to the death in defense of whatever he happens to regard as his rights. The mountaineer may be poor and illiterate and shiftless, but he is a free man, and is likely to remain so for some time to come.

Except for the ties of family and clan relationships, the hill people are individualistic and non-social in the extreme. They are so suspicious of one another that they cannot be organized. They recognize no community of economic interest, and it is almost impossible to get them to work together for their common welfare. Most of them will have no dealings with labor unions, or with organized efforts to market their crops more advantageously; they will not even combine to work the roads, which are obviously for the benefit of the whole neighborhood. When the hillman is reduced to day labor on public works he is a constant source of trouble to the "furrin" bosses, and cannot compete with imported workmen. He is unused to contin-

uous labor, he is unable to take orders or endure any sort of
discipline, and he will quit work and demand his wages at the
slightest provocation. Time is of no importance to him, and a
man who is expected to report for work on Monday may show
up the following Wednesday, cheerful and without any apology or explanation. . . . A friend of mine who built a cottage
in northwestern Arkansas obtained carpenters from Kansas,
paying them eight dollars per day and transportation, although
local carpenters could have been hired for about three dollars
per day. The hillmen would probably have done just as good
work, too, but they are so exasperating to manage, and so trying
to the temper of anyone not accustomed to dealing with them,
that he preferred to bring in craftsmen from outside.

It is no wonder that the best minds among the hill people
resent the invasion of outside interests. Great corporations are
taking their timber and their water-power, and their neglected
little farms are fast falling into alien and more efficient hands.
Their old neighbors are moving out, and new and unwelcome
ones are coming in. Many of the most prosperous farmers and
the most enterprising merchants in the Ozarks nowadays are
not natives at all. The rapidly growing tourist and resort business is practically controlled by "furriners". The best of the
mountain boys and girls leave this under-privileged region and
go to the cities; only the culls are left in the hill country, and
these are regrettably prone to imitate the follies and vices of the
skylarking-tourists. Recent attempts to educate the children of
the hills have not been conspicuously successful; the schools of
which they are so pathetically proud are among the poorest in
America, and many graduates of the village high-schools have
little learning beyond the bare ability to read and write.

I do not pretend to know what is to become of these people,
but I cannot believe that, as a class, they will be able to adapt

themselves to the complex requirements of modern civilization, or that they will ever again play any important part in the development of the region in which they live. It may be that the native Ozarkers will soon give place to "furriners", and vanish like the Indians and the Bluff-Dwellers who kept these wilds in other years. . . . Nothing is to be gained by becoming sentimental about such matters, of course. If the Ozark hill-billy has done his work and outlived his usefulness, he must inevitably go the way of all primitive people who stand in the way of economic progress. To those of us who know the old-timers, however, the transition is not without a touch of melancholy and regret. The gods of the hills are not the gods of the valleys, and the old-time hillfolk are very different from the efficient but comparatively uninteresting people who are replacing them. . . . The valleys raise corn, perhaps, but the Ozark hills produced extraordinary men and women. Their passing definitely closes one of the most romantic and colorful chapters in the history of our country.